World Economy
and World Politics,
1924–1931

World Economy and World Politics, 1924–1931

From Reconstruction to Collapse

Gilbert Ziebura

Translated from the German by
Bruce Little

BERG

Oxford / New York / Munich

Distributed exclusively in the US and Canada by
St Martin's Press, New York

English edition first published in 1990 by
Berg Publishers Limited
Editorial offices:
150 Cowley Road, Oxford OX4 1JJ, UK
165 Taber Avenue, Providence, RI 02906, USA
Westermühlstraße 26, 8000 München 5, FRG

English translation © Berg Publishers 1990
Originally published as *Weltwirtschaft und Weltpolitik 1924 bis 1931. Zwischen Rekonstruktion und Zusammenbruch.*
Translated from the German by permission of the publishers, Suhrkamp Verlag, Frankfurt am Main
© Suhrkamp Verlag 1984

British Library Cataloguing in Publication Data

Ziebura, Gilbert
    World economy and world politics, 1924–1931: from reconstruction to collapse.
    1. Economic conditions, history. International political aspects
    I. Title   II. Weltwirtschaft und Weltpolitik 1922/24–1931:
    Zwischen Rekonstruktion und Zusammenbruch. *English*
    330.9

ISBN 0-85496-646-3

Library of Congress Cataloging-in-Publication Data

Ziebura, Gilbert.
    [Weltwirtschaft und Weltpolitik 1922/24–1931. English]
    World economy and world politics, 1924–1931: from reconstruction to collapse / Gilbert Ziebura: translated from the German by Bruce Little.
        p.   cm.
    Translation of: Weltwirtschaft und Weltpolitik 1922/24–1931.
    Includes bibliographical references.
    ISBN 0-85496-646-3
    1. Economic history—1918–1945.   2. World politics—1919–1932.   3. Depressions—1929.   I. Title.
HC57.Z5413   1989
330.'042—dc20   89-35884

Printed in Great Britain by
Billing & Sons Ltd, Worcester

Contents

List of Tables

List of Tables

Abbreviations

AER	American Economic Review
AHR	American Historical Review
APSR	American Political Science Review
EHR	Economic History Review
FAZ	Frankfurter Allgemeine Zeitung
HZ	Historische Zeitschrift
JAH	Journal of American History
JCH	Journal of Contemporary History
JMH	Journal of Modern History
NPL	Neue Politische Literatur
RHMC	Revue d'histoire moderne et contemporaine
VfZ	Vierteljahrshefte für Zeitgeschichte
VSWG	Vierteljahrschrift für Sozial- und Wirtschaftsgeschichte

Foreword

This book has had a long gestation. The questions that it poses arose for the first time in connection with a research project which I headed between 1963 and 1974 at the Central Institute 6 of the Free University of Berlin. We set out to study the foreign policy of the four most important European countries, Germany, France, Italy and Great Britain, during the 1930s with special attention to the critical year of 1936. The aim was to elaborate further on the reasons for the eventual collapse of the international system. We abandoned the well-worn paths of traditional political and diplomatic history to the extent that we focused attention from the outset on the domestic factors and the global economic factors that conditioned the foreign policy of these countries. This meant, among other things, that we needed to determine the impact of the Great Depression on the ability of the major parties to the Versailles System to steer a particular foreign policy. This was a pivotal question that previously had not received the consideration it deserved.

It quickly became apparent that this would only be possible if a clear understanding was gained of the structural flaws inherent in attempts in Europe between 1924 and 1929 to reconstruct the world economy and political system. At the same time, the situation in south-east Asia had also to be considered, in no small measure because the United States acted here, as well as in Europe, as a stabilising force. Furthermore, an explanation needed to be found as to why the Versailles and Washington Systems – the very foundation of the reconstruction attempt – both collapsed in 1931. This was crucial to any understanding of why the great economic crisis of 1929 so devastated the global economy and political system.

Two colleagues, Fritz Luther and Reinhard Mayer, worked on this aspect of the project and presented a number of working papers in which they cogently summarised the international research. This contributed immeasurably to refining the questions we wished to pose and to confirming their suitability for the project as a whole. Without these papers, which were often the object of passionate discussion, this book would not have been possible. For this, both colleagues deserved our deepest gratitude.

The original project ended before the results of this aspect were ready for publication. Several years later, Gustav Schmidt, who had formerly been involved in the project and in the meantime had taken up a position as professor of international politics at the University of Bochum, asked me to read the opening paper at an international conference he had organised. The conference was held in September 1981 in Dortmund under the heading, 'Political Nationalism and the International Financial and Trade System: Constellations of International Policy 1924–1931/32'. The book containing the fruits of this conference (see the Select Bibliography) provides an excellent supplement to this volume. The purpose of this volume is to make the ideas outlined in my opening paper, which are based on the results of the previous research project, available to a wider audience.

In contrast to the series published by H.-U. Wehler in the Neue Historische Bibliothek, this volume does not intend to provide a didactic overview of a certain topic. Instead, it attempts to elucidate global structures using the example of a particularly fateful era of contemporary history. The acceptance of this volume in the Neue Historische Bibliothek series points up the soundness of this approach, something that is not always taken for granted nowadays. For this and for reading the manuscript I am indebted to H.-U. Wehler. I would also like to express my gratitude to Dr Birgit Pollmann and Gerhard Becher, my colleagues in Braunschweig who read the manuscript and offered suggestions. Thanks are due as well to Christiane Dill who wrote parts of it.

I would like to dedicate this volume to my parents. They struggled through the era described here as witnesses to, or better, victims of history. And yet, despite deprivations that today are scarcely imaginable, they did their utmost to provide their three sons, born in 1924, '25 and '34, with a happy childhood and a solid education.

Gilbert Ziebura
Braunschweig, January 1984

Foreword to the English Edition

This book may well be received with some surprise in English-speaking countries, where many readers will find that it pushes theory too far. Historical and political science research in these countries has been particularly inclined to detailed descriptions of a limited subject matter and rather leery of audacious attempts to discern underlying structures. I have certainly learned an enormous amount from the often admirable empirical studies of British and American authors, as the notes and bibliography will testify. Without them, this book could not have been written.

I remain convinced, however, that the present state of research into the 1920s enables us to set more ambitious goals. The essential features of the so-called 'interwar years' are becoming ever more apparent, and we can no longer be satisfied with not being able to see the woods for the trees. We know that the attempt to build a new, peaceful world order using the political, economic and ideological methods of the prewar era was doomed to failure as a result of the massive changes spawned by the First World War. The dominant political forces wished to restore a world that had disappeared forever. In attempting to do so – and this is the central thesis of my book – they only aggravated the structural defects inherent in the new order in Europe and the Far East. First and foremost was the Great Depression of 1929, whose *combined* effects on the evolution of world politics and the global economy are still not fully recognised.

This is all the more reason why the questions that now arise require at least some minimal amount of theoretical analysis. The most important of these questions is the relationship between politics and economics – a relationship which took on a whole new quality because of the huge increase in state intervention in the economy during the Great War and the resulting economic, financial and social effects. What were the effects of mounting political influence in the economy and mounting economic influence in the world of politics, on both the domestic and international levels? What was the role of the United States, which needed a reconstructed world economy and yet implemented strict and necessarily counter-productive protectionism. The United States took it upon itself to intervene in the economic affairs of both Europe and the Far East, but it did little to foster political stability. How was it that Germany and Japan, the countries that were to become America's bitterest enemies in the 1930s, developed into her privileged partners of the 1920s?

This book not only poses some of these questions but attempts to answer them. It will surely provoke controversy, which I trust will only help to deepen our basic understanding of this dramatic era which still remains something of a mystery. This book is certainly not intended as the final word. It will have fulfilled its purpose if it serves to broaden our horizons and impart new impulses. It is intended first and foremost as a contribution to our thinking about the present state of historical-political research into this era and to the question of whether traditional research methods, which continue to play a major role, still suffice to enable us to understand the mounting interdependence of economics, politics and strategic planning on both the domestic and international levels. Only then will we be able to understand the margin for ma-noeuvre of the leading figures of the 1920s and the bounds within which they were compelled to operate. The interdependence of our subject matter necessarily requires an interdisciplinary approach. Much of what we take for granted today began during the 1920s. This is the essence of the challenge which this book attempts to address.

Gilbert Ziebura
Braunschweig, April 1989

1
Questions,
Gaps in the Research and
Development of a Theory

I. The Lessons of History?

The era between the two world wars has recently assumed heightened significance in light of the worldwide political and economic crisis which began in 1974–5 and grew increasingly severe after 1979–80. Even practising politicians continually draw analogies to the interwar period, especially to the great economic crisis of 1929, whether out of fear and alarm or in order to bolster confidence.

All this is new. After 1945 the United States set out to forge a postwar order which would prevent the catastrophes of the 1930s from ever recurring. Washington's policies were legitimised with the argument that one must learn from history.[1] But comparisons with the 1930s degenerate into sheer demagoguery when the West's futile appeasement of Hitler is trotted out in order to prove that the Soviet Union must now be dealt with from a position of strength. The mere mention of 'Munich' suffices to set the hawks of all countries to full oratorical flight, while easing their consciences.

But history does not provide ready-made answers. Comparisons between the crisis of that time and the present international crisis give rise to a host of theoretical and methodological problems that have not been clearly recognised, let alone solved, by historians and social scientists of any particular stripe or ideology. No theory has been advanced which explains the entire relationship between politics, economics and ideology, between the multitude of domestic and inter-

1. From the abundant literature see: J.B. Condliffe, *The Reconstruction of World Trade* (New York, 1940) and H.W. Arndt, *The Economic Lessons of the Nineteen-Thirties* (London, 1944).

national factors that play a role in the crisis. Those who are willing to take the easy way out simply throw up their arms and claim that no such theory can possibly exist. The better part of wisdom, they say, is to moderate one's ambition. However, scholars must then accept the fact that they will be driven onto the defensive and even marginalised by active politicians with no such scruples. They will not wait for academia to come to a determination, and even if it has, are perfectly prepared to ignore it if they sense that dubious historical comparisons will help to 'sell' their policies. They may claim only to draw on the lessons of history, but in fact are simply picking out whatever best serves their purposes.[2] In plain language, they are manipulating the truth.

The high priests of academe reply that such abuses are inevitable, that there will always be a certain discrepancy between their pristine research results and the political hurly-burly. These lofty observers may appear very distinguished as they scoff at politicians and their fellow researchers who allow themselves to be diverted from the path of righteousness, but they contribute in their own way to the general confusion. There is good fishing in troubled waters.

Historical experience is not an objective standard, though everyone points to it and employs it to best advantage in class struggles. But it is a treasure-house of experience on which we can draw in judging the events of the present. The perfidy of historical experience can be illustrated by a simple example. For reasons that are all too apparent, banking circles continually assert that the contemporary banking system could not possibly collapse as it did in 1931. The salient mistake of the 1930s – the restrictive monetary policies of the central banks that greatly exacerbated the depression – would not be repeated. What is more, the financial 'security nets' in place on both the national and international levels are now far more sophisticated than before.[3] There is no doubt that bankers have learned a great deal from the trauma of 1931; but what they have learned is how to cope with the same kind of crisis. Much has changed in the meantime. Most importantly, the amount of

---

2. See for instance M. Debré, '1929–1983' in *Le Monde*, 15 September 1982. The first of President de Gaulle's prime ministers made use of the crisis of 1929 in this way in order to attack the policies of François Mitterand. None the less, the article contains a noteworthy sentence: 'In 1929 an economic depression got out of control and eventually plunged the world into war; in 1983 it is an uncontrolled state of war (the arms race between the super powers is meant) that is condemning us to economic depression.'

3. From the abundant literature see: T. Wilson, '1929–30, Could It Happen Again?', *The Three Banks Review* (London, December 1980), p. 128; W. Fautz, 'Wiederholt sich die Depression von 1929–1933?' in Schweizerischer Bankverein, *Der Monat* 10 (1982); much less optimistic is 'The Last Great Depression and the Next', *International Currency Review* 4 (London, 1979).

outstanding credit has risen enormously, leading, to mention only one aspect of the present financial crisis, to astronomical foreign debts in many countries of the first, the second and above all the third world.[4] Can the banks contend with this type of crisis (which they brought on themselves to a certain extent)? When they make confident reference to the years between 1929 and 1931, are they not simply trying to spread a self-serving sense of optimism? What are we to make of the Cassandra cries of the German banker von Bethmann in an interview granted to the newsmagazine, *Der Spiegel* on 1 August 1983:

> Bethmann: I am convinced that the world monetary system and therefore the world economy have never been so unstable as at the present time.
> *Der Spiegel*: Things will get even worse than in the 1930s?
> Bethmann: I think so. And the reason is that we are doing far too little in order to deal with the crisis. We seem to think, despite the worldwide explosion of debt, that things won't really be all that bad.

What makes these lines so shocking is that similar warnings were voiced in the late 1920s – but to no avail. Do bankers, like so many generals, learn only how to fight the battles of yesteryear?

Another, even more fateful error arises when lessons are drawn from the crash of 1929. In seeking to explain the causes of the Great Depression in order to help devise a strategy for dealing with the present difficulties, researchers fasten upon a single factor in isolation from all the others. The best example of this practice is the still influential monetarist school, embodied in its purest form by Milton Friedman. In his view, ill-advised monetary policies were largely responsible for the 1929 crisis,[5] and 'correct' monetary policies would solve the present predicament. Though plausible at first blush, this analysis soon proves to be little more than an attempt on the part of political conservatives to influence social policy in favour of the wealthy by restricting the money supply and reducing state intervention in the economy. Once again, history is abused in order to legitimise a certain social agenda.

It is better advised to adopt the view of the British economic historian Derek H. Aldcroft who sees the primary cause of the 1929 crisis not in monetary policies but in 'structural imbalances'[6] – a cautious phrase

---

4. Cf. A. Schubert, 'Von der Verschuldungskrise zum internationalen Finanzchaos?' [From the Debt Crisis to International Financial Chaos?] in U. Albrecht et al. (eds), *Weltpolitik. Jahrbuch für internationale Beziehungen* 2 (Frankfurt, 1982).
5. M. Friedman and A.J. Schwartz, *A Monetary History of the United States, 1867–1960* (NY, 1963); see as well Friedman's foremost work under the revealing title, *Capitalism and Freedom* (Chicago, 1962).
6. D.H. Aldcroft, 'Britische Währungspolitik und Wirtschaftstätigkeit in den 1920er Jahren' [British Monetary Policy and the Economy in the 1920s] in H. Winkel (ed.), *Finanz- und wirtschaftspolitische Fragen der Zwischenkriegszeit* (Berlin, 1973), p. 120.

which provides sufficient scope. One can only learn from history when time is taken to understand the true nature of an event by analysing the social forces which brought it about. Who derived advantage from the event in order to advance which interests? These questions arise over and over again. The responses to them are not only fundamental to a genuine understanding of history; they also provide the methodological basis on which specific, historically unique circumstances can be determined and distinctions drawn, as well as comparisons and general truths.

Beneath the superficial fluctuations in the economy, long-term structural factors must be analysed. Only then can the response of contemporaries be understood and not before, as Wolfram Fischer tries to do when he asks: 'Did contemporaries not recognise the crisis in time, did they misjudge its causes or were their opinions too diverse? Were their methods for coping with the crisis appropriate or were they so hedged in by circumstances that they were unable to implement the proper policies even though they knew what they were?'[7] All these incessant but ultimately inappropriate questions about perception and margin of manoeuvre! As if the Depression was an illness which needed only to be accurately diagnosed in order to prescribe the proper cure – so long, to be sure, as 'circumstances' did not upset the calculation.

The ease with which sagacious historians and social scientists 'solve in hindsight the problems of previous eras' (Borchardt) does little to advance our historical understanding. Fischer even suggests that it is possible to learn how to solve these crises through rational analysis. But this is far from true. An economic crisis, as André Gunder Frank has pointed out,[8] is an ultimatum to effect certain essential adjustments to the system, without which serious consequences or even a great catastrophe could result. For the Chinese, the word 'crisis' means 'a combination of danger and opportunity'. Crises, therefore, are 'critical' periods in which tensions reach particularly acute levels. These tensions evolve according to the way in which the crisis is handled. In the course of such crises, frequent reference is often made to historical experience. It may help us find our bearings, but it is also continually misused and manipulated, especially by those in power.

Though there are many obvious differences between the 'first' global economic crisis in the twentieth century and the 'second', striking

---

7. W. Fischer, 'Lehren aus der Geschichte. Wirtschaftspolitik einer vergangenen Epoche im Speigel unserer Zeit' [The Lessons of History. The Economy Policy of a Former Era in the Mirror of the Present], *Frankfurter Allgemeine Zeitung*, 16 October 1982, p. 15.
8. A.G. Frank, 'Die gegenwärtige Krise und die Perspektiven des Weltsystems' [The Present Crisis and the Prospects of the World-System] in J. Blaschke (ed.), *Perspektiven des Weltsystems. Materialien zu I. Wallerstein, 'Das moderne Weltsystem'* (Frankfurt, 1983), p. 230.

parallels continually appear, less in regard to specific causes than to the strategies that are proposed in order to overcome the crisis. In both cases, governments pursued deflationary austerity policies, a stable currency and balanced budgets, at least as the ideal. The most important difference in the political approach to the two economic crises is that today every attempt is made to encourage manufacturers to invest by granting them special concessions, though no one has the slightest idea whether the necessary restructuring can be achieved in this way. (Between 1929 and 1931, this kind of strategy played a relatively minor role.) During both economic slumps, conservative political forces held power in virtually all the leading western industrial nations.

All these similarities are overshadowed, however, by a cardinal distinction. The Great Depression eliminated the United States, then as now the world's leading economic power, as the motive force behind the global restructuring process. During the second great crisis, on the other hand, the United States appears to be recovering some of the economic and military–strategic hegemony she had attained in the 1950s and '60s. In 1929–31, each country was thrown back on its own resources; today, all depend on developments in the United States.

Are attempts to strengthen competitiveness, on both the political and economic levels, by means of austerity programmes all that we have learned from history? This would be a very poor lesson indeed, though it is still too early in the day to draw such depressing conclusions. The restructuring process is not yet over. One of the salient lessons of history is that this approach to the economic situation after 1929 ended in a disastrous failure and opened the door to even worse calamities.

II. The Relationship between Politics and Economics

Deeply ingrained in our perception of that era, which richly deserves its label of the 'interwar years', is the notion that 1924 to 1929 was a period of 'relative stability'. Yet neither surveys, like the early and now classic study of Edward H. Carr, *The Twenty Years Crisis 1919–1939* (London, 1939),[9] nor the rising tide of monographs are able to explain how an era of 'relative stability' could have spawned a profound political and economic crisis that not only scotched all attempts at reconstruction but totally demolished the 'postwar order' that had been so carefully cobbled together. This study investigates why reconstruction and col-

---

9. In this book the interwar era serves primarily as a paradigm for the purpose of developing a theory of international relations. The best, still unsurpassed presentation of the entire era can be found in P. Renouvin, *Les crises du XXe siècle*, vol. 1: *De 1914 à 1929* (Paris, 1957) and vol. 2: *De 1929 à 1945* (Paris, 1958).

lapse were so proximate, indeed intertwined. What factors were responsible? Our central thesis is that the structural flaws inherent in the world economy and political system in consequence of the Great War were in fact growing more serious beneath the surface of seeming reassurance throughout the era of 'relative stability'. This is the major reason why the global economic crisis touched off by the stock-market crash of 1929 proved so utterly devastating.

Conclusions such as these are only possible when one has the courage to undertake an analysis of the underlying structures. This alone provides sufficient perspective, though contemporary political history has largely forsworn such broadly based approaches in favour of the 'insipid positivism',[10] about which it even boasts. But the challenge remains of elucidating the developments that shaped an era beneath its relatively placid exterior. No elaborate or well-polished theories are necessary; all that is required is an appreciation of structures and their composition.

A central feature of the 'interwar period' was the extensive intermingling of politics and economics – a fact which contemporaries did not fail to notice with some amazement. Developed societies have always experienced this to some degree of course, but it now grew to previously unimagined proportions. In contrast to the period before the First World War, the realms of politics (the state) and economics no longer seemed in any way autonomous from one another. The economy was coloured by politics, and politics, both domestic and international, were coloured by economics to an extent never previously experienced. Everyone knew that a healthy economy was essential to political stability; but it was also becoming increasingly apparent that political decisions were increasingly influenced by economic and especially monetary conditions.[11] As Walter Rathenau, the great German indus-

10. Cf. the (by no means new) criticism of F. Furet, the leading historian of the French Revolution and president of the celebrated *Ecole des Hautes Etudes en Sciences Sociales*: 'To a certain extent historians are inclined to a somewhat insipid positivism, the cult of bare facts, sources and archives. This is important, but not sufficient. The task remains of organising the facts, interpreting them, and this is often the weakness of contemporary historiography.' *Le Monde*, 14 May 1982, p. 24.

11. C.S. Maier, in H. Mommsen et al. (eds), *Industrielles System und politische Entwicklung in der Weimarer Republik* (Düsseldorf, 1974), p. 932. For the relationship between politics and economics see as well W. Fischer, *Weltwirtschaftliche Rahmenbedingungen für die ökonomische und politische Entwicklung Europas 1919–1939* (Wiesbaden, 1980), pp. 5–12. Fischer quite rightly points out the remarkable propensity of political historians to emphasise the constraints imposed by economic circumstance while economic historians emphasise the political constraints, both domestic and international, that 'prevented politicians from implementing the appropriate economic policies'. Fischer escapes this problem by claiming that far-reaching theories are impossible in the social sciences and consciously confining himself to 'description'.

trialist and foreign minister, commented: 'Our fate is economics!'
Where could economics be said to end and politics to begin in regard
to the great questions of the day: currencies, restructuring, economic
growth and adjustment, international economic relations, reparations,
and inter-Allied debt? The highest priority after the war had to be
accorded to economic reconstruction as a result of the dislocation
suffered by both domestic economies and international trade – a situation which was only aggravated by the terms of the peace treaties, as
John Maynard Keynes never tired of pointing out.[12] In consequence,
the state and the economy became far more dependent on one another
than ever before. The controversy over whether politics or economics
was most important is therefore not very appropriate in regard to the
1920s. It only becomes crucial in the 1930s when the tendency to politicise
economics reached full force in response to the Great Depression.[13]

The postwar intermingling of politics and economics needs to be fully
analysed because it provides so many insights into the social structure of
various nations, the distribution of political power and above all the way
in which capitalist reproduction was carried out. The turning point in
this relationship occurred during the First World War. The war economy greatly enhanced the power of the state relative to the other
elements in society everywhere in the world, but first and foremost in
the warring nations. At the same time, big business succeeded in
harnessing the state to its ends.[14] After 1919, large industrial interests in
all the capitalist countries succeeding in shaking off many of the state
controls placed on them during the war[15] and in reinforcing their

---

12. In his celebrated work, *The Economic Consequences of Peace* (London, 1920).
13. Cf. the well-known controversy about the nature of fascism provoked by T. Mason,
'Der Primat der Politik,' *Das Argument*, Heft 6 (1966) and Heft 3 (1968). Much food for
thought can be found in E. Stanley, *World Economy in Transition. Technology vs.
Politics. Laissez-Faire vs. Planning. Power vs. Welfare* (NY, 1939; 1971²).
14. No systematic comparative study yet exists. Bits and pieces in: A. Delemer, *Le bilan
de l'étatisme* (Paris, 1922); P. Renouvin, *Les formes du gouvernement de guerre* (Paris,
1925); A. Schröter, *Krieg, Staat, Monopol 1914–1918. Die Zusammenhänge von im-
perialistischer Kriegswirtschaft, Militarisierung der Volkswirtschaft und staatsmonopolis-
tischem Kapitalismus in Deutschland während des Ersten Weltkrieges* (Berlin, 1965); K.
Gossweiler, *Grossbanken, Industriemonopole, Staat. Ökonomie und Politik des staats-
monopolistischen Kapitalismus in Deutschland* (Berlin, 1971); G. Hardach, *Der Erste
Weltkrieg 1914–1918* (Munich, 1973), esp. Chapter 4; *idem*, 'Französische Rüstungs-
politik 1914–1918' in H.A. Winkler (ed.), *Organisierter Kapitalismus. Voraussetzungen
und Anfänge* (Göttingen, 1973); D.M. Kennedy, *Over Here. The First World War and
American Society* (NY, 1980); J. Kocka, *Klassengesellschaft im Krieg. Deutsche Sozialgeschichte 1914–1918* (Göttingen, 1978²); G. Feldman, *Army, Industry and Labour in
Germany, 1914–1918* (Princeton, 1966).
15. See R.H. Tawney, 'The Abolition of Economic Controls, 1918–1921' in *EHR* 13
(1943).

political influence after a period of struggle with revolutionary workers. None the less, the state retained much more economic clout than it had possessed prior to the war.

This was true above all for monetary policy. The decline in the value of money drove home to every citizen, in graphic and often painful fashion, the extent of the damage caused by the war. This was the most obvious evidence that the old, prewar world had indeed disintegrated. The era before 1914 took on a new aura as a 'golden age' of stability and middle-class prosperity, while volatile currencies came to symbolise the fallen state of postwar society. Entire classes were robbed of their wealth and suffered even greater hardship in return for all the sacrifices they had made on behalf of their country. As a result, the legitimacy of the state and of traditional political elites was called into question. These elites, in return, believed that this was where stabilisation had to begin, which explains why monetary policy assumed such all-encompassing significance in the 1920s. Consequently, our analysis shall begin with it (Chapter 2, I).

The postwar economic situation was very confused and uneven. In the United States, the most highly developed and powerful capitalist country, the *laissez-faire* economy reasserted itself under the aegis of Republican administrations; in Europe however, there was a continuing tendency to replace 'the invisible hand of the market with the visible hand of the state'.[16] The trend to the welfare state deepened, though to differing extents in individual countries. Working-class uprisings compelled governments on all sides to make social concessions in order to offset some of the burdens of the war and reconstruction. These developments widened the rift between the European and American economies and after the mid-1920s fuelled ever more vehement complaints on the part of European industrialists about wage rates, benefits and public deficits which, in their view, were hobbling productivity. As a result, the pressure on the interventionist state began to mount, especially in the years of 'relative stability'.

At the same time, the liberal, parliamentary states in Europe were confronted with a completely new challenge stemming from a fierce struggle over the distribution of income – a challenge which the defeated countries in particular proved less able to meet than the victorious powers.[17] In many cases, the 'social block in power' (Poulantzas) was

16. G. Arrighi, 'Der Klassenkampf in Westeuropa im 20. Jahrhundert' in F. Fröbel et al. (eds), *Krisen in der kapitalistischen Weltökonomie* (Reinbek, 1981), p. 63.
17. This was already apparent in a book that is still worth reading: E. Trendelenburg, *Amerika und Europa in der Weltwirtschaftspolitik des Zeitabschnitts der Wirtschaftskonferenzen*, Part 1: *Bis zum Dawes-Plan 1924* (Berlin, 1943), pp. 42–7. Trendelenburg was

not strong enough to withstand the politicisation of the distribution of income, which was carried out in Germany, for instance, through state intervention in wage disputes. In this way, the certain autonomy which the state requires *vis-à-vis* political pressure groups was greatly diminished. This went so far in some cases that the state was unable to carry out its crucial function of maintaining a minimal social balance, opening the door to authoritarian alternatives in many countries, including Germany. Why Great Britain or France were not pushed down this path remains one of the key questions of contemporary history, which this study hopes to elucidate (Chapter 3, II).

The troubling relationship between politics and economics, so characteristic of the 1920s and a primary source of domestic and international instability, reached much further. The collapse of the relatively liberal world economy as a result of the Great War compelled all countries to adopt firm, even nationalistic economic, trade and monetary policies in the hope of sustaining their own economy as the international division of labour shifted and competition heated up on stagnating world markets. This task too could not be left to 'market forces'. Confidence was rapidly waning on all sides, even among industrialists, in the resilience of national economies and in their ability to survive. A return to 'neo-mercantilism' therefore became inevitable.

But what was the state to do? The antagonism had deepened between those sectors of the various national economies that depended on the domestic market and those that were oriented toward exports. What has been called (with some exaggeration) the 'rationalisation boom'[18] of the 1920s encouraged the spread of monopolies, particularly in the areas of raw materials, heavy industry and the chemical industry. These monopolies in turn sought to reduce competition by concluding international, state-sanctioned agreements known as 'ententes'.[19] The traditional export-oriented industries, some of which still faced stiff competition on world markets, were handicapped by high tariff policies. At the same time,

---

a secretary of state in the imperial ministry of economics and headed the ministry for a time under Brüning. K. Borchardt claims ('Die deutsche Katastrophe. Wirtschaftshistorische Anmerkungen zum 30. Januar 1933', *FAZ*, 29 Jan. 1983, p. 13) that the Weimar Republic would have been 'relieved' of many of its problems if it had allowed the market to solve them, but this is misguided. International economic circumstances rendered such an approach impossible, not to mention the fact that economic leaders themselves were continually calling for state action. In addition, a strong distinction between society and the state would have been necessary, though this would not have helped in any case as is demonstrated by the presidential cabinets after 1930.

18. Cf. A. Sohn-Rethel, 'Ökonomie und Klassenstruktur des deutschen Faschismus', J. Agnoli et al. (eds) (Frankfurt, 1973), p. 45f.

19. Cf. E. Minost, *Aux confines de la politique et de l'économie internationales. Les coopérations interétatiques* (Paris, 1929).

they lacked the necessary political clout to counteract older domestic industries which were already in decline and therefore clamouring all the more vehemently for state protection. These trends varied somewhat from country to country but were present to some degree virtually everywhere. In all the European countries, economic concentration and the formation of strong cartels in important industrial sectors facilitated the translation of economic interests into political action.

This tendency increasingly drove the state onto the defensive, where it could no longer play the role of a more or less impartial referee between antagonistic interest groups. As will later be shown in greater detail, the balance of social forces had shifted in favour of the upper middle class as a result of currency stabilisation, global deflationary policies, and last but not least the decline of the labour movement. As Charles S. Maier has commented, the second half of the 1920s proved to be crucial years in the conservative transformation of society.[20] And conservative forces understood reconstruction only in the narrowest sense of the term: it was the past they attempted to rebuild, even though circumstances had changed radically after the war.

Many contemporary academics and others sought to analyse the new relationship between politics and economics. However, their conclusions remained unsatisfactory, as so often is the case, because they generalised the experience of a single country or because they were one-sided or formulated their conclusions primarily as a stimulus to action, as a weapon in the social struggle. This was true of Lenin for instance when he described 'state monopoly capitalism', or of the Social Democrat R. Hilferding when he spoke of 'organised capitalism'. Significantly, both terms emerged almost simultaneously during the Great War. So much has already been written about their analytical value that very few additional comments are needed here.[21] The great virtue of these writers no doubt is that they saw the changes in the production system, in relations between the classes and in the role of the state as an interrelated whole. The concepts of 'state monopoly capitalism' and 'organised capitalism' were predicated quite correctly on the conviction that liberal, competitive capitalism had either been supplanted (Lenin)

20. Cf. the pioneering work of C.S. Maier, *Recasting Bourgeois Europe. Stabilization in France, Germany and Italy in the Decade after World War I* (Princeton, 1975), esp. the introduction, 'From Bourgeois to Corporate Europe'.
21. See above all H.A. Winkler (ed.), *Organisierter Kapitalismus*; H. Staudinger, 'Die Änderungen in der Führerstellung und der Struktur des organisierten Kapitalismus' in C. Böhret and D. Grosser (eds), *Interdependenzen von Politik und Wirtschaft. Beiträge zur politischen Wirtschaftslehre*, Festschrift for G. von Eynern (Berlin, 1967); E.W. Hawley, 'New Deal und "Organisierter Kapitalismus" in internationaler Sicht' in H.A. Winkler (ed.), *Die grosse Krise in Amerika* (Göttingen, 1973).

or had undergone a far-reaching transformation (Hilferding) as a result of the increasing concentration of economic power.[22]

However, both Lenin and Hilferding were less interested in pure theory than in its application to the political fray. For this reason, their arguments were too linear and simplistic from an academic point of view.[23] Neither of them took time to deal with national distinctions and peculiarities or to assess fully the influence of the international situation. Both subscribed to a rough-hewn economism. And both drew very different conclusions from their theoretical observations, depending on the political strategies they wished to pursue.

According to Lenin, the interpenetration of industrial monopolies and the state aggravated the inherent contradictions in capitalism and hastened its collapse. As a result, the development of a revolutionary strategy for the working class became all the more imperative.

Hilferding, on the other hand, understood 'organised capitalism' as the mounting tendency for financial capitalists to work hand in hand with the state in order to alleviate the anarchy of the productive system, thereby diminishing the internal contradictions within capitalism and enhancing its chances of survival. In Hilferding's view, the susceptibility of capitalist economies to slumps and depressions would be mitigated by the concentration of capital and a willingness to plan and lead the economy. As a result, the confrontation between labour and capital could only be curtailed by democratising the economy through a reformist strategy. Here too the fatal flaw is evident: Hilferding's concept of 'organised capitalism' vastly underestimated the likelihood and scope of an economic crisis. This explains the ideological and political helplessness of the German Social Democrats and the trade unions before and, above all, after the onset of the Great Depression.[24] Hilferding's analysis overlooked the serious structural problems inherent in capitalist production in the 1920s on both the domestic and international levels. As H.A. Winkler remarked, this analysis suffered from 'excessive harmonisation'.[25]

German academics, particularly Jürgen Kocka,[26] sought to divest the term 'organised capitalism' of its historic meaning in order to invest it

---

22. H.A. Winkler in H. Mommsen et al. (eds), *Industrielles System*, p. 961.
23. Cf. the neo-Marxist approaches evincing further development and differentiation, esp. N. Poulantzas, *Klassen im Kapitalismus heute* (Berlin, 1975).
24. Cf. M. Held, *Sozialdemokratie und Keynesianismus. Von der Weltwirtschaftskrise bis zum Godesberger Programm* (Frankfurt, 1982), pp. 107ff.
25. Winkler, in Winkler (ed.), *Organisierter Kapitalismus*, p. 15.
26. J. Kocka in ibid., pp. 19–35; and in Mommsen et al. (eds), *Industrielles System*, p. 958f. There is good reason, therefore, why the term 'organized capitalism' has not made much headway in historical writing in either English or French.

with a new, more accurate content that could be used to describe the changing nature of relations between the society and the state. This led, as was quite correctly pointed out,[27] to an overloading of the term. However, the crucial and finally fatal objection was that the term 'organised capitalism' had no real meaning prior to the 'Keynesian revolution' because capitalism had been organising itself ever since the demise of the Manchester School. The term is even less useful for describing the post-Keynesian period, which in any case hardly affected the 1920s.[28]

Charles S. Maier has suggested the term 'corporative pluralism' to describe the evolving relations between politics and economics, society and the state, which became apparent during the 1920s, especially during the so-called 'stabilisation phase'.[29] He too, like Lenin and Hilferding, sees a transformation of traditional liberal, democratic, competitive capitalism, though in the direction of a new kind of crisis management epitomised by a joint attempt on the part of the state, industry and the labour unions to restructure the capitalist economy. Each of these three parties carried out certain tasks, and the entire attempt was predicated, as Maier points out, on a vision of class collaboration in the public interest. The result was a blurring of the demarcation line between public and private interests, which in turn eroded the authority of parliaments and political parties as the embodiment of the public will and brought about a decline in the representative system. As the labour movement lost ground, the state and industrial interests grew increasingly interconnected.

According to Maier, 'corporative pluralism' was the institutional expression of the 'stabilisation offensive' conducted by the conservative bourgeoisie in Europe in the second half of the 1920s. It was apparent everywhere, though to varying degrees: it was strongest in Germany,

27. G.D. Feldman in Winkler (ed.), *Organisierter Kapitalismus*, pp. 150–71, esp. p. 166.
28. On the widespread acceptance of Keynesianism see, besides M. Held: W. Grotkopp, *Die Grosse Krise. Lehren aus der Überwindung der Weltwirtschaftskrise* (Düsseldorf, 1953); G. Kroll, *Von der Weltwirtschaftskrise zur Staatskonjunktur* (Berlin, 1958); G. Garvey, 'Keynes and the Economic Activists of Pre-Hitler Germany,' in G. Bombach et al. (eds), *Der Keynesianismus*, vol. II (Berlin, 1976); R. Campbell, 'The Keynesian Revolution 1920–1970' in C.M. Cipolla (ed.), *The Fontana Economic History of Europe*, vol. 5/1 (London, 1976).
29. C.S. Maier, *Recasting Bourgeois Europe*, passim; idem, 'Between Taylorism and Technocracy: European Ideologies and the Vision of Industrial Productivity in the 1920s', *JCH* 5 (1970/2), pp. 27–61; idem, 'Strukturen kapitalistischer Stabilität in den zwanziger Jahren. Errungenschaften und Defekte' [The Structures of Capitalist Stability in the 1920s. Achievements and Defects] in H.A. Winkler (ed.), *Organisierter Kapitalismus*; idem in H. Mommsen et al. (eds), *Industrielles System*, pp. 950–84 (with discussion).

weakest in France, and in Italy immediately assumed the guise of Fascism.[30] At bottom, 'corporative pluralism' denotes a combination of technocratic planning and 'social partnership' in an attempt to reinforce social control at a time of saturated markets and deflationary pressure on wages. Production had to be curtailed because opportunities to compete on export markets were very limited, not least because of currency stabilisation. Many European manufacturers were unable to adopt the Ford model of capitalist production being developed in the United States, and to them 'corporative pluralism' represented a safe haven.[31] If any restructuring was to occur at all, it would always be on the backs of the workers. To this extent, 'corporative pluralism' represented an authoritarian attempt to consolidate political power. It emerged in Europe, according to Maier, as soon as the masses realised that no one could escape the deflationary pressures which were emanating from the international economy and political system and to which national governments were rapidly succumbing.

Maier's views deserve more attention as well in regard to the present debate about 'neo-corporatism'.[32] The similarities in the two situations are striking, and astute observers during the 1920s came to comparable conclusions. Moritz J. Bonn for instance described the Germany of the day as a 'land of capitalist estates'.[33] The concept of 'corporative pluralism' is therefore very close to the mark, though its limitations are also evident. Maier himself is far from exaggerating its theoretical importance and with fetching modesty ascribes it only illustrative value.[34] 'Corporative pluralism' has the advantage of focusing attention

---

30. Since Italy does not play a central role in our analysis, a pioneering work of T. Rafalski should be pointed out in addition: *Italienischer Faschismus in der Weltwirtschaft. Zur Interdependenz von innerer und äusserer Politik, 1925 und 1935* (Opladen, 1984). The work resulted from the research project mentioned in the Foreword.

31. This did not obviate a violent debate everywhere in Europe on 'Americanism', 'Fordism', 'rationalisation', 'scientific management', 'Bedaux system', etc. The debate had its origins not least of all in the discovery by business interests that they could use it as a weapon against the labour movement, which was divided in its reaction to these phenomena. Cf. Maier, *Taylorism*, pp. 28, 35. From the plethora of contemporary literature on the reception of 'Fordism' in Germany, see F. v. Gottl-Ottlilienfeld, *Fordism? Von F.W. Taylor zu H. Ford* (Jena, 1925²).

32. For the discussion of 'neo-corporatism' see: U. von Alemann (ed.), *Neokorporatismus* (Frankfurt, 1981); K. von Beyme, 'Der Neo-Korporatismus und die Politik des begrenzten Pluralismus in der Bundesrepublik' in J. Habermas (ed.), *Stichworte zur 'Geistigen Situation der Zeit'* (Frankfurt, 1979), vol. 1.

33. M.J. Bonn, *Das Schicksal des deutschen Kapitalismus* (Berlin, 1930); D. Stegmann, 'Die Silverberg-Kontroverse 1926, Unternehmerpolitik zwischen Reform und Restauration' in H.-U. Wehler (ed.), *Sozialgeschichte heute. Festschrift für H. Rosenberg* (Göttingen, 1974), p. 595.

34. Maier in Mommsen et al. (eds), *Industrielles System*, p. 960.

on *strategies for solving conflict* rather than on the nature of the conflicts, their origins and development. But too little is said about the nature of the main protagonists and about the frictions within classes and social groups, especially the middle class.[35] The strength of this approach is largely a function, however, of its limitations.

The theories and approaches above, as well as other, similar attempts,[36] share an important characteristic regardless of their value in other respects. They all point to two structural features of the so-called 'stabilisation phase': the greatly weakened condition of European capitalism and the attendant vulnerability of the democratic, parliamentary order. As a result, antidemocratic movements arose on all sides, though with varying success in different countries. Eugen Varga, the foremost economic theorist of the Third International, spoke about the 'declining, collapsing capitalist order'[37] of the 1920s in an attempt to justify the confrontational strategy of the Communist Party, but this characterisation vastly overshoots the mark. The weakness of European capitalism was temporary, not fundamental. It resulted, as M. Dobb has pointed out,[38] from rigidities in the national economies. This structural

35. As Maier himself admits for instance, the extremely thorny question of the extent to which the currency would be revalued as part of stabilisation caused a great deal of conflict within the bourgeois parties.

36. E.g. 'politischer Kapitalismus' (Kolko); 'kollektiver Kapitalismus' (Feldman); 'corporate capitalism' (Dobb); 'geplantes oder administriertes kapitalistisches System' (Staudinger); 'Managed Economy' (Aldcroft). A good overview can be found in B. Ward, 'National Economic Planning and Policies in Twentieth Century Europe 1920–1970' in C.M. Cipolla (ed.), *The Fontana Economic History of Europe*, vol. 5/1 as well as the works of F. Blaich, ' "Garantierter Kapitalismus". Subventionspolitik und Wirtschaftsordnung in Deutschland zwischen 1925 und 1932' ['Guaranteed Capitalism'. Subsidies and the Economic Order in Germany between 1925 and 1932], *Zeitschrift für Unternehmensgeschichte* 22 (1971); idem, ' "Kapitalistische Planwirtschaft". Ein ordnungspolitischer Versuch zur Überwindung der Weltwirtschaftskrise' [' "The Planned Capitalist Economy". An Attempt at Restructuring in order to Overcome the Great Depression'] in *Schmollers Jahrbruch* 90 (1970).

37. E. Varga, *Aufstieg und Niedergang des Kapitalismus* (Hamburg, 1924); idem, 'Die Krise des Kapitalismus und ihre politischen Folgen', E. Altvater (ed.) (Frankfurt, 1969); A.H. Hansen, *Full Recovery or Stagnation?* (London, 1938). For the theory that economic stagnation was caused by a lack of technical innovation see D.S. Landes, *Der entfesselte Prometheus. Technischer Wandel und industrielle Entwicklung in Westeuropa von 1750 bis zur Gegenwart* [Prometheus Unbound. Technical Change and the Industrial Revolution of Western Europe from 1750 to the Present] (Cologne, 1973), especially Chapter 6. A similar approach in G. Mensch, *Das technologische Patt. Innovationen überwinden die Depression* [Technological Stalemate. Innovations overcome the Depression] (Frankfurt/M, 1975). For a critique of these views: W. Fischer, *Weltwirtschaftliche Rahmenbedingungen*, pp. 22ff. The best introduction based on sound empirical fact can be found in I. Svennilson, *Growth and Stagnation in the European Economy* (Geneva, 1954).

38. M. Dobb, *Studies in the Development of Capitalism* (London, 1946), pp. 320ff.

defect was social in origin and found expression in a preference for restricting production rather than reducing costs and prices. So long as stable profit margins were maintained through inelastic prices, the salient problem of these years could not be solved, namely overcapacity and the related curse of 'technological unemployment'. Neo-mercantilist policies and the extreme importance attached to monetary stability compelled politicians and manufacturers alike to be very cautious in their approach, that is, to be conservative. The price of this approach was high as entire branches of the economy 'ossified' in Dobb's colourful phrase.

The economies of the capitalist countries were therefore very vulnerable, both internally and externally. Contrary to what the term 'corporative pluralism' might lead one to believe, politicians and economic leaders, though interdependent, ended up doing everything they could to weaken one another. Manufacturers called upon the state for help; but at the same time they refused to allow it to carry out a somewhat fairer distribution of income, a measure which was all the more imperative in that the living standards of many workers as well as middle-class and lower middle-class people were declining in the wake of the conservative reorganisation. Finally, politicians and economic leaders together were unable to generate a rate of growth sufficient to maintain the stability of society and the state in a capitalist order. This eventually lead, with the assistance of the Great Depression, to either social disintegration, as in Germany, or to stagnation, as in France and Great Britain.[39]

III. The Relationship between the World Economic System and International Politics

The deficiencies in the research and in theoretical analysis are most evident when it comes to elucidating the relationship between the global economic system and international politics. It is fashionable of course to refer to the rising 'interconnectedness' of domestic and foreign policy and of developed and underdeveloped nations, or to the mounting 'interdependence' of the industrial countries, or indeed, to the emergence of 'one world'. Even the phrase 'international domestic policy' is occasionally heard. However, there is no satisfactory theoretical explanation of these widely recognised phenomena. Such an undertaking may be destined to fail from the outset because it overtaxes

---

39. For theories about the 'stagnant society' in France, see S. Hoffmann et al., *A la recherche de la France* (Paris, 1963), p. 15f.; for Great Britain see M. Abrams, *The Condition of the British People 1911–1945* (London, 1945).

any individual. But when scholars confine themselves to facets of the problem, they greatly limit the import of their conclusions, as evidenced for instance by the classic theory of imperialism and its modern successors.[40] Researchers first limited their studies either to the motives of the imperialist nations or to the impact on the conquered countries, and it is only recently that the relationship between the two has been evaluated. This requires, to be sure, a comprehensive view of the entire system. Even then, light is only cast on a small if important part of what is tending to become a 'global society'.

The first step towards imparting a fresh impulse to our theoretical understanding must consist in some kind of rapprochement between the widely differing interests and approaches of economic history and political history. Hyperspecialisation and the resulting impermeability of the various disciplines is an enormous impediment to the advancement of knowledge. Reality cannot be broken into discrete pieces and compartmentalised under various headings.[41] To the political historian, international politics is the sum total of all the conflict and compromise perpetrated by the major players on the world stage, the nation states. They have a more or less clearly defined 'national interest' which their governments defend to the extent which their means will permit. As a result, political historians concentrate on inter-governmental relations and assume that the 'constraints of the international system' limit each government's margin for manoeuvre, regardless of how this is perceived by the politicians involved. Whether explicitly or not, a belief in *Realpolitik* underlies this approach, which in practice accords supreme importance to geostrategic planning.

As economists and economic historians liberate themselves from the strait-jacket of neo-classical theories, they inquire ever more persistently into the position of various national economies in the international division of labour, i.e. in the structure of the world economy, and into what that connotes for their further development.[42] It soon becomes

40. Cf. R. Owen and B. Sutcliffe (eds), *Studies in the Theory of Imperialism* (London, 1972).
41. See in this regard S. Strange, 'International Economic Relations: The Need for an Interdisciplinary Approach' in R. Morgan (ed.), *The Study of International Affairs* (London, 1972); idem, 'International Monetary Relations' in A. Shonfield (ed.), *International Economic Relations of the Western World 1959–1971* (London, 1976), pp. 19ff. For an early attempt to combine history and economics see C. Brinkmann, 'Weltpolitik und Weltwirtschaft im 19. Jahrhundert', *Weltwirtschaftsarchiv* 16 (1920–1), pp. 186–201.
42. Cf. G. Simonis, 'Der Staat im Entwicklungsprozess peripherer Gesellschaften. Die Schwellenländer im internationalen System' [The Role of the State in the Development of Peripheral Societies. The Developing Countries in the International System], PhD thesis, Konstanz, 1981; W. Hein, 'Kapitalakkumulation im Weltmassstab. Nationalstaat und nationale Entwicklung: Das Beispiel des Öllandes Venezuela' [Capital Accumula-

16

apparent that accumulation of the factors of production and hence a nation's level of economic development depends on both domestic and international circumstances and that these circumstances influence one another. This may sound very abstruse but is really rather simple. The position which a national economy is able to occupy in the international division of labour depends on its ability to manufacture products which are in demand on world markets. This ability is developed through a continuous economic struggle on two fronts: the struggle on the domestic market between sectors, branches and individual firms with greater or lesser productivity and the struggle on world markets with other national economies. The competition in exports becomes increasingly important to national economies as their share of world markets increases. In this way the various national economies determine the international division of labour and attempt to turn it to advantage in order to protect their own industries (perhaps, if they are very successful, by prescribing production and consumption standards). At the same time, the extent to which the national economy is integrated into the world economy as a whole has a crucial impact on the relative strength of various domestic political forces.[43]

Consideration of these relationships can greatly benefit both theoretical understanding and practical analysis. First, it is possible to define more clearly the role of the state. In so doing, all the talk of 'international domestic policy' proves to be nonsense. One of the most important functions of the state is to mediate between two usually contradictory requirements: the need to strengthen the position of one's own economy in the international division of labour and the need to mitigate the negative effects which an opening to world markets inevitably has on a nation's internal stability. Only the state is in a position to accomplish this task, which is an important source of its autonomy. A good part of its legitimacy in the eyes of its own people depends on its success (that is, the success of the forces which support it) in accomplishing this task. So far as academic analysis is concerned, this highlights a realm which political historians have virtually ignored and the domestic importance of which economic historians have largely underestimated: economic foreign policy. It is crucial to the relationship between the nation state and the world economy and is an important link between domestic policy and foreign policy. It plays an essential

---

tion on a World Scale. The State and National Development: the Example of the Oil-Exporting Country of Venezuela], PhD thesis, Konstanz, manuscript.
43. Unfortunately only a formal model of the domestic effects of an 'open economy' can be found in D. Cameron, 'The Expansion of the Public Economy: A Comparative Analysis', *APSR* (1978), p. 1256.

role in struggles for political power on both the domestic and international levels for the reason that power depends to a large extent on which 'share of the production for the world market each nation state manages to bring under its control'.[44]

This is the prime reason why the following study focuses on international economic policy. It affords a highly informative opportunity to draw a *causal* link between the evolution of the global system and forms of domestic political rule and in this way to determine the key structural features of a given era. After the First World War, 'politics' and 'economics' melded, not only domestically but also on an international level. This could not have been otherwise at a time when control over the restructuring of the world economy had become the central prize in the struggle for political power. It is therefore not surprising that international relations became largely economic in nature. This holds true above all for the world's greatest economic power, the United States. It is not by chance that the phrase, 'economic diplomacy', figures so prominently in the titles of many recent as well as coeval studies of the American role in the world economy and political system.[45] There is more to this of course than that politics and economics simply began to serve one another[46] – a concept which in the end implies a considerable degree of autonomy in both realms.

No illusions should be harboured about the chances for success of this approach. The daunting magnitude of the problems which arise can be demonstrated using the example of monetary policy, which became extremely important both for individual nations and for the reconstruction of the international economy. Economists and economic historians, whether Marxist or not, espouse very different and indeed contrasting views of such crucial questions as the social, economic and political impact of currency revaluations. Aldcroft goes even further when he claims that in spite of the enormous literature published in the 1920s on monetary questions 'none of the fundamental problems was really satisfactorily explained'.[47] In circumstances such as these, what are the chances for success of those historians and political scientists who wish

---

44. W. Hein, 'Kapitalakkumulation in Weltmassstab . . .', p. 85.
45. In addition to the classic works of H. Feis, see *inter alia* M. Trachtenberg, *Reparation in World Politics. France and European Economic Diplomacy, 1916–23* (NY, 1980); F.C. Adams, *Economic Diplomacy: The Export–Import Bank and American Foreign Policy, 1934–39* (Columbia, 1976); M.E. Falkus, 'U.S. Economic Policy and the "Dollar Gap" of the 1920s', *EHR* (1971); above all, C.P. Parrinni, *Heir to Empire. United States Economic Diplomacy, 1916–23* (Pittsburgh, 1969).
46. According to S.A. Schuker, *The End of French Predominance in Europe. The Financial Crisis of 1924 and the Adoption of the Dawes Plan* (Chapel Hill, NC, 1978[2]), p. 35.
47. D.H. Aldcroft, 'Britische Währungspolitik', p. 93.

to understand a nation's monetary policy in its full context of the domestic situation and global economic and political circumstances? But not to despair. The academic debate has received fresh impulses, this time from I. Wallerstein, who offers an undogmatic, neo-Marxist approach which seems to surmount many of the previous theoretical difficulties.[48] Wallerstein attempts to subsume the realms of international politics and economics in his concept of the 'world system', which evolved during 'the "long" sixteenth century' (1450–1640). Unlike previous human societies, the new world system was strongly interdependent, that is, the evolution of each of its components was heavily influenced by the evolution of all others. This interdependence has only intensified with time. The originality of Wallerstein's concept lies in the claim that the world system was held together by the triumphant, expansionist 'capitalist world economy', that is to say, by the fact that accumulation now took place, and by its very nature had to take place, on a worldwide level.[49] This resulted in the emergence and progressive evolution of an international division of labour, which created within the world system a hierarchical order of 'core-states', 'semiperipheries', and 'peripheries'. These were all integrated into a single world economy, directed at first from Europe. This then was the 'arena' in which all social activity and change took place. The capitalist world economy developed its own natural history of cyclical periods of expansion and contraction during which the relative strength of the core-states evolved, while at the same time the balance between the more dominant and dependent states in the semiperiphery and periphery also changed. Since the capitalist world economy formed the driving force behind the 'global structure', our analysis must focus on it. However, this primary

---

48. I. Wallerstein, *The Modern World-System. Capitalist Agriculture and the Origins of the European World-Economy in the Sixteenth Century* (NY, 1974); idem, *The Modern World-System*, vol. 2: *Mercantilism and the Constitution of the European World-Economy 1600–1750* (NY, 1980); idem, *The Capitalist World Economy* (Cambridge, 1979) (a collection of essays); T.K. Hopkins and I. Wallerstein, 'Grundzüge der Entwicklung des modernen Weltsystems' in D. Senghaas (ed.), *Kapitalistische Weltökonomie. Kontroversen über ihren Ursprung und ihre Entwicklungsdynamik* (Frankfurt, 1979); I. Wallerstein, 'Aufstieg und künftiger Niedergang des kapitalistischen Weltsystems' in ibid. This omnibus volume contains further trenchant contributions by A.G. Frank and H. Elsenhans; for a discussion of Wallerstein's views see J. Blaschke (ed.), *Perspektiven des Weltsystems*.

49. For this Wallerstein relies on the works of S. Amin, *L'accumulation à l'échelle mondiale* (Paris, 1970); A.G. Frank, *L'accumulation mondiale 1500–1800* (Paris, 1977). Cf. as well M. Massarat, *Hauptentwicklungsstadien der Weltwirtschaft* (Lollar, 1976). For a more liberal, neo-classical view see W. Woodruff, *The Emergence of an International Economy, 1700–1914* (London, 1974); A.G. Kenwood and A.L. Lougheed, *The Growth of the International Economy, 1820–1960* (London, 1971).

19

organising force behind the world system was soon confronted by another force: the global system of national states, characterised above all by the struggle of each state to establish its hegemony. An essential ingredient in Wallerstein's concept of a world-system is the contradiction that inevitably exists between a single world economy and a politically decentralised system of states. However, this inherent tension does not threaten the overriding importance of the world economy since each state's political strength is ultimately derived from its place in the international division of labour.

Wallerstein's concept of a world system left a number of questions unresolved[50] and was therefore severely criticised. Stanley Hoffmann denounced it as a 'majestic fiction', at least so far as historians and political scientists are concerned. 'The world economic system is not a prime mover, nor a God-like distributor of roles and divider of labour', according to Hoffmann, 'but the outcome of discrete political decisions made by the separate units'.[51] Again the old dispute resurfaces about the primacy of either politics or economics – though this sort of discussion has little purpose because those who champion politics also absolutise only one aspect of power. None the less, four criticisms of Wallerstein should be mentioned, criticisms which also indicate the direction in which the future discussion should evolve.

First, it cannot be emphasised enough that the capitalist world economy has always represented far more than the sum of the exchanges between individual countries. However, it is not clear how this fact, perceived and described of course by Wallerstein, can be reconciled with the fact that a *single* dominant centre has always emerged which is able to impose an international division of labour serving, first and foremost, its own interests. The struggle of the various national economies to carve out a place for themselves in the centre, 'in the sun', cannot be explained solely by the increasingly global utilisation of capital. This would underestimate a key feature of the capitalist world economy, namely the characteristic dialectic between unification and division which lends it its dynamism. In addition, the evolution of a 'transnational' world economy was, at least in the narrow sense, a long-term process. The trend toward the 'internationalisation of capital' until full global interdependence of production was reached was qualitatively and quantitatively a very slow process which did not reach its climax until after the Second World War at a time when the American

50. Especially the age-old question, which we cannot pursue here, of the point at which the world-economy could be described as 'capitalist'.
51. S. Hoffmann, 'Reflections on the Nation-State in Western Europe Today', *Journal of Common Market Studies*, (Sept.–Dec., 1982), p. 30.

economic model had reached full maturity and was emulated around the world.[52] During the 1920s, this tendency was still in its infancy, as we shall see.

Secondly, there is still a great deal of justified controversy in regard to the relationship between the core-states and the periphery, about the assertion, taken over from the classical theory of imperialism and its modern successors, that capitalist accumulation in the core-states could not have taken place without an enforced surplus flowing in from the periphery. The counter-argument is no less plausible and is supported by better empirical evidence: the most significant stimulus to economic expansion came from the core-states themselves as a result of the social conditions prevailing there and the mass demand, innovations, etc. which they stimulated.[53] This controversy illustrates once again the importance of a thorough analysis of the relationship between the internal social conditions in a nation and its position on world markets.

Thirdly, Wallerstein maintains that the 'world economy' and the 'world system of the states' each have their own inner logic. But their relationship with one another, which in the end forms the basis of the single 'world system', remains largely unexplained. The conviction that the 'world economy' ultimately predominates ('the world economy can survive on its own; the national state cannot'), does not solve the problem. The internal dynamics of a nation are not determined solely by the role it plays on world markets,[54] and even Wallerstein must acknowledge the extreme importance of the state. The state apparatus influences the allotment of economic tasks, he says, by interfering in the natural evolution of the world market. It creates monopolies or dissolves them, subsidises some kinds of production or makes them more expensive, destroys products or erects tariff barriers to protect them. As a result, the power of the state (understood as its ability to impose its will despite domestic and foreign opposition) is a critical variable in the on-going realignment of functions within the world economy.[55] The matter becomes even more complex when we leave the level of the individual state to discuss the 'world system of states', as indeed a

---

52. Cf. C. Deubner et al., *Die Internationalisierung des Kapitals. Neue Theorien in der internationalen Diskussion* (Frankfurt, 1979).

53. Cf. in particular the position of H. Elsenhans in D. Senghaas (ed.), *Kapitalistische Weltökonomie*. One of the sharpest critics of Wallerstein and Frank is R. Brunner, 'The Origins of Capitalist Development: A Critique of Neo-Smithian Marxism', *New Left Review* 104 (1977); for a critical view of this see J.A. Marino, 'Matrices of Materialist Historiography', *JMH* (1979), p. 106.

54. See the criticism of P. Worsley in J. Blaschke (ed.), *Perspektiven des Weltsystems*, pp. 32–79.

55. Hopkins and Wallerstein in D. Senghaas (ed.), *Kapitalistische Weltökonomie*, p. 175.

system'. The relationship between the 'world economy' and the 'world system of states' has been of the utmost significance in contemporary history and, thanks in small part to Wallerstein, has become a salient subject of research and theoretical conjecture.[56]

This leads to a fourth criticism. Is Wallerstein's approach at all able to explain the relationship between economic depressions (the contraction phase), the restructuring of core economies, and expansion with the goal of changing both the international division of labour and the 'world-system of states'. The last three periods of economic crisis (1873–95; 1929–32; after 1974–5) are typified by three entirely different sets of characteristics. The social sciences are confronted by the difficult but not impossible challenge of developing a theory which is able to explain 'only' these three great crises without escaping to such levels of abstraction as to be virtually meaningless.[57] The essence of the discussion is not the extent to which Wallerstein or his critics are 'right'; rather, a discussion is needed in order to broach new paths of research and theoretical conjecture. A theoretical approach like Wallerstein's always runs the risk of toppling into economism or a monistic, highly deterministic theory of history[58] and for this reason alone needs to be continually questioned. Fortunately, Wallerstein himself would be the last to claim such a degree of perfection for his 'world system' that all alternative or contradictory forces are disqualified *a priori*.[59] This is where historiography, theoretical conjecture and practical politics must meet.

Regardless of the state of economic analysis in the 1920s, the clarity with which contemporaries, supported by experts from the League of Nations, recognised the unity of the world economy and the extent of its

56. Interesting attempts in this direction have been undertaken by G. Modelski, 'The Long Cycle of Global Politics and the Nation State', *Comparative Studies in Society and History* (1978) and idem, 'Long Cycles, Kontratieffs, and Alternating Innovations: Implications for U.S. Foreign Policy' in Ch. W. Kegley, Jr. and P. McGowan (eds), *The Political Economy of Foreign Policy Behavior* (Beverly Hills, 1981). In these works, Modelski attempts to develop an alternative to Wallerstein based more on the international system of states. Where the *political* dimension is lacking in Wallerstein's approach is shown by A.R. Zolberg, 'Origins of the Modern World System: A Missing Link', *World Politics* (1981), pp. 253–81. I am indebted to G. Junne (Amsterdam) for this information.

57. The accusation of over simplification immediately launched by historians certainly salves their historical consciences but is of little use. See H. Kellenbenz's discussion of Wallerstein's Modern World-System in *JMH* 48 (1976), pp. 685–92.

58. This criticism of Wallerstein is justified. See Worsley in J. Blaschke (ed.), *Perspektiven des Weltsystems*, pp. 10–12 and 32–79.

59. I. Wallerstein, 'Die Zukunft der Weltökonomie' in J. Blaschke (ed.), *Perspektiven des Weltsystems*, pp. 215–29. He fails to exhaust the complex dialectic relationship in the system between inertia and change, but then who could?

interconnection with politics is nothing short of amazing. The consequences of the war,[60] the postwar slump, monetary stabilisation, reparations, inter-Allied debts and trading relations all seemed to be facets of an overarching problem afflicting the world economy as a whole.[61] For this reason, a world economic conference was convened in 1927 (see Chapter 2, IV). Its president declared in his opening address:

> It is evident that many, perhaps most, of the matters which we shall be emphasizing are more or less European in nature. But we must not forget that the undoubted, and indeed perfectly obvious interdependence of nations signifies that every situation or measure affecting the economic life of one nation or group of nations also has an influence on all other nations, perhaps slight but still appreciable.[62]

However, such statements remain mere abstractions so long as the crucial features of the world-economy at each stage of its development – the dialectic of unification and division, of dominance and dependence – are not clearly described. During the 1920s, the impulse toward unification and domination clearly emanated from the United States which, as contemporaries already realised and modern research is confirming, had become 'the political and economic cornerstone of the international system'.[63] The political elite in the United States was well aware of this development, and the deep recession of 1921 strengthened the consensus in the leadership of both parties that the prosperity of the United

60. According to H.G. Moulton and L. Pasvolsky in *War Debts and World Prosperity* (Washington, 1932), p. 374, the economic losses resulting from the destruction of the international economic system extended to the 'ends of the world'. Cited in D.H. Aldcroft, *From Versailles to Wall Street, 1919–1929* (London, 1977).

61. W. Link, *Die amerikanische Stabilisierungspolitik in Deutschland 1921–32* [American Stabilisation Policies in Germany 1921–32] (Düsseldorf, 1970), p. 576.

62. Cited in E. von Bastineller, 'Die Genfer Weltwirtschaftskonferenz des Jahres 1927. Ihr Verlauf, ihre Ergebnisse,' [The 1927 International Economic Conference in Geneva. Its Proceedings, its Results] PhD thesis, Würzburg, 1927, p. 18f.

63. According to Maier in Mommsen et al. (eds), *Industrielles System*, p. 951. A host of recent monographs underline the pivotal role the United States played in international politics and economics and help lay to rest the old conflict in American historiography between 'traditionalists' and 'revisionists'. See the works of: W. Link, *Die amerikanische Stabilisierungspolitik*; M.P. Leffler, 'Political Isolationism, Economic Expansionism, or Diplomatic Realism: American Policy toward Western Europe, 1921–1933', *Perspectives in American History* 8 (1974); idem, *The Elusive Quest. America's Pursuit of European Stability and French Security 1919–1933* (Chapel Hill, NC, 1979); F.C. Costigliola, 'The Other Side of Isolationism: The Establishment of the First World Bank, 1929–1930', *JAH* (1972); idem, 'The United States and the Reconstruction of Germany in the 1920s', *Business History Review* (1976); idem, 'The Politics of Financial Stabilisation. American Reconstruction Policy in Europe, 1924–1930', PhD thesis, Cornell University, 1971; M.J. Hogan, 'The United States and the Problem of International Economic Control,' *Pacific Historical Review* (1975); and many more.

States in an interdependent world was contingent on the re-establishment of a healthy world economy.[64]

The attempt of some industrialised European countries to begin adopting the Ford economic model marked the first step down the path toward a global society, which was not finally reached until after the Second World War. Under the circumstances prevailing in the 1920s, this emerging trend only aggravated the existing difficulties because, as we shall see in Chapt. 2, II, the United States failed to fulfil the stabilising role which fell to her as the dominant economic power in the world (in the way which Britain had done in the middle of the nineteenth century under the banner of free trade). This lapse strengthened the already strong hand of those forces in Europe which wished to pursue nationalistic foreign and economic foreign policies in order to remedy the deteriorating position of their own nations in the international division of labour. Not surprisingly, those sectors and branches of the economy which had profited most from the war now became the most vocal advocates of protectionism in the profoundly irrational hope of prolonging wartime conditions. The resulting tendency to fence each nation off from its fellows was immeasurably strengthened by the cultural, ideological and ethnic animosities which had taken on truly pathological proportions during the war.

IV. The Connection between the Versailles System and the Washington System

The global system of states that arose after the First World War exhibited a political and strategic structure which was incompatible in many ways with the structure of the world economy. This was one of the major reasons for the mounting instability of the world system. The fundamental incompatibility was especially true of the most important of the peace arrangements, the Versailles System created by the series of treaties signed in the Paris suburb and reinforced by the French system of alliances known as the 'Little Entente'. This system was tailored to meet the security needs of a single nation, France, which thereby assumed primary responsibility for maintaining the status quo and, if possible, consolidating it. France possessed the requisite military muscle but could not develop sufficient economic power, which greatly weakened her position when economic reconstruction became the cornerstone of a stabilised world order. As a result, the United States seized the initiative.

64. F.C. Adams, *Economic Diplomacy*, pp. 3ff., 36. Adams cites the concurring views of Wilson, Hull, Harding, Hughes, Hoover and the influential Senator Lodge.

The Washington System was the product of another series of treaties signed at the Washington Conference of 1921–2 among various combinations of nations, above all, the United States, Great Britain, France, Italy, Japan and China (see Chapt. 4, I). Unlike its Versailles counterpart, the Washington System sought to stabilise south-east Asia by coupling a military and strategic balance with restructured trading relationships in such a way that each reinforced the other. Abundant literature is available on both systems, and it is not the intent of this study to contribute more details. Instead, we shall focus on three problem areas which have not been sufficiently considered in the literature, though they can only be outlined here.

Firstly, if the world system of states in the 1920s is to be adequately understood, the connections between the Washington and Versailles Systems must be more thoroughly explored than has previously been done. Events in south-east Asia, especially those involving the great powers of the United States, Japan and China, were of the utmost concern to the European countries.[65] Great Britain was most directly affected, for obvious reasons, and her concerns have often been studied.[66] The research shows that Britain, in spite of all her differences with the United States, needed and sought American support in Europe in order to foil the French attempt to dominate the continent. London accordingly felt constrained to pursue a policy in the Far East which was at least compatible with American interests, which meant in the end following Washington's lead. This raised the danger of provoking the Japanese. Under pressure from the United States, Britain renounced her 1902 treaty with Japan, in the hope that the Washington System would prove successful. However, by supporting the Washington System, Britain found that she was drawn into the quarrels of the Far East and accordingly found it impossible to devote full attention to Europe. Britain's ties to the Dominions also prevented her from ignoring for a moment the power struggles in south-east Asia, quite apart from her own traditional economic and financial interests which needed to be defended against mounting pressure from Japan and the United States.

Secondly, America's position as 'the political and economic cornerstone of the world system' stemmed largely from the fact that she played a pivotal role in upholding both the Versailles and Washington Systems. One of the most fateful political consequences of the Great Depression

65. Ibid., p. 11f. There are noteworthy attempts here as well to investigate the connections between the Versailles and Washington Systems.
66. Cf. *inter alia* R.A.C. Parker, 'Probleme der britischen Aussenpolitik während der Weltwirtschaftskrise' [Problems of British Foreign Policy during the Great Depression] in J. Becker and K. Hildebrand (eds), *Internationale Beziehungen in der Weltwirtschaftskrise 1929–1933* (Munich, 1980), p. 4.

was that it destroyed the economic basis of this function, thereby greatly hastening the collapse of both systems in the early 1930s. Only this sort of comprehensive view of America's role in the world makes it possible to assess adequately her extraordinary pre-eminence in the 1920s – a pre-eminence which was not only economic but political as well.

The achievement of a dominant position in both systems was an essential prerequisite of Washington's long-term aspiration to expel Great Britain from her traditional position of political and economic domination in order to reinforce America's own claim to hegemony, including such other areas of the world as Latin America.[67] In the 1920s (as well as after the Second World War) the United States counted on special partners to help her assert her leadership of both systems: Germany in Europe and Japan in south-east Asia. The relationship went so far as to include attempts to influence the internal balance of forces in both these countries.

This situation gives rise to another of the central theses of this study: when the United States took over the critical stabilising function in both systems, she became the 'hinge' of the global political system and the only true world power of the 1920s. The crucial remaining questions pertain, not to the sterile debate about 'isolationism' or 'interventionism',[68] but to whether a discrepancy existed between America's claim to pre-eminence and her willingness to assume the resulting responsibilities, and if so, to what extent and for what reasons. In other words, were America's political leaders up to the responsibilities they had assumed? Did they develop any long-term vision beyond immediate economic advantage? Were they at all prepared to do so?

Thirdly, the preceding remarks give rise to an observation which can

67. See M. Beloff, 'The Special Relationship: An Anglo-American Myth' in M. Gilbert (ed.), *A Century of Conflict, 1850–1950. Essays for A.J.P. Taylor* (London, 1966); see as well M.D. Goldberg, 'Anglo-American Economic Competition', *Economics and History* 16 (Lund, Sweden, 1973), pp. 15–36.
68. For the present state of the discussion see from the abundant literature available: R.F. Smith, 'American Foreign Relations, 1920–1942' in B.J. Bernstein (ed.), *Towards a New Past* (NY, 1969); R.A. Divine, *The Illusion of Neutrality* (Chicago, 1962); K. Schwabe, *Der amerikanische Isolationismus im 20. Jahrhundert. Legende und Wirklichkeit* (Wiesbaden 1975); J.H. Wilson, *American Business and Foreign Policy, 1920–1933* (Lexington, 1971); W. Link, *Die amerikanische Stabilisierungspolitik*, p. 36f.; idem, *Die Aussenpolitik der USA, 1919–1933*; W.A. Williams, 'The Legend of Isolationism in the 1920s' in R.M. Abrams and L.W. Levine (eds), *The Shaping of Twentieth-Century America* (Boston, 1965); this is a chapter from the book *The Tragedy of American Diplomacy* (NY, 1959). For sources and recent American literature see: *NPL* 12 (1967); E.C. Bolt Jr., 'Isolation, Expansion and Peace: American Foreign Policy Between the Wars' in G.K. Haines and J.S. Walker (eds), *American Foreign Relations. A Historiographical Review* (London, 1981); cf. above note 63.

scarcely be overlooked, though it has seldom been noted heretofore: the evolution of the Versailles and Washington Systems was strikingly similar. Both systems passed through three phases at almost identical times: a difficult incubation period before 1923–4, during which the United States played a much more active political and strategic role in south-east Asia than in Europe; a so-called 'stabilisation' phase till the onset of the Great Depression; and finally a period of progressive disintegration after 1930–1 during which Washington's special partners became her bitterest enemies. These similarities can only be explained if the world economy, the world system of states and their mutual influences are understood as a dynamic whole.

2
The Weaknesses in the Capitalist World Economy 1924–9

I. The Illusion of the Gold(-Exchange) Standard

From the outset, attempts to reconstruct the world economy were vitiated by two fateful errors in judgement stemming largely from the attitude and interests of the political and economic elites. First, economic reconstruction was understood in the narrowest sense, namely, as restoration of the conditions prevailing before the war. It should seem, in the view of these elites, as if the war had never happened. This ultimate aspiration pervaded all the criteria and goals underlying economic and monetary policy. However, as so often happens, the historic model to be recaptured was greatly idealised and romanticised. Before the war, signs of an impending economic crisis (such as the depression of 1913–14) and shifts in the international division of labour were becoming increasingly apparent and were intensified by the war. The determination of the political and economic elites to restore the world to its former glory blinded them to the changes, substantial in many cases, which were occurring.[1] Not until the end of the 1920s did contemporaries begin to realise that the material devastation of the war, on which they lavished so much attention, was in fact much less significant than the disruption of the world economy.[2]

Secondly, the impact of the war caused national governments to be

1. Contemporary economic historians on the other hand analysed these changes quite extensively. See for instance the standard work of A. Sartorius von Waltershausen, *Die Umgestaltung der Weltwirtschaft. Ein geschichtlicher Rückblick 1914–1932* [The Restructuring of the World Economy. An Historical Review 1914–32] (Jena, 1935).
2. D.H. Aldcroft, *Die Zwanziger Jahre: Von Versailles zur Wall Street 1919–1929* (Munich, 1978), p. 62; a translation of *From Versailles to Wall Street 1919–1929* (London, 1977).

far more concerned about the domestic costs of international stability than they had been prior to 1914 or indeed should have been.[3] In practice, this meant that the attempt to achieve international stability was subordinated to all kinds of national restrictions regarding trade, the movement of capital, labour mobility, etc. This precluded from the outset reconstruction of the world economy as a unified system encompassing all national economies.

Nothing after the First World War can compare with the American efforts after the Second World War to put the world economy back on its feet (which was in her own interest, too, of course) with the help of an international monetary system based on firm exchange rates, convertibility and the dollar as the world's leading currency (Bretton Woods) as well as the promotion of free trade through institutions such as the GATT. The conviction after the First World War that salvation lay in a return to prewar conditions was nowhere so prevalent as in the monetary sphere. All the nations agreed with dogmatic certainty that a return to 'normalcy' could only be achieved by reverting to the gold standard. Unshakable was their faith, based on classic economics, that this was the only way in which domestic and international 'imbalances' and economic aberrations could be corrected thanks to 'automatic' adjustment processes.[4] This attitude is not surprising, given that monetary stability lay at the heart of middle-class economic virtue, then as well as now, and seemed to provide the best guarantee that business interests would be defended. But a price had to be paid for returning to the gold standard, and it was not long in coming. Whenever nations ascribe a high priority to achieving particular monetary goals (and thus satisfying certain financial interests), regardless of other economic and social considerations, the overall cost of the policy is largely ignored, and the danger rises of ultimately provoking instability – the precise opposite of what one was trying to achieve. As a result, the monetary policies of the 1920s were characterised by the same dilemma that bedevilled the entire attempt at economic reconstruction.

In fact, none of the reasons why the gold standard had functioned fairly well before 1914 pertained any longer.[5] Postwar inflation had

3. Ibid., p. 17.
4. See the pioneering work of A.W. Brown Jr., *The International Gold Standard Reinterpreted, 1914–1934*, vol. 2 (NY, 1940).
5. The international gold standard is a currency system characterised by the establishment of fixed rates of exchange, the so-called 'exchange parity', between gold-standard countries (or countries which have legally bound their money supply to gold). The exchange parity corresponds to the gold value of the national currency unit. The most important prerequisite of the gold standard is the free international flow of gold. If a country develops a deficit in its balance of payments, gold is exported in order to restore

caused the price of goods to rise more quickly than that of gold,[6] which was one of the reasons why gold production declined appreciably for a while. In addition, gold reserves were distributed much more unevenly than they had been before 1914. The extent to which circumstances had changed is indicated by the fact that the United States held over half the world's reserves as early as 1920. Above all, the gold standard, as A. Predöhl has pointed out, is a 'fair weather standard'.[7] It assumes free competition in world markets, the unimpeded play of supply and demand and an equilibrium in the balance of payments. Furthermore, it requires central banks to abstain from independent credit policies, since credit must depend exclusively on available gold stocks. Finally, before 1914 no serious discrepancies existed between domestic and international economic imperatives, as they did in the 1920s. This was due to a large extent to the City of London which provided a very flexible and effective world financial centre based on the position of the pound sterling as the world's leading currency.

This role should have been assumed in the 1920s by the United States which had been transformed by the war from a debtor nation into the world's greatest creditor.[8] The United States certainly endeavoured

---

equilibrium. In theory, prices rise in countries which are net recipients of gold and decline in those which are net exporters. This causes the exports of countries that run a deficit to become less expensive and therefore more attractive. Their balance of payments swings into a positive position and gold flows back. In this way, international economic equilibrium is maintained. As a result of the gold standard, world prices tend to converge. This means that national economies are tightly integrated into the international system, leaving little room for national economic policy. The maintenance of equilibrium in the balance of payments becomes the highest goal of national economic policy. This monetary system only functions properly so long as an international financial and banking centre exists to regulate the movements of gold. Before 1914, the City of London fulfilled this task. See in this regard the classic work of unparalleled clarity by W. Bagehot, *Lombard Street* (new edn, London, 1915). The best critique of the gold standard can be found in R. Triffin, *Our International Monetary System: Yesterday, Today and Tomorrow* (NY, 1968).

6. See D. de Laubier, *Les relations financières internationales. Mécanismes, idéologies et rapport de force* (Paris, 1975), p. 79f.

7. A. Predöhl, *Das Ende der Weltwirtschaftskrise. Eine Einführung in die Probleme der Weltwirtschaft* (Reinbek, 1962), pp. 51ff.

8. From the plethora of literature, see for this and what follows the outstanding work by D.H. Aldcroft, *Zwanziger Jahre*, chapters 6 and 7; J. Schiemann, *Die deutsche Währung in der Weltwirtschaftskrise 1929–1933. Währungspolitik und Abwertungskontroverse unter den Bedingungen der Reparationen* [The German Currency during the Great Depression. Monetary Policy and the Devaluation Controversy in the Conditions created by Reparations] (Bern, 1980), pp. 15–56; G. Haberle, 'Die Weltwirtschaft und das internationale Währungssystem in der Zeit zwischen den beiden Weltkriegen' [The World Economy and the International Monetary System in the Interwar Period] in Deutsche Bundesbank (ed.), *Währung und Wirtschaft in Deutschland 1876–1975* (Frankfurt, 1976).

throughout the 1920s to squeeze Great Britain out of her traditional position as the world financial centre, but proved unable to fulfil the City of London's function as the regulator of the international monetary system and therefore of the world economy. The first step on the road to perdition came in 1919 when the United States returned to the gold standard and began to do everything in her power to persuade as many other nations as possible to follow her example, since the health of her own currency depended on it. Washington hoped thereby to reduce the pressure on its gold reserves (which was contributing to inflationary tendencies on the domestic market) but above all to gain an even more advantageous position from which to carry on the struggle to control the world monetary system.

Though the United States was able to introduce the full gold standard without much difficulty, the same cannot be said of the vast majority of countries, which in general were highly indebted. Many could not even contemplate returning to prewar parity levels, and some sought escape in a variation on the prewar system: the gold-*exchange* standard. None the less, the American model was still considered to be the ideal. Accordingly, all the countries participating at the international conference of experts in Genoa in 1922 pledged to return to the gold standard as quickly as possible. Researchers, despite their other differences, largely agree that the return to the gold standard played a major role in destabilising the world economy during the 1920s and that it then contributed to the collapse of what remained of the international monetary system during the Great Depression.[9]

Many contemporaries, especially the experts at the League of Nations,[10] agreed by and large on the reasons for this catastrophic outcome. Their unanimously critical and even devastating assessment of the new monetary system stands in curious contrast to the self-assurance and complacency of those responsible for the world monetary system. Unfortunately, no research has ever been undertaken from the viewpoint of *social* history into the way in which these decisions, especially those related to the new parities, were made. The eventual breakdown of the monetary system can be ascribed on the whole to four closely related causes.

First, the gold-exchange standard proved to be 'more a source of weakness than of strength'.[11] When monetary reserves in key currencies

9. Cf. D.H. Aldcroft, *Zwanziger Jahre*; Haberle, 'Die Weltwirtschaft . . .'; C.P. Kindleberger, *Die Weltwirtschaftskrise 1929–1939* (Munich, 1973).
10. The most important publications are cited in D.H. Aldcroft, *Zwanziger Jahre*, pp. 371ff. In addition, see the publications of the Royal Institute of International Affairs, e.g. *Monetary Policy and the Depression* (London, 1935).
11. D.H. Aldcroft, *Zwanziger Jahre*, p. 196.

(dollars and sterling) replaced gold as the basis of convertibility (in order to counteract the shortage of gold), the currency holdings of central banks naturally shot up. However, since these were largely short-term credits, the central money markets came under pressure. When interest rates changed, for whatever reason, large sums of money flowed between New York and London as well as Paris after 1927–8. When currencies were stabilised, advantage was taken of the right to convert currency into gold, further increasing the pressure on the main financial centres in New York and London. The latter suffered more than the former due to its smaller gold reserves and high liabilities. This further weakened the pound sterling and increasingly shifted responsibility for maintaining a viable world monetary system to New York. However, the Americans proved less and less equal to the task.

Secondly, enormous, indeed insurmountable, difficulties were created by the fashion in which various countries stabilised their currencies. The process was largely completed only in 1928 (with the exception of Japan), through adoption of either the full gold standard (the United States, Sweden, the Netherlands and some Latin American countries) or the gold-exchange standard. The baleful but alluring tendency was for each country to carry out this process without any regard for the national interests of others. No accords or even general understandings were reached. Successful currency stabilisation came to be viewed as a symbol of full national sovereignty,[12] even though it was a fiction in most cases. Nationalist passions were especially aroused by the level at which a country's currency would be stabilised. This was indeed a crucial question with ramifications for the entire economy; but not surprisingly, exchange rates or parities were actually established more in response to domestic political pressures than to technical financial considerations.[13] The result can only be described as chaotic. Some nations returned to prewar exchange rates (the United States, Great Britain and the Dominions, Switzerland, the Scandinavian countries and finally Japan in 1930). Others had to create new monetary units because their former currencies had been ravaged (Germany, the Soviet Union, Austria, Hungary and Poland). Most countries devalued their currencies before stabilising them, with the steepest devaluations in central and eastern Europe. No one considered whether the new exchange rates reflected actual costs and prices. In consequence, some currencies were undervalued (e.g. the French franc before stabilisation) and others were overvalued (the pound sterling).[14] This created fertile

12. According to a League of Nations study by R. Nurkse, *International Currency Experience: Lessons on the Inter-War Period* (Geneva, 1944).
13. Cf. C.P. Kindleberger, *Die Weltwirtschaftskrise 1929–1939*, pp. 48–53.
14. For the uses to which these differences in exchange rates were put, see S. Glynn and

ground for speculation, hectic capital movements and price discrepancies on world markets. The new gold standard was accordingly marred from the outset by a host of unresolved economic difficulties and by the deep gulf between creditor and debtor nations. It is not surprising that it failed to make the expected contribution to the recovery of the world economy and to the expansion of world trade in particular.

Thirdly, no less disturbing were the domestic economic and social effects of this chaotic method of stabilising currencies. Previously, gold inflows and outflows had served to correct imbalances in the balance of payments; now, however, central banks (especially in France and the United States) were compelled to protect the economy against unexpected money movements, and currency reserves were built up to offset inflows of gold. When the gap between countries with a gold surplus and those with a deficit failed to narrow, the distribution of global monetary reserves became extremely imbalanced. By the end of the 1920s, approximately two-thirds of these reserves were held by the United States, France and the neutral European countries alone. In an absurd spectacle, gold flowed into countries like the United States, which did not need it, while the other countries such as Great Britain had far too little to cover their existing liabilities. This of course weighed heavily on their balance of payments. Most importantly, however, the domestic economies of all countries were compelled to conform to unrealistic exchange rates. In countries with overvalued currencies, prices and costs had to fall. This was hardly possible in Britain and elsewhere, however, because unemployment would have been further aggravated and because there was very little margin for manoeuvre in so far as wages and prices were concerned. Currency stabilisation therefore raised a major obstacle to the necessary economic restructuring.

The related question of internal political advantage has not been adequately studied. To what extent was this method of currency stabilisation intended not only to improve a country's position in the international division of labour but also to export financial burdens and thereby relieve social tensions?[15] In fact, the opposite usually resulted, at least in Europe. The difficulty can best be described using Great Britain as an example. Scarcely anyone doubts that the adoption of prewar exchange rates in 1925 was an 'atavistic' move[16] in light of the general abandonment of free trade. It exacerbated all the structural

---

A.L. Lougheed, 'A Comment on United States Economic Policy and the "Dollar Gap" of the 1920s', *EHR* 26 (1973).

15. For France, see W.A. McDougall, 'Political Economy versus National Sovereignty: French Structures for German Economic Integration after Versailles', *JMH* 51 (1979).

16. A. Predöhl, *Das Ende der Weltwirtschaftskrise*, p. 54.

defects in the British economy and deepened its perennial sluggishness. With the benefit of hindsight, it is easy to confirm the wisdom of Keynes's views and laud his passionate but lonely attacks on the policies of the Conservative chancellor of the exchequer, Winston Churchill.[17] These policies were adopted by the British government primarily as a matter of prestige in order to reinforce the claims of the City of London to be the financial capital of the world. One must admit, however, that Britain's declining economy made it desirable to encourage such an important source of wealth by attempting to restore confidence in London.

However, the return of sterling to its former exchange value, in deference to international trade and financial interests, came at a steep price: strong deflationary policies carried out on the backs of the broad masses. The vicious circle was complete: the high exchange value of the pound diminished the competitiveness of British products on world markets. Exports declined, and imports increased, further damaging domestic industries. At the same time, demand weakened so that manufacturers did not invest sufficient funds to modernise the means of production. As a result, the British economy became very sluggish, creating structural unemployment that had risen to 10 per cent even before the Great Depression even began.[18] Under conditions such as these, social conflict grew more bitter, culminating in the great general strike of 1926. However, the government formed a common front with business interests and quickly overwhelmed the labour unions. To this extent, the view is justified that currency stabilisation in Britain and elsewhere played a major role in the 'conservative offensive' of the mid-1920s. None the less, the governor of the Bank of England, Sir Montagu Norman, was moved to declare that in his opinion the domestic upsets occasioned by the return to prewar parities were relatively insignificant compared to the external advantages that it brought.[19]

Fourthly, a major weakness of the international monetary system (which did not really deserve to be termed a 'system' at all) stemmed from the fact that monetary issues and policies were an integral part of the struggle for world economic and, especially, political power. The

17. J.M. Keynes, *The Economic Consequences of Mr. Churchill* (London, 1925); see above all D.E. Moggridge, *British Monetary Policy 1924–1931. The Norman Conquest of $4.86* (Cambridge, 1972); cf. as well D. de Laubier, *Les relations financières internationale*, pp. 81ff.
18. E.J. Hobsbawm, *Industrie und Empire. Britische Wirtschaftsgeschichte seit 1750* (Frankfurt, 1972), vol. 2, pp. 42–59, 72ff. Aldcroft claims ('Britische Währungspolitik', p. 93) that the widespread view that the British pound was overvalued by some 10 per cent after the return to the gold standard in April 1925 has never been clearly demonstrated.
19. Cited in D. de Laubier, *Les relations financières internationales*, p. 82, note 13.

spate of 'difficulties', as they were called, could have been surmounted if the major central banks had cooperated more closely, or even at all. However, a complex mixture of political, personal and financial factors prevented regular policy coordination. The very nature of the currency stabilisation process induced central banks to show much less interest in forging the best possible international monetary system than in tending to domestic problems, especially in the realm of monetary policy. As these problems intensified, the banks had even less margin for manoeuvre.[20] The situation could not even be improved by the fact that the central banks were headed by such stubborn and powerful men as Norman in Britain, Moreau in France and Strong in the United States till his death in October 1928.[21] This trio was joined by the president of the German *Reichsbank*, Hjalmar Schacht, who strove not without success to glean advantage for Germany from the mounting rivalry between the three leading central banks.

This rivalry casts a telling light not only on the world monetary system but also on the international scene in general. The struggle between New York and London for control of the monetary system flared up continually despite frequent high-level contacts,[22] though this did not prevent them from forming a common front against the Bank of France on particular occasions. The French feared, not without reason, that the Anglo-Saxons were conspiring to drive them back to the second rank.

20. This has been thoroughly investigated. See R.H. Meyer, *Banker's Diplomacy: Monetary Stabilization in the Twenties* (NY, 1970); S. Strange, *Sterling and British Policy. A Study of an International Currency in Decline* (Oxford, 1971); M. Wolfe, *The French Franc Between the Wars 1919–1939* (NY, 1957); St.V.O. Clarke, *Central Bank Cooperation, 1924–1931* (NY, 1967); D.H. Aldcroft, 'The Impact of British Monetary Policy, 1919–1939', *Revue internationale d'histoire de la Banque* 3 (1970); and a summary by idem, *Zwanziger Jahre*, pp. 205–8.

21. The activities of these three central bank governors has been thoroughly investigated. Besides the titles in note 20, cf. L.V. Chandler, *Benjamin Strong. Central Banker* (Washington, DC, 1958); Sir H. Clay, *Lord Norman* (London, 1957); A. Boyle, *Montagu Norman* (London, 1967); E. Moreau, *Souvenirs d'un gouverneur de banque. Histoire de la stabilisation du franc* (Paris, 1954).

22. In early July 1927 a conference was held on Long Island for the express purpose of improving cooperation among the central banks. The conference induced the Federal Reserve System to lower interest rates in order to diminish the pressure on Britain and Germany. However, in this case too, the main motivation was the domestic American recession of 1927 rather than concerns about the international monetary system. Cf. C.P. Kindleberger, *Die Weltwirtschaftskrise 1929–1939*, pp. 66–9. The struggle between London and New York to dominate the monetary system was described very lucidly by contemporary observers. See for instance the notable book by the Zurich banker F. Somary, *Wandlungen der Weltwirtschaft seit dem Kriege* [Changes in the World Economy since the War] (Tübingen, 1929) and the very favourable review by W. Röpke in the *Frankfurter Zeitung*, 12 January 1930; see as well G. Bienstock, *Deutschland und die Weltwirtschaft* (Berlin, 1931), p. 105f.

The French also believed that their former allies had betrayed them in respect to German reparations. Paris, which had risen after the franc was stabilised to become the third most important financial centre in the world, accordingly did all it could to break the financial dominance of the Anglo-Saxons. As we shall see, the Bank of France made a major contribution in 1931 to undermining the British currency and causing its devaluation (and hence the end of the gold standard) by deciding to liquidate its substantial sterling holdings.

In his memoirs, Emile Moreau has given us a colourful but nevertheless scarcely exaggerated depiction of the bitter struggle between the central banks of Britain and France.[23] Moreau openly admits that he detested Norman and accuses him of cooperating too closely with the president of the German *Reichsbank*, Hjalmar Schacht. He repeatedly calls Norman an 'imperialist' who used all available means to strengthen British influence on international trade and on the financial committee of the League of Nations (and hence on various national currencies) with the help of the pound sterling. Moreau found his colleague 'complicated' and 'mysterious' and he criticises Norman's profoundly pessimistic views about the economic and financial outlook in Europe. Finally, Moreau freely acknowledges that his determination to defend the gold standard in France would necessarily threaten it in Britain.[24]

Moreau's memoirs also reveal that the tensions between Britain and France always reached their zenith when they were actively seeking to consolidate or extend financial and therefore political influence in the countries of eastern and south-eastern Europe. This, it seems, was an extremely sensitive point. The attempt to divide the Balkans into two zones of financial interest failed, and the competition among the great financial powers grew especially intense when the Romanian currency was being stabilised. New York threw its weight behind London in this case, and the Bank of France barely managed to prevail in the end, even though Romania was one of France's most important allies. After Paris had succeeded in re-establishing itself as a key financial centre, it usually managed to break up the common Anglo-Saxon front whenever it began to form. The three major central banks did not begin to cooperate until 1936, when it was already far too late, and even then only the bare minimum was done.[25]

23. E. Moreau, *Souvenirs*, esp. pp. 40, 48f., 322, 331f., 489ff., 491–511, 515ff.

24. Ibid., p. 322.

25. Three-power agreement of 25 September 1936 which allowed the Popular Front government under Léon Blum to devalue the franc. However, even then the three governments made only vague declarations of intent. The agreement neither established fixed exchange rates, nor did it guarantee that the currencies would be bound to one another. Cf. G. Haberle, *Die Weltwirtschaft*, p. 220f.; H.V. Hodson, *Slump and Recov-*

As Keynes had warned early on,[26] no country was pursuing policies compatible with a return to the gold standard.[27] Economic facts did not permit it, let alone the political realities. These were clearly not the times for a 'fair-weather monetary system'. The belief that the gold standard would right the many imbalances proved to be misguided; in fact, imperfect adherence to the gold standard only exacerbated the existing problems. The international monetary system finally revealed its many flaws, indeed its inexistence, at a time when it was most needed, for it was during the so-called 'stabilisation phase' that floods of international capital and transfer payments surged back and forth in the form of reparations, debt repayments, loans and direct investments, thereby increasing international economic interdependence and the vulnerability of individual national economies.

All this had occurred before 1929, and it is therefore not surprising that monetary and financial policies played a major part in the onset of the Great Depression. Fittingly enough, the gold standard was one of its most prominent victims. As long as the gold standard remained in place, the crisis could not possibly be resolved, as each country eventually discovered – though some, such as France, clung a little longer to the old illusions. No one has pictured developments more vividly and accurately than Aldcroft who compared the gold standard to an old, damp fire-cracker that, when relit, sparked and sputtered a while before finally hissing away.[28]

II. American Dominance of the World Economy and its Consequences

According to Wallerstein, the evolution of the capitalist world economy should never be interpreted solely in the light of the policies pursued by any one country, no matter how powerful. It is a simple truth, he says, that no single state can transform either the international political system or the world economy. It is not easy to elbow all the rest of the world aside.[29] The validity of this assertion is limited, however, so far as the 1920s are concerned. In the years following the First World War, the weight of the American economy in the international system can

---

ery 1929–1937. A Survey of World Economic Affairs (London, 1938), pp. 414–24; R. Girault, 'Léon Blum, la dévaluation de 1936 et la conduite de la politique extérieur de la France', *Relations internationales* 13 (1978).

26. J.M. Keynes, *Ein Traktat über Währungsreform* (Munich, 1924).
27. J. Schiemann, *Die deutsche Währung*, pp. 40ff.
28. Aldcroft, *Zwanziger Jahre*, p. 181.
29. Wallerstein in J. Blaschke (ed.), *Perspektiven des Weltsystems*, pp. 223, 225.

scarcely be exaggerated. As we have seen, America's new-found position as the world's greatest creditor greatly assisted her in imposing the gold(-exchange) standard – which she believed would create a climate in which the dollar would rise to become the world's leading currency. The pressure which the United States exerted to this end played a crucial role in the period of currency stabilisation.

All this would scarcely have been possible without a major transformation of the American economy which began before 1914 but did not achieve a real breakthrough until the war years: a prodigious expansion of the forces of production in what was now by far the world's most developed capitalist economy. In order to consolidate this growth, especially by easing economic adjustment to postwar conditions, it was imperative that the United States attempt to take control not only of the international monetary system but also of the entire world economy during the reconstruction period.

The situation differed from that after the Second World War in two critical ways: first, American overseas involvement was chiefly economic and not overtly political (in regard to Europe at least, if not the Far East). This was not necessarily a great disadvantage in that the United States was so overwhelming economically that she could afford a certain political restraint.[30] Furthermore, military and strategic considerations were not nearly as important as they became after the Second World War during the super-power confrontation. In a world consumed with economic reconstruction, political influence was largely equated with economic influence. In addition, what we shall call the 'Ford' model of economic growth remained largely confined to the United States. Other capitalist economies, especially Germany, attempted to adopt the 'Ford' model, but with limited success. Indeed, these attempts were rather counterproductive on the whole since they exacerbated many of the existing economic imbalances. In the 1960s there was a gradual narrowing of the economic gap that had separated the United States from all other advanced capitalist economies after the war; but in the 1920s nothing of the sort occurred. The impact of the continuing economic disparity on attempts to reconstruct the world economy has not been adequately studied, and we shall now look into it, though only in outline.

The statistics draw an impressive picture of the economic might of the United States during the 1920s, a might of which contemporaries were fully cognisant both inside and outside the United States.[31] The United

---

30. Cf. D.E. Baines, 'Die Vereinigten Staaten zwischen den Weltkriegen' in W.P. Adams (ed.), *Die Vereinigten Staaten von Amerika* (Frankfurt, 1977), p. 283f.
31. A raft of data, which cannot all be discussed here, is available in the classic work

Table 1 Share of World Industrial Production (as a %)

Year	Germany	GB	France	USA	Russia/USSR	Japan
1870	13.2	31.8	10.3	23.3	3.7	–
1913	15.7	14.0	6.4	35.8	5.5	1.2
1913[1]	14.3	14.1	7.0	–	4.4	–
1926–9	11.6	9.4	6.6	42.2	4.3	2.5
1936–8	10.7	9.2	4.5	32.2	18.5	3.5

[1]in the borders established in 1918

Sources: Société des Nations (ed.), *Industrialisation et commerce extérieur* (Geneva, 1945), Tab. 1.14; cited in part by W. Fischer in H. Mommsen et al. (eds), *Industrielles System*, p. 27f.

Table 2 Share of World Exports (as a %)

	1913	1927–9
USA	13.3	15.7
Germany	13.2	9.1
GB	13.9	11.0
France	7.2	6.5

Source: D. Petzina and W. Abelshauser in H. Mommsen et al. (eds), *Industrielles System*, p. 70.

States held 'the working capital of the world economy', as was so aptly stated,[32] and overtook the Europeans as 'banker to the world'.[33] Moreover, she was unquestionably the world's greatest industrial and commercial power (Tables 1 and 2). The annual index of industrial production (Table 3) shows that the United States not only always surpassed the world average during the 1920s but far outstripped the

---

published by the U.S. Dept. of Commerce, H.B. Lary et al., *The United States in the World Economy. The International Transactions of the United States during the Interwar Period* (Washington, DC, 1943); cf. the informative contemporary studies by J. Klein, *Frontiers of Trade* (NY, 1929); B.H. Williams, *Economic Foreign Policy of the United States* (NY, 1929); valuable data can also be found in the *Commerce Yearbook* and the *Hoover Committee Report on Recent Economic Changes* (1929). For developments in the domestic economy and international economic relations see as well: B. Anderson, *Economics and the Public Welfare. Financial and Economic History of the U.S., 1914–1946* (NY, 1950); L. Frank, *Histoire économique et sociale des Etats-Unis de 1919 à 1949* (Paris, 1950); R.F. Mikesell, *U.S. Economic Policy and International Relations* (NY, 1952). The concept of the 'dominant economy' employed here is based on the works of F. Perroux: *L'économique du XXe siècle* (Paris, 1961) and *Indépendance de l'économie nationale et interdépendance des nations* (Paris, 1972).

32. E. Trendelenburg, 'Bis zum Dawes Plan,' pp. 50ff.

33. For Europe's role as the 'world's banker' before 1914 see the classic work of H. Feis,

leading European nations of Germany, Great Britain and France. Only Fascist Italy and the rapidly industrialising countries on the periphery such as Japan and the Soviet Union (after the implementation of the first Two-Year Plan in 1929–30) achieved higher rates. The growth rates of industrial production (Table 4) also demonstrate the vigour of American business. By 1923 the United States had become the world's greatest exporter and second-largest importer.[34]

The extraordinary preponderance of the United States in the world economy is illustrated by the fact that it consumed 39 per cent of the world production of the nine most important minerals and fertilisers in 1927–8. With a 7 per cent share of the world population in 1927–8, the United States consumed 75 per cent of crude oil production, 48 per cent of iron and steel production, 55.4 per cent of copper production, 75 per cent of raw rubber production and so on. Table 5 illustrates the enormous capacity of primary industry in the United States and also the extent of her productivity advantage, in tonnes per man-shift in the coal industry, over Germany, Britain and France. The magnitude of the difference is illustrated by the fact that gross annual manufacturing output per capita was on average almost twice as high in the United States as in the three European countries in the years 1926–9. By 1929 the real growth in her gross national product had made the United States the wealthiest nation on earth (Table 6).

1. Contradictions in the Ford Model of Economic Growth
The enormous expansion of the forces of production in the United States, as reflected in these figures, was only possible because the capitalist mode of production had reached an entirely new stage in its evolution.[35] Most significantly, the American economy began a phase of intensive growth, though the acceleration was not completed until after the Second World War. New standards of consumption and production were set on the basis of a new kind of mass production and 'economy of scale'. The most important prerequisite was the reorganisation of labour in order to achieve far-reaching, indeed revolutionary, increases in

Europe: the World's Banker 1870–1914 (NY, 1930); also: W. Woodruff, *Impact of the Western Man. A Study of Europe's Role in the World Economy 1750–1960* (NY, 1966), Chapt. IV: 'Europe: The Banker of the World'; P. Bairoch, *Commerce extérieur et développement économique de l'Europe au XIXe siècle* (Paris, 1976), Chapt. V.

34. For this and what follows: W.P. Adams (ed.), *Die Vereinigten Staaten von Amerika*, pp. 33ff.
35. The best analysis of this can be found in M. Aglietta, *Régulation et crises du capitalisme. L'expérience des Etats-Unis* (Paris, 1976), pp. 94ff. A satisfactory but rather impressionistic and descriptive overview can be found in H. Jaeger, *Geschichte der amerikanischen Wirtschaft im 20. Jahrhundert* (Wiesbaden, 1973).

Table 3 Annual Index of Industrial Production (1920–31) (1913 = 100)

Year	World	USA	Germany	GB	France	USSR	Italy	Japan
1920	93.2	122.2	59.0	92.6	70.4	12.8	95.2	176.0
1921	81.1	98.0	74.7	55.1	61.4	23.3	98.4	167.1
1922	99.5	125.8	81.8	73.5	87.8	28.9	108.1	197.9
1923	104.5	141.4	55.4	79.1	95.2	35.4	119.3	206.4
1924	111.0	133.2	81.8	87.8	117.9	47.5	140.7	223.3
1925	120.7	148.0	94.9	86.3	114.3	70.2	156.8	221.8
1926	126.5	156.1	90.9	78.8	129.8	100.3	162.8	264.9
1927	134.5	154.5	122.1	96.0	115.6	114.5	161.2	270.0
1928	141.8	162.8	118.3	95.1	134.4	143.5	175.2	300.2
1929	153.3	180.8	117.3	100.3	142.7	181.4	181.0	324.0
1930	137.5	148.0	101.6	91.3	139.9	235.5	164.0	294.9
1931	122.5	121.6	85.1	82.4	122.6	293.9	145.1	288.1

Source: Same as Table 1, p. 160. Very similar figures can be found in I. Svennilson, *Growth and Stagnation in the European Economy* (Geneva, 1954). For the reliability of these data, see Aldcroft, *Zwanziger Jahre*, p. 118. According to other sources, the figures for Germany were even worse, cf. D. Petzina, *Die deutsche Wirtschaft in der Zwischenksriegszeit* (Wiesbaden, 1977), p. 14.

Table 4 Growth Rates of Industrial Production

	1896/1900–1911/13	1911/13–1926/29	1926/29–1936/38
USA	+5.2	+3.5	+0.2
Germany	+4.0	+0.9	+2.2
GB	+1.6	−0.03	+2.9
France	+3.5	+2.0	−0.1
Japan	+9.0	+7.6	+6.6

Source: Same as Table 1, p. 66.

Table 5 Productivity of American Industry in International Comparison (Second Half of the 1920s)

	USA	Germany[a]	GB	France
Hard Coal Production (1928)				
– Annual Production in Mill. of Tonnes	522.6[b]	150.1	241.3	51.4
– Tonnes per Man-Shift	4.3	1.2[c]	1.1	0.7
Pig Iron Production (1928)				
– Annual Production in Thousands of Tonnes	38,768	11,804	6,716	9,981
– Average Annual Production per Blast Furnace in Thousands of Tonnes	–	119	47	67
Electricity Production in 1927 in mill. of kWh	102,760	25,135	13,828	11,875
Annual Gross Value of Manufactured Goods Average for the Years 1926–9 in mill. of Dollars	42,200	11,500	9,400	6,600
Ditto per capita in Dollars	350	180	190	160

[a]without the Saar area
[b]including a small amout of brown coal
[c]only the Ruhr area

Sources: Same as Table 1, p. 69; I. Svennilson, *Growth and Stagnation*, pp. 252ff.; *Statistisches Jahrbuch für das Deutsche Reich* (1930), pp. 42ff. I am indebted to J.-O. Spiller (Berlin) for this compilation.

Table 6 Evolution of the Real Gross National Product (1913 = 100)

Year	France	German Reich/FRG	GB	USA
1890	72.2	51.3	68.0	41.3
1913	100	100	100	100
1925	110.6	90.3	108.5	142.6
1929	130.6	106.2	122.8	164.5
1932	115.3	89.5	123.4	120.4
1938	109.4	149.9	149.5	162.6
1950	130.3	157.3	170.4	291.2

Source: A. Maddison, 'Growth and Fluctuation in the World Economy, 1870–1960', *Banco Nazionale del Lavoro Quarterly Review* (1962), p. 194f, cited in D. Petzina and W. Abelshauser, *Deutsche Wirtschaftsgeschichte im Industriezeitalter. Konjunktur, Krise, Wachstum* (Königstein, 1981), p. 57.

productivity. This went so far as to 'subordinate the market to the needs of the factors of production'.[36] The process had been initiated late in the nineteenth century when the system known as 'Taylorism' was gradually introduced. After the First World War, this system was further developed in the guise of 'Fordism'. During the 1920s the semi-automatic assembly line began to take over the mass production of consumer durables (e.g. automobiles, radios and home appliances). The reasons are not hard to find. Manufacturers realised that they could kill two birds with one stone: productivity could be increased by dividing work into separate tasks, and at the same time individual workers lost their autonomy as separate tasks and increased specialisation made it possible to oversee what they were doing and to employ less-skilled labour. The appalling dreariness of the resulting jobs was portrayed by Charlie Chaplin in the first part of the comedy, *Modern Times* (1932–5). 'Technical progress' was thus achieved primarily by clamping down on the workforce. However, 'Fordism' distinguished itself from the older 'Taylorism' in one key area: faster production was closely related to improved living standards for the broad masses because the 'Ford model' of economic growth required high levels of consumption and even faster circulation of mass-produced goods.

However, the Ford model as practised in the United States harboured certain internal contradictions, which soon began to eat away at the economy, thereby assuming international significance because of American domination of the world economy. Republican administrations continually favoured capital over labour, and over production inevitably resulted as mass purchasing power failed to keep pace. An

36. The succinct phrase of A. Sohn-Rethel, 'Ökonomie und Klassenstruktur des deutschen Faschismus', p. 45f.

early sign of this tendency was a further widening of the already substantial income differential.[37] The Mellon tax reform, typical of Republican economic policy, was designed to reduce taxes in such a way that the lion's share of the benefit accrued to high-income earners and industry. Whereas in 1920 the top 1 per cent of the population received 12 per cent of disposable personal income, this proportion rose by 1929 to 18 per cent. During the same period, income from profits, interest and rent increased by 45 per cent while income from wages and salaries mounted by only 13 per cent.[38] The real hourly wage-rate of the industrial workforce stagnated (a 2 per cent increase between 1920 and 1929). This was a major reason why some 40 to 45 per cent of all American households were unable to satisfy more than their most basic needs.

The mounting inequality of income distribution was inconsistent with the economic necessity to expand the market for the flood of goods resulting for mass production. It also tended to aggravate the macro-economic structural defect endemic to the Ford system: the widening discrepancy between the production of capital goods and consumer goods.[39] Between 1923 and 1926 alone, production of capital goods increased twice as fast as general industrial production. Contemporaries already wondered 'whether too much of the productive energies of the country are going into the manufacture of capital goods'.[40] Indeed, sales of consumer durables were already reaching their limits by 1926, as can be seen in Table 6a.[41]

These developments indicate that the linkage between mass production and mass consumption, so essential in order for the 'Ford model' of economic growth to function properly, had not yet been established. Overaccumulation, which certainly played a key role in the crisis of 1929, was a sign of the fundamental imbalance in the system resulting from the fact that wages had not kept pace with mounting productivity. A balance could have been restored if prices had fallen sufficiently to spur domestic demand, but in reality prices rose between

---

37. See T. Wilson, *Fluctuations in Income and Employment* (NY, 1949[3]); W.P. Adams (ed.), *Die Vereinigten Staaten von Amerika*, p. 38; H. Jaeger, *Geschichte der amerikanischen Wirtschaft*, p. 69; M. Aglietta, *Régulation et crises du capitalisme*, p. 74.
38. The figures vary. According to H.R. Guggisberg, *Geschichte der USA*, vol. 2: *Die Weltmacht* (Stuttgart, 1979[2]), p. 179, the return on investment and company profits increased between 1923 and 1929 by 60 to 65 per cent while the incomes of workers and white-collar employees rose by only 11 per cent. In any case, farm income was definitely stagnant.
39. M. Aglietta, *Régulation et crises du capitalisme*, p. 74f.
40. M. Dobb, *Studies in the Development of Capitalism*, p. 328.
41. M. Aglietta, *Régulation et crises du capitalisme*, p. 75.

Table 6a American Growth Rates (as a %)

	1920 to 1926	1926 to 1929
Housing Construction	215	37
Consumption of Durables	66	5

Source: M. Aglietta, *A Theory of Capitalist Regulation. The US Experience* (London, 1979).

1922 and 1926 and declined by only 3 per cent between 1926 and 1929. This reinforces the view that the Great Depression would not have been so severe if the benefits of prosperity had been distributed more widely.[42] Massive production of expensive consumer goods could not possibly have continued much longer in view of the increasing disparity in income distribution.

The tendency of Republican governments to favour capital over labour found expression in attempts to undo the very modest social reforms implemented by the Democrats. When labour strife erupted, the justice system clearly came down on the side of employers. As was the case in all the advanced capitalist countries, the American labour movement suffered severe setbacks in the immediate postwar period.[43] Economic slumps, for instance that of 1927, immediately produced vast armies of unemployed (over 2 million by 1928), though this warning signal was ignored. Moreover, Republican administrators supported the trend in big business toward vertical and horizontal integration by means of numerous tax advantages and tariff policies which most benefited those industries that had expanded enormously during the war. As a result, fifty companies in the finished-goods sector employing only one-sixth of all workers generated 28 per cent of total production in terms of value. The 200 largest firms, employing 26 per cent of all workers, generated 41 per cent of total production.[44] Anti-cartel legislation, the symbol and assurance of free-market competition, was continually subverted to the great disadvantage of working people, at times even with the knowledge and approval of the government which hoped that this would strengthen America's international competitiveness. The crassest example (of which contemporaries were well aware)[45] was the support which the government provided the great American oil companies

42. According to H.R. Guggisberg, *Geschichte der USA*, vol. 2, p. 198.
43. For the details see T.R. Brooks, *Le labeur et la lutte. Histoire du mouvement ouvrier américain* (Paris, 1983); J.B. Rayback, *A History of American Labour* (London, 1966).
44. M. Dobb, *Studies in the Development of Capitalism*, p. 340f.
45. See for instance K. Hoffmann, *Ölpolitik und angelsächsischer Imperialismus* (Berlin, 1927).

in their struggle with British and some French interests in the Middle East.

2. Contradictions during the Prosperity Phase

Frantic investment and easy money were an integral part of the Ford model of economic growth. Economic euphoria quickly led to a vast speculative boom that typified the overly-opulent 'age of prosperity' beginning in 1922. Observers were filled with awe and admiration, especially between 1925 and 1929, that is, during the supposed stabilis-ation of the Versailles and Washington Systems. Some clear-sighted commentators, however, especially foreigners,[46] were moved to express their doubts and fears.

The wave of prosperity in the United States stoked economies around the world, and should therefore be analysed in greater detail. First, it appears to run counter to the Kontratieff cycles according to which the entire interwar period should have been a time of economic downturn. The years of prosperity were fuelled not by another outpouring of technical inventions but by changes in the production process, as we have seen. This was one of the main reasons, as numerous studies have shown,[47] why they were shot through with imbalances and dangers, which were only papered over by boundless optimism that an era of progress towards ever higher standards of living had been achieved by virtue of the 'American way of life.' How much more painful, then, was the great crash of October 1929.

During the prosperity phase, the American gross domestic product ballooned from 74,200 million dollars in 1919 to 104,400 million in 1929 (real dollars in stable prices). Per capita income increased in this period by about 20 per cent. Total output in 1929 surpassed that of 1922 by 34 per cent and that of 1913 by 65 per cent.[48] The originators and main beneficiaries of this prosperity were a small number of industries which thoroughly implemented the new production techniques and stoked the Ford model of economic expansion: the automobile, electrical and chemical industries. They achieved the highest growth rates in pro-

46. See for instance the criticism of P. Claudel, French ambassador in Washington from 1927 to 1933, of a prosperity wave 'that tends to unbalance the planetary economic system' in L. Garbagnati (ed.), *Cahiers P. Claudel*, vol. II (Paris, 1982).
47. For the prosperity phase in detail, see W.E. Leuchtenburg, *The Perils of Prosperity, 1914–1932* (Chicago, 1960); J.W. Prothro, *The Dollar Decade. Business Ideas in the 1920s* (Baton Rouge, 1954); G. Soule, *Prosperity Decade: From War to Depression* (NY, 1947); R. Sobel, *The Great Bull Market. Wall Street in the 1920s* (NY, 1968); J. Dorfmann, *The Economic Mind in American Civilization* (NY, 1959), Chapt. IV; H. Feis, *The Diplomacy of the Dollar. First Era, 1919–1932* (Baltimore, 1950).
48. Cf. H. Jaeger, *Geschichte der amerikanischen Wirtschaft*, pp. 57–71.

duction and productivity and their share of world output spurted ahead, leading in the case of the automobile industry to a virtual American monopoly on international markets.[49] The automobile industry prompted the emergence of a skein of supply industries and greatly stimulated road construction, which in turn encouraged the construction of new housing. All in all, a cycle of economic growth was generated such as the Europeans would only experience in the golden years following the Second World War. The much-cited Hoover Report determined that in the automobile industry alone an average of 750 million dollars was invested annually in order to rationalise production further.[50] According to an expert observer, 'It is hardly possible to estimate the huge sums that are being invested in order to adapt society to the automobile'.[51]

Success on the domestic market was seen from the very beginning as a springboard toward world markets, as can be observed for example in the case of consumer electrical products, especially newly popular radio sets. The radio industry was particularly important because the United States hoped to utilise it in order to achieve a dominant position in international communications and in the distribution of news as a means of extending and reinforcing her economic and cultural influence. Washington sought a cable monopoly for the same reasons (as well as for military reasons) and attempted to develop an international telecommunications system under exclusive American control despite the British, French and German competition in south-east Asia (China) and Latin America.[52]

---

49. In 1929 American automobile production represented 81 per cent of the world total. By 1919 a total of 6.7 million automobiles had already been sold. In 1921 alone, 1.47 million were sold and in 1923 alone, 3.62 million. From then until 1928 annual sales lay between 3 and 4 million. In 1929 a new record was established of 4.46 million sales. In this year, a total of 26.5 million automobiles were registered, in other words one vehicle for every five people. This proportion was not attained in the industrialised countries of Europe until the 1960s. Cf. M. Roy, *1929: La grande crise* (Paris, 1969), p. 43; T.C. Cochran, *Wirtschaft und Gesellschaft in Amerika. Von der Jahrhundertwende bis zur Gegenwart* (Stuttgart, 1964), pp. 36–45. G. Maxcy, *Les multinationales de l'automobile* (Paris, 1982), p. 50 affirms that the American share of world automobile production had risen to 84 per cent by 1929. World production that year was 5.3 million.
50. *Hoover Committee Report*, Note I/31.
51. T.C. Cochran, *Wirtschaft und Gesellschaft in Amerika*, p. 44.
52. Cf. the informative contemporary study by L.B. Tribolet, *The International Aspects of Electrical Communications in the Pacific Area* (Baltimore, 1929), cited in M.D. Goldberg, 'Anglo-American Economic Competition', pp. 25ff. where lengthy excerpts can be found. This was the first example of a symbiosis between modern technology and American cultural and ideological imperialism. See in this regard: R. Elder, *The Information Machine* (Syracuse, 1968); E. Rosenberg, *The American Dream. American Economic and Cultural Expansion, 1890–1945* (NY, 1982).

The construction industry expanded as never before, though it later suffered a particularly cruel fate as a result of this general scramble to expand capacity. The great American cities took on the aspect familiar to us today as skyscrapers mushroomed upwards by the hundreds in a hectic building spree. It was their appearance above all that fuelled the optimistic belief in the boundless opportunity of America, while distracting attention from the unevenness of the boom. 'Old' industries such as ship building, textiles, leather, etc. and primary industries such as coal mining never participated in the prosperity, despite all attempts at rationalisation. The 'adaptation of society to the automobile', as the most important of the new articles of consumption, certainly stimulated road construction, but it also ruined the railway. The foremost victim of this era was agriculture, which never recovered from the deep recession of 1920–1 despite rapid mechanisation.[53] The price stagnation between 1925 and 1929, high indebtedness (especially in the Middle West), and the refusal of the Harding and Coolidge administrations to grant federal aid all contributed to an ongoing crisis in agriculture which greatly increased the vulnerability of the American economy as a whole, especially during and because of the prosperity phase.

What most impressed contemporaries, however, and what many already labelled the cancer of the society of mass consumption was the almost unlimited extension of consumer credit. Individual indebtedness rose between 1920 and 1929 from 22,000 to 29,000 million dollars, while the volume of short- and medium-term loans climbed to almost 6,500 million dollars. Automobile purchasers alone owed 1,400 million dollars. The government failed to implement any counter-measures because it feared that efforts to restrict credit and combat inflation would precipitate another recession. Not surprisingly under the circumstances, the economy experienced a serious recession in 1927, though no one took this as a warning of worse things to come. Quite to the contrary, a decision was made that very year to loosen the money supply. This restored economic growth, while at the same time it fuelled a speculative boom which reached enormous proportions but had no other effect than to send huge quantities of capital swooshing back and forth among the wealthy.[54] The euphoria was therefore highly artificial. Exports of American capital began to dry up as early as summer of 1928 because of the speculative boom at home, thereby contributing to the domestic

---

53. See the most penetrating study in this regard: G. Fite, 'The Farmer's Dilemma, 1919–1929' in J. Braeman et al. (eds), *Change and Continuity in Twentieth Century America: The 1920's* (Columbus, 1968), pp. 67–102. This important omnibus volume contains a profusion of further information about the prosperity phase.
54. M. Aglietta, *Régulation et crises du capitalisme*, p. 303f.

euphoria. This led to an economic downturn in Latin America and in many European countries, especially Germany. The discount rate was raised dramatically in the summer of 1929, but it was already far too late to have a substantial impact on speculation.

Finally, the extreme weakness of the American banking system, which even the creation of the 'Federal Reserve System' (FED) failed to repair, must bear a good part of the blame for the ensuing financial catastrophe. Already between 1921 and 1929, no fewer than 5,400 banks collapsed, especially smaller institutions in rural areas. The archaic system of individual banks (25,000 independent banks in June 1929 and still 15,000 in 1933) was not protected by an effective deposit insurance system and was therefore likely to collapse in case of a liquidity crisis. The FED, moreover, failed to institute an energetic monetary policy, and no further bulwarks were added on this front. Conservative Republican administrations had made *laissez-faire* their dogma and saw no reason to attempt to brake the run-away boom.

3. Contradictory Position in the International Division of Labour

The previous analysis leaves the impression that the American economy of the 1920s was a mighty colossus with feet of clay. Indeed, the tumultuous expansion had generated forces that threatened to destroy it. The situation was all the more serious in that the huge American economy had a major impact on the structure and evolution of the world economy. The entire attempt to reconstruct the world economy and hence the international political system depended largely on the enduring vitality of the American economy. However, the United States was seriously handicapped by the underlying weaknesses of the prosperity phase and the imbalances in the Ford model of economic growth on which it was based.

Much of the blame must be ascribed to the inner circles of the Republican administrations. What international political and economic goals were they pursuing, in view of America's new position of economic dominance and also of the highly divergent interests of her economy and society? The salient and in many ways typical representative of Republican leadership during the 1920s was Herbert Hoover. He held influential positions throughout this period, first as Secretary of Commerce (1921–8) and then as President of the United States (1929–33) during the Great Depression. He lent continuity to these years and exemplified the Republican conviction that the political and economic realms – especially foreign policy and 'big business' – should be as closely interwoven as possible. He, as well as Secretaries of State Hughes (1921–5) and Kellogg (1925–9), believed that the most important task of diplomacy was to open channels of trade.[55] All championed America's traditional 'open door' policy which, as soon as the domestic market proved too small to absorb the entire output of the American economy, became the guiding principle behind all of Washington's political and economic dealings on the international stage.[56]

However, the 'business community' was anything but a homogeneous group, as many studies have demonstrated.[57] Again and again the conflicting views of various banking interests, of industries serving mainly the domestic or foreign markets, and of big business and the mass of small and medium-sized companies fuelled intense power struggles which were further aggravated by regionalism and the contest between the two political parties. As a consequence very few united fronts emerged. The notion that the 'world of business' was able to dictate its demands to the government is far from true: to the contrary, the heterogeneity of American economic and financial interests was the major reason why Washington was unable to establish a clear, convincing foreign policy on both the political and economic levels on many different occasions during the 1920s, at times even in regard to fundamental questions (e.g. China). In addition, a contradiction emerged between the political restraint which the United States wished to practise in order to maintain her independent foreign policy, and the need to become deeply involved in specific economic issues in order to maintain her domination of the world economy. The political and strategic interests of the United States were often at variance with her economic interests until the era after the Second World War, especially during the Cold War, when they largely coincided.

All this is not to deny one factor that served to unite business circles

55. To the inner circle of American policy makers in regard to foreign policy and international economic relations belonged, in addition to Hoover, Hughes and Kellogg, the powerful industrial and financial magnate, A. Mellon. He held the post of Secretary of the Treasury for almost the entire duration of the Republican administration. For many he incarnated the intimate relationship between politics and the economy. Further members of this circle were W.G. Harding, President of the United States from 1921 to 1923 and C. Coolidge, Vice-president in 1921–3 and President in 1923–9. All these men had assets valued in the millions. From the host of biographies, see J. Brandes, *Herbert Hoover and Economic Diplomacy. Department of Commerce Policy 1921–1928* (Pittsburgh, 1962).
56. W.P. Adams, (ed.) *Die Vereinigten Staaten von Amerika*, pp. 22–6 (on Hughes); cf. note I/68. For foreign trade as 'an absolute economic necessity' see the *Report of the 6th National Foreign Trade Convention, 1924*, which according to W. Link in *Die amerikanische Stabilisierungspolitik*, p. 264 proclaimed 'the creed of the American business world'.
57. See the lengthy analysis of J.H. Wilson, *American Business* (Introduction). Wilson criticises authors who in his view exaggerated the influence of business on political policy such as B.H. Williams, *Economic Foreign Policy of the United States* (NY, 1929).

and to reconcile their fundamental interests with the goals of the Republican administrations, namely, the deeply-held belief that the specifically American blend of capitalism and democracy was uniquely suited to ensure freedom and prosperity at home and throughout the world. This conviction provided the ideological and rhetorical basis for America's claim to economic and moral leadership. It also underlay Hoover's attempts as Secretary of Commerce to unite American business interests under his aegis in order to advance America's claim to economic paramountcy. These efforts earned Hoover the sobriquet of America's 'super businessman',[58] though he failed by and large to achieve his goals. None the less, many decisions were facilitated by turning the Department of Commerce into a kind of clearing house between politics and economics and a centre for reconciling opposing economic interests.

How did the United States employ its financial and economic clout? The first aspect of this question is how it fulfilled its new role as 'world banker' and supplier of the 'working capital of the world'. The dollar had already become the leading international currency, and New York had taken over in a bruising struggle with the City of London as the world's most important financial centre and stock market. In contrast to the City of London's priorities before 1914, the United States did not consider the stability of the world's leading currency to be of utmost concern, though this would scarcely have been possible any case because the average profit ratio of American capital was far superior to that of European capital. Of greater immediate concern, however, was the fact that the discount rate policies of the Federal Reserve Board were not as clear and decisive as those of the City of London. However, the dilemma in which the American central bank found itself should be appreciated: the United States already held huge monetary reserves, and if interest rates were raised, more foreign capital would be drawn in, thereby further distorting the worldwide distribution of capital so essential to the stabilisation of the world economy. But if rates were kept low, run-away speculation would continue. New York was the most important market for securities of all kinds, and the atmosphere of prosperity even lured capital from countries with higher interest rates whose investors were more attracted by speculative profits than by interest rates alone. As a result, the New York Stock Exchange became the major source of disorder in the world monetary system.

In addition, the New York bank rate[59] became extremely important

58. J.H. Wilson, *American Business*, p. xv.
59. The terms 'bank rate', 'discount rate' and 'prime rate' are often used interchangeably, though this is not quite exact. Basically, they refer to the annual interest rate which a central bank uses in calculating discount interest.

to Europeans since its influence on discount rates abroad was far greater than the other way around. No European central bank, not even the Bank of England, could remain unaffected by fluctuations on the American money market. This was the problem with short-term loans, which necessarily spread nervousness and uncertainty to European money and stock markets.

On a fundamental level, the principle governing American capital exports, which were so vital to the development of the world economy, was never codified. Though such a step may seem unlikely in view of the dominant philosophy of *laissez-faire*, Hoover, Mellon, Hughes and Kellogg did try repeatedly to establish something akin to a firm policy.[60] It was accepted that capital exports lay within the province of the private banks, not the government, but Washington claimed the right at least to supervise their activity. Though bankers often objected to even very loose controls, the administration was eager to retain this effective means of exercising political clout. According to very general guidelines, those countries which lived up to their 'obligations' towards the United States, especially in regard to inter-Allied loans, were to be allowed access to American capital. Foreign governments which failed to collect sufficient taxes would be barred from taking out American loans in order to balance their budgets. This incidentally is the origin of the policies practised by the International Monetary Fund after the Second World War. At times, foreign companies were even refused American capital if the price of their products was judged to be too high for the American consumer.

The main purpose of American capital exports, as contemporaries realised,[61] was to strengthen the international competitiveness of large American firms, mainly in comparison with their European competitors. The war-debt criterion meant in the end that former allies of the United States such as France, Belgium, Greece, Romania, Yugoslavia and Italy could not receive any loans until they had arrived at bilateral agreements on how their debts would be discharged. Under these conditions, Germany soon found herself in a privileged position, leading to the absurd monetary cycle so often described:[62] the United States lent Germany funds, enabling her to pay reparations to America's former allies, which in turn were supposed to enable them to pay off their debts to Washington (though in actual fact they usually postponed payment).

60. Cf. H. Feis, *The Diplomacy of the Dollar*; J.-B. Duroselle, *De Wilson à Roosevelt. Politique extérieur des Etats-Unis 1913–1945* (Paris, 1960), p. 185 (where he refers to Kellogg as a tool of big business in the realm of capital exports) and pp. 188ff.
61. According already to F. Somary, *Wandlungen der Weltwirtschaft*, pp. 55ff.
62. E.g. C.P. Kindleberger, *Die Weltwirtschaftskrise 1929–1939*.

A major consequence of this credit policy was that the United States became a divisive force within the club of victorious powers, which certainly did not contribute to the stability of the Versailles System.

A few figures will help to illustrate the stupendous volume of American capital exports.[63] Between 1919 and 1929, the long-term foreign investments of the United States rose by almost 9,000 million dollars. In 1929 they represented two-thirds of all new investment in the world. As a result, American foreign holdings rose to a total of 15,400 million dollars, consisting of 7,800 million dollars in net portfolio investments and 7,600 million in direct investments, of which 1,800 million went to foreign subsidiaries of American companies. A total of 7,500 million dollars flowed into Germany alone, giving Europe as a whole 31.4 per cent of all American capital exports. Latin America and Canada were the next largest recipients. Then as now, the lion's share of this capital went to highly developed or industrialising countries, while most peripheral countries received very little. The mounting proportion allotted to Germany is indicative of the fact that Americans wished to exercise tighter control over their exported capital and were eager to establish foreign subsidiaries and thereby strengthen their position on foreign markets.

This strategy too strongly distinguishes the United States from Europe. Leading German, French, British, Italian and Swiss concerns (Bayer, Daimler, Michelin, Lever, Fiat, Nestlé) had originated attempts to internationalise capital by establishing foreign subsidiaries in the era before the First World War; but these initiatives stagnated or even receded during the 1920s when American firms really become involved for the first time.[64] Most of their efforts were concentrated on Europe,

63. For a detailed analysis of American capital exports see C. Lewis, *America's Stake in International Investments* (Washington, DC, 1938), pp. 447, 450; idem, *The United States and Foreign Investment Problems* (Washington, DC, 1948); United Nations, *International Capital Movements during the Inter-War Period* (NY, 1949); J.H. Wilson, *American Business*, p. 103; W.P. Adams (ed.), *Die Vereinigten Staaten von Amerika*, p. 32; D.H. Aldcroft, *From Versailles to Wall Street*, Chapt. 10.

64. For a detailed description of the emergence of American multinational companies see A.G. Kenwood and A.L. Lougheed, *The Growth of the International Economy 1820–1960*; B. Thomas, 'The Historical Record of International Capital Movements to 1913' in J.H. Adler (ed.), *Capital Movements and Economic Development* (London, 1967); M. Wilkens, *The Emergence of Multinational Enterprise. American Business Abroad from the Colonial Era to 1914* (Cambridge, Mass., 1970); J.M. Stopford et al., *The World Directory of Multinational Enterprises* (London, 1980); M. Ghertman, *Les multinationales* (Paris, 1982); J.M. Dunning, *American Investment in British Manufacturing Industry* (London, 1958); F.A. Southard, *American Industry in Europe* (Boston, 1931); C.P. Kindleberger, 'Les origines des investissements directs des Etats-Unis en France' in M. Lévy-Leboyer (ed.), *La position internationale de la France. Aspects économiques et financiers XIXe–XXe siècle* (Paris, 1977).

where this kind of investment was often far from eagerly received. When ITT won a lucrative contract to modernise the French telephone system, there was an explosion of resentment toward the United States, not only in the French electrical industry but even in the German.[65]

The American invasion was led, not surprisingly, by the most important of the expanding sectors in the economy: the automobile industry.[66] Mass automobile production in the United States had reached a scale which no European manufacturer could hope to equal, especially production of Henry Ford's legendary 'Model T' selling for some $900. European manufacturers, especially the technically advanced French, were convinced that the automobile should remain an expensive luxury item for the upper classes, an attitude which reflects the whole concept of an upper-middle-class restoration after the war. A curious division of labour was even reached, according to which the Europeans exported an occasional expensive automobile – some even to the United States – while the Americans conquered the world market and reinforced their paramountcy in this domain. Automobile production reached such heights in the United States that plants had to be constructed abroad in order to further decrease costs. At first these were simple assembly facilities, but in the second half of the 1920s full-fledged, autonomous plants were built.

Ford led the way. By 1920 it had already constructed assembly plants in twenty different countries (Europe, South Africa, Australia, Japan, Latin America and even India). When capital exports to Europe increased after 1926, full-fledged production plants were built primarily in Great Britain and Germany, but also in France.[67] It is instructive to note that Ford's foreign connections went back almost as far as the founding of the company itself in 1903. General Motors stood second on foreign investment, followed at a distance by Chrysler. In 1939, 23.2 per cent of their total production took place abroad, despite the devastating impact of the Depression. The monopoly position of the American firms is illustrated by the fact that Ford was able to raise European capital for its new subsidiaries at substantially lower interest rates than its European competitors![68] Under conditions such as these, the trend towards the

65. C.P. Kindleberger, 'Les origines des investissements directs', p. 349.
66. For the internationalisation of the automobile industry see M. Wilkens and F.E. Hill, *American Business Abroad: Ford on Six Continents* (Detroit, 1964); G. Maxcy, *Les multinationales de l'automobile*; M. Ghertman, *Les multinationales*, pp. 26–9; for the American automobile industry's penetration of Germany see W. Link, *Die amerikanische Stabilisierungspolitik*, pp. 377ff.
67. For Ford's activities in France, see J.M. Laux in M. Lévy-Leboyer (ed.), *La position internationale de la France*, p. 373f.
68. Cf. the perspicacious observations of F. Somary, *Wandlungen der Weltwirtschaft*, pp. 55ff.

internationalisation of American capital soon spread to the large banks. While only four of them had moved abroad by 1913, establishing a total of six foreign branches, the total number of foreign branches rose to over one hundred during the 1920s, a level that remained unchanged until 1950.[69]

These few statistics give an inkling of the extent to which the Ford model of economic growth had begun to traverse national borders. However, what served the United States and its economic interests seldom conferred permanent benefits on the foreign recipients of American capital. The fateful effects of American capital exports on the world economy, especially on Europe, have been exhaustively explored.[70] It will therefore suffice to recapitulate the most important findings. The United States always loaned the Europeans less capital than it received in return. Capital flows during this period show a clear imbalance, both quantitative and qualitative, in favour of the United States. America acted as a giant magnet for capital, and huge quantities of gold arrived in return for the relatively cheap industrial and agricultural products she exported to Europe. Since the dollar was the most sought-after currency in the world, all European banks maintained large holdings in New York. Moreover, the opportunities for investment in the United States, especially short-term investment in securities, was always much more diverse and profitable than elsewhere.

All this served to augment the already strong financial position of American companies, enabling them to widen their productivity advantage over European firms – though their rate of capacity expansion was becoming dangerous. The United States totally dominated its most dangerous economic competitors during the 1920s to an extent far outstripping anything which Great Britain had achieved even at the height of her economic glory between 1815 and 1875. These tendencies were reinforced by the fact that a substantial proportion of the American credits was short-term, intended as speculative rather than productive investment. However, this did not prevent the Europeans, especially the Germans, from increasingly using short-term credits to finance long-term projects. This necessarily sowed instability and the danger of a battery of bankruptcies. Regardless of how these credits are regarded, the United States always emerges in the end as the prime beneficiary.

69. M. Ghertman, *Les multinationales*, p. 32; for the history of the internationalisation of banks see United Nations, *Transnational Banks: Operations, Strategies and their Effects in Developing Countries* (NY, 1981).

70. For Germany, already A. Rosenberg, *Geschichte der Weimarer Republik* (Frankfurt, 1961), Chapt. VIII; W. Link, *Die amerikanische Stabilisierungspolitik*; C.P. Kindleberger, *Die Weltwirtschaftskrise 1929–939*; and many others.

The situation changed in the late 1920s, though the Americans had only themselves to blame. Even genuine investors were swept up in the speculative wave sweeping the United States, and everybody began to play the stock market. The funds they required were withdrawn from normal business investments, and their foreign partners were the first to suffer the effects. Long before the great stock-market crash, the abrupt decline in American capital exports after June 1928[71] seriously undermined the European economy, which had grown addicted to the regular influx of American capital. Thus Europe was drawn into the domestic maelstrom in the United States.

Even more disastrous for Europe was the illusion of economic vigour conjured up by inflows of American capital. In reality, this capital not only masked the existing structural difficulties but exacerbated them.[72] The widespread impression of economic stability was therefore highly illusory. This is illustrated by the fact that at the end of the 1920s many debtors owed more in interest than they were receiving in new credits. When the flow of capital dried up and prices fell, many debtors could no longer keep their heads above water. Latin America was the second largest recipient of American investment, and the difficulties it caused were even more serious than in Europe.[73] In the second half of the 1920s, the foreign debt of many Latin American countries reached dangerous proportions. Payments on the principal and interest reached almost three times as much as the amount of inflowing capital. On all sides, the acceptance of American loans after currency stabilisation caused more problems than it solved, because little attention was paid to ensuring that the loans were invested in export-oriented sectors of the economy that would earn foreign exchange. In any case, rearing foreign competitors was hardly one of the objectives of the American investors.

Many economies were caught in a vicious circle. It was widely believed, especially in southern and south-eastern Europe, that deflationary policies would attract foreign capital and make it possible, as one major objective, to service the debt at a highly advantageous exchange rate. In reality, however, these policies proved self-destructive because they hobbled domestic capital accumulation. This in turn hampered the process of structural adaptation of the economy. If economic restruc-

71. C.P. Kindleberger, *Die Weltwirtschaftskrise 1929–1939*, p. 71.
72. Cf. J.B. Condliffe, *Les changements fondamentaux dans la vie économique* (Paris, 1939), p. 8; C.W. Guillebaud, *The Economic Recovery of Germany* (London, 1939), pp. 11–13.
73. For the mounting debt burden of the East European countries, which reached the brink of bankruptcy even prior to 1929, see the impressive case study by V.N. Bandera, *Foreign Capital as an Instrument of National Economic Policy. A Study Based on the Experience of the East European Countries Between the World Wars* (The Hague, 1964).

Table 7 Foreign Trade of the United States (Percentage Share According to Degree of Processing)

Year	Exports Minerals	Agricultural Products	Processed Raw Materials	Semi-Manufactures	Industrial Finished Goods	Imports Minerals	Agricultural Products	Processed Raw Materials	Semi-Manufactures	Industrial Finished Goods
1910	33.6	6.4	15.1	15.7	29.2	37.1	9.3	11.7	18.3	23.6
1920	23.3	11.4	13.8	11.9	39.7	33.8	10.9	23.5	15.2	16.6
1925	29.5	6.6	11.9	13.7	38.3	41.4	11.7	10.2	17.9	18.8
1926	26.8	7.1	10.7	13.9	41.5	40.5	12.2	9.4	18.1	19.8
1927	25.1	8.8	9.7	14.7	41.6	38.2	12.1	10.8	17.9	21.0
1928	25.7	5.9	9.3	14.2	44.9	35.8	13.4	9.9	18.6	22.1
1929	22.2	5.2	9.4	14.1	49.1	35.4	12.2	9.9	20.1	22.6
1930	21.9	4.7	9.6	13.6	50.2	32.7	13.1	9.6	19.9	24.7
1931	23.8	5.3	10.4	13.4	47.1	30.7	14.6	10.6	17.8	26.3
1932	32.6	5.7	9.6	12.5	39.6	27.1	17.6	13.1	16.4	25.7

Source: W.S. and E.S. Woytinsky, *World Commerce and Governments* (NY, 1955), Table 42, p. 129.

turing had been carried out, it might have brought about greater diversification of both industry and agriculture, as in less developed countries, which in turn would have made it possible to reduce costs of production that were now too high in order to compete effectively on international markets. Many contemporaries understood the situation, especially, as was so often the case, the experts on the League of Nations financial committee.[74] A leading economist of the day, G. Haberle, summed up the matter in a pregnant formula: 'The mounting inflexibility of the economy hampered restructuring, and the maladjustments multiplied until the bubble finally burst in the Great Depression.'[75]

The United States contributed to the destabilisation of the world economy not only through capital exports but also through merchandise exports. In contrast to the periods before 1914[76] and after 1945, capital and merchandise exports were much less balanced, as contemporaries already noted.[77]

This presented two distinct dangers to the world economy. The United States had played a dominant role in world trade before the war, but during the 1920s she became totally overpowering. Between 1925 and 1930, the proportion of total American exports covered by finished goods soared from 38.3 per cent to 50.2 per cent while imports of finished goods rose only from 18.8 per cent to 24.7 per cent (Table 7).[78] It is therefore not surprising that the American portion of international exports of industrial goods rose sharply until 1929, primarily at the expense of British industry but also of German (Table 7a). The United States thereby carried on the tendency of the formerly dominant European powers, especially Britain and Germany, to enhance the classical international division of labour between the industrialised countries at the core of the world system and the producers of raw materials on the periphery.

Secondly, the United States' heavy surplus in foreign trade between 1920 and 1929 helped to keep domestic prosperity superficial and uneven, and it aggravated the fundamental economic imbalances be-

---

74. In spite of a great abundance of source materials, there is no satisfactory study of the League of Nations' financial committee.
75. G. Haberle, 'Die Weltwirtschaft', p. 227; for the theory of maladjustments see as well H.W. Arndt, *The Economic Lessons*, p. 287ff.; I. Svennilson, *Growth and Stagnation*.
76. Cf. P. Bairoch, *Commerce extérieur*, Table 34, p. 106.
77. See H. Truchy, *La reconstruction économique de l'Europe* (Paris, 1932), pp. 83ff.; report by T.E. Gregory in Comité Mixte (ed.), *Reconstruction économique internationale* (Paris, 1936), pp. 179ff.
78. See as well C.P. Kindleberger, 'International Trade and the United States Experience' in R.E. Freeman (ed.), *Postwar Economic Trends in the United States* (NY, 1960).

Table 7a Finished Goods Share of World Exports

	Ger	F	GB	USA	Japan
1911–13	21.4	11.8	27.5	9.2	1.3
1926–9	16.1	10.9	21.6	16.3	1.9
1936–8	19.8	6.0	18.6	16.3	7.0

Source: League of Nations; cited in R. Lasserre et al. (eds), *Deutschland–Frankreich – Bausteine zum Systemvergleich*, vol. 2: *Wirtschaft und Soziale Beziehungen* (Stuttgart, 1981), p. 28.

tween the leading industrial countries.[79] This tendency was reinforced by the high tariff policies practised by Republican administrations (instituted in the form of the infamous 'Fordney–McCumber Tariff' of 1922), which made it very difficult for countries that ran a deficit with the United States or were indebted to her to export more goods and services and thereby improve their trade figures and balance of payments.

This represented of course a particularly egotistical assertion of American national interests, though it all seemed very logical to the ruling Republicans. High tariffs protected those industrial sectors which had prospered during the war but were now in some difficulty. At the same time these tariffs insulated the entire domestic economy from the vicissitudes of the world economy, while simultaneously stimulating exports of American goods and capital. The Republicans were convinced that they had discovered an economic panacea which would strengthen the American position in world markets while simultaneously protecting uncompetitive sectors. Expansion and protection were two sides of the same coin. The resulting harm to the trading partners of the United States and to the stability of the world economic system did not enter into Washington's calculations. There is therefore much truth to the assertion that the United States proved unable to fulfil the role she had assumed as the world's leading economic power primarily because she failed to understand that war debts, high protective tariffs and exports of capital and merchandise were all aspects of an all-encompassing whole.[80]

Americans found this difficult, if not impossible to comprehend so long as they ascribed absolute priority to domestic economic concerns, a tendency that was reinforced by the rapidly changing social structure within the United States. The upper classes looked with horror on the revolutionary events in Europe in the early 1920s. The depth of their

79. See Baines in W.P. Adams (ed.), *Die Vereinigten Staaten von Amerika*, pp. 304–8.
80. See J.H. Wilson, *American Business*, p. 112.

feeling can be seen among other things in the sharp reductions in immigration quotas[81] undertaken not least of all in order to prevent Marxist ideology from infecting the United States and stirring up social unrest. These concerns proved totally unfounded, but not before they had prompted a rather extreme response from the United States. Further rationalisation of industry and fear of declining standards of living led to cutbacks in the labour force, further hampering the international mobility of labour which had played a crucial role in the era of prosperity before the war.[82] This aggravated the already serious social and economic problems in the countries of eastern, south-eastern and southern Europe, which were the traditional source of immigrants to the United States.[83]

This clarifies many of the inconsistencies in the American attitude to the international division of labour. On the one hand, the United States adopted a unique combination of deflationary economic policies and the Ford model of economic growth in order to entrench the position of the ruling classes (especially *vis-à-vis* the trade unions), though in reality, as we have seen, this approach unleashed a spate of destabilising forces, both domestic and international. On the other hand, American policies such as the gold standard, capital exports and a balanced budget bolstered the 'conservative offensive' in Europe while at the same time Washington's trading relations with Japan strengthened the political power of the business-oriented, liberal-conservative middle classes in Japan, as we shall see in Chapter 4, II. Conservatives in both Europe and Japan operated in the framework of the pseudo-stability largely created by the United States which markedly reduced their margin of political and economic manoeuvrability within their own countries. Under these conditions, the conservatives failed to solve the problems of their own societies or did so at a great social cost, thereby further hindering reconstruction of the world economy, which as a result had few chances of success. It is therefore not surprising that an enormous economic crisis eventually erupted, marking the beginning of the end of the 'postwar order'.

81. Laws passed in 1921 and 1924 limited immigration to 165,000 in 1925 and 150,000 in 1927. In 1913 by comparison, it had almost reached 1.2 million. Another argument which was advanced was prevention of the bastardisation of the race by Slavs and southern Europeans.
82. For the period prior to 1914, see in this regard P. Bairoch, *Commerce extérieur*, pp. 111–22.
83. For a pertinent analysis see E. Trendelenburg, 'Bis zum Dawes Plan', pp. 55, 75f., 122f. F. Somary, *Wandlungen der Weltwirtschaft*, has a similar view, pp. 33–9.

III. Reduced World Trade, the Decline of Europe and Economic Hard Times

American capital exports certainly contributed to the expansion of world trade between 1924 and 1929, a phase which in many people's minds heralded a permanent recovery. However, the negative repercussions of American economic dominance also set tight limits on the volume of world trade, as we have seen. Further factors, largely unrelated to the United States, help to explain why world trade, though clearly expanding in these years, failed to develop anything like the momentum generated before 1914 (not to mention the era following the Second World War).[84] At no time did world trade act as a real additional stimulus to national economies. Since this structural flaw was directly related to the economic paramountcy of the United States, it proved impossible in the second half of the 1920s to attempt to consolidate and coordinate national and international economic conditions.

The evolution of world trade during this period reveals a number of shortcomings, of which many contemporaries were well aware. The export volume index surpassed its prewar level in 1924, but then grew very tentative and halting, especially in 1925–6, in response to another recession in many countries (Table 8). None of the highly industrialised countries achieved growth rates between 1913 and 1929 equalling prewar growth. However, characteristic discrepancies did emerge: while Europe suffered major reverses (especially Germany, Britain and Switzerland; France least of all), the United States and Canada approached their prewar performances.[85]

The state of international trade is best indicated by the fact that it was growing more slowly than international production, in stark contrast to the pre-1914 and post-1945 periods.[86] This held true throughout the 1920s for finished goods. So far as agriculture and minerals are concerned, a turning point was reached in 1925 when production surpassed the 1913 level by 17 per cent, though world population had risen by only 6 per cent and total world trade by 7 per cent. The situation was

84. See E.S. and W.S. Woytinsky, *World Commerce and Government* (NY, 1955); A. Maizels, *Industrial Growth and World Trade* (Cambridge, Mass., 1963); P.L. Yates, *Forty Years of Foreign Trade, 1913–1953* (London, 1959).

85. The growth rate figures are contradictory. The Woytinskys give 39 and 35.1 per cent for the period between 1913 and 1929; other authors give higher or lower figures (cf. A. Maizels, *Industrial and World Trade*, P.L. Yates, *Forty Years of Foreign Trade*). Cf. in this regard D.H. Aldcroft, *Zwanziger Jahre*, p. 345 (Table 17) and pp. 346–54.

86. G. Bienstock, *Deutschland und die Weltwirtschaft*, pp. 18ff.; Ohlin Report in Comité Mixte (ed.), *Reconstruction économique internationale*, p. 37f.; League of Nations, *Industrialisation et commerce extérieur*, p. 17.

Table 8 World Trade: Exports, Imports, Export Volume Index (1913; 1920–32; and for comparison, 1938, 1949 and 1951)

Year	Exports (in millions of gold dollars)	Imports	Export Volume (Index 1929 = 100)
1913	19,800	20,800	74.0
1920	31,600	34,200	53.5
1921	19,700	22,100	55.0
1922	21,700	23,600	59.0
1923	23,800	25,900	65.5
1924	27,850	28,980	75.7
1925	31,550	33,150	83.2
1926	29,920	32,120	85.2
1927	31,520	33,760	91.9
1928	32,730	34,650	95.2
1929	33,024	35,595	100.0
1930	26,480	29,080	93.0
1931	18,910	20,800	85.5
1932	12,885	13,970	74.5
	(in millions of US dollars)		
1938	20,700	23,200	89.0
1949	53,700	58,500	100.1
1951	75,400	80,200	124.2

Source: W.S. and E.S. Woytinsky, *World Commerce and Governments* (NY, 1955), p. 39.

quite different in the period between 1926 and 1929, when international trade increased more rapidly than production. However, even this was not particularly auspicious, since the productive capacity of the peripheral countries (the 'white Dominions' and the countries of Latin America thanks to the new strategy of import substitution) was rising more rapidly than the demand in the highly industrialised core. The resulting decline in the price of primary products was one of the most important reasons for the collapse of the international agricultural market.[87]

These weaknesses are of cardinal importance in that they indicate that the international division of labour, that is, the extent to which various national economies were interwoven, had suffered a considerable setback. As a result, international trade failed for the most part to contribute to the expansion of the world economy. Many countries, especially in Europe, experienced a reduction in their export ratio, that is, the

87. See D. Landes, *The Unbound Prometheus*, pp. 339–41. The collapse of agricultural prices aggravated the general depression in agriculture caused by over production after the First World War. See the classic work by V.E. Timoshenko, *World Agriculture and Depression* (Ann Arbor, 1953). The countries of southern and south-eastern Europe were especially hard hit.

share of national income attributable to foreign trade. Even more dangerous in the long term was the tendency towards the regionalisation of international trade which became apparent already in 1928 well before the onset of the Great Depression. International trade was increasingly confined to preference zones or even trading 'blocks', and intra-regional trade became more important than inter-regional. By the end of the 1920s, four such zones were beginning to emerge: Europe and its colonies, the sterling-zone, the dollar-zone (the United States, Canada and Latin America) and, even earlier, the Soviet Union. This too was a sign that the world economy was disintegrating.[88] The process was hastened by the depressed prices for agricultural products and raw materials, which cast further doubt on the 'complementary' but already highly unjust international division of labour,[89] while failing to provide an alternative.

Europe's declining importance in world trade marked another momentous change, that was also much lamented by contemporaries.[90] In contrast to the United States, per capita income in the three most important European economies, Britain, Germany and France, was stagnant. Each country's share of international industrial production was dwindling (Table 1, p. 40). France declined least, though she began to suffer heavy losses in the 1930s as a result of the Great Depression, deflationary policies and the fact that she had directed her reconstruction efforts during the 1920s toward modernising primary industry, machine building and the automobile industry while neglecting the 'old' consumer goods industries. None of these three countries adapted very successfully to the new conditions on world markets, among which numbered the rapid and occasionally explosive expansion of productive capacity not only in the United States but also in a series of peripheral countries such as Canada, Australia, New Zealand, Japan, Argentina, Brazil and even India.[91] There were differences in the rate of

88. M. Byé and G. Destanne de Bernis, *Relations économiques internationales* (Paris, 1977[4]), vol. 1, p. 436.
89. G. Hardach, *Deutschland in der Weltwirtschaft 1870–1970* (Frankfurt, 1977), p. 106f.
90. From the abundant literature see I. Svennilson, *Growth and Stagnation*; W. Fischer, 'Die Weimarer Republik unter den weltwirtschaftlichen Bedingungen der Zwischenkriegszeit' [The Weimar Republic in the Economic Conditions of the Interwar Era] in H. Mommsen et al. (eds), *Industrielles System*, pp. 25–50; E. Lundberg, *Instability and Economic Growth* (New Haven, 1968). Of interest is H. Gaedicke and G. v. Eynern, *Die produktionwirtschaftliche Integration Europas* [The Integration of Production in Europe] (Berlin, 1933); for the 'de-Europeanisation tendencies' in the world economy see the extensive analysis by H. Lewy, *Der Weltmarkt 1913 und heute* (Berlin, 1926), pp. 75–100.
91. See in detail D. Rothermund (ed.), *Die Peripherie in der Weltwirtschaftskrise. Afrika, Asien und Lateinamerika 1919–1939* [The Periphery in the Great Depression. Africa, Asia and Latin America 1919–1939] (Paderborn, 1983).

productivity growth of course between the various European economies and between the various branches and sectors of each national economy.[92] On the whole, though, no European country managed to regain, let alone surpass, the position it had held prior to 1914 in the international division of labour. What is more, none of them managed to avoid a severe structural crisis in agriculture. In this, they were no different from the United States, apart from the important strides the Americans had made towards mechanising their huge farms.[93]

It is therefore not surprising that Europe's share of world trade was in decline (Table 9). The loss of exports relative to 1913 could not be recouped even in the years of relative recovery. While intra-European trade comprised some 40 per cent of world trade in 1913, this share had shrunk to 29.2 per cent by 1928. In those same years, the share of world trade carried on by non-European nations rose from 23.3 per cent to 28.9 per cent (Table 9a). North America (especially the United States) and Asia (especially Japan) experienced considerable success, though it could not be fully maintained in the late 1920s when the Europeans began to win back market share (without approaching, however, their prewar levels). None the less, the non-Europeans still recorded an improvement on their prewar record. The trend towards a 'de-Europeanisation' of world trade was unmistakable. The slide could not even be halted by the partially successful attempts of Germany and Great Britain to 'reopen' the Soviet market. Noteworthy as well is the declining share of American exports absorbed by Europe while all other regions were increasing their intake (Table 10). France and Great Britain compensated for their loss of exports by intensifying trade with their colonies, in keeping with the tendency discussed above toward regionalisation of world trade. Even within Europe, the leading exporting nations of Britain, Germany and France lost ground to their smaller competitors (Table 11).

The deterioration of Europe's position in the international division of labour is particularly apparent if the two countries most intensely involved in world trade, Britain and Germany, are studied more closely.[94] The economic competitiveness of both countries was blunted by an over-valued currency. Neither, when stabilising its currency, had taken into account its reduced productivity after the war in comparison with the United States. Their trade balance, which had always been un-

92. Unfortunately, no systematic comparative study of this exists.
93. In 1930 there were over one million tractors in the United States and only 130,000 in Europe (without the Soviet Union). For more extensive analysis see V.E. Timoshenko, *World Agriculture and Depression*, C.P. Kindleberger, *Die Weltwirtschaftskrise 1929–1939*, Chapt. 3.
94. G. Hardach, *Deutschland in der Weltwirtschaft 1870–1970*, pp. 105–11.

Table 9 a) Regional Share of World Exports (World = 100)

Year	North America	Central America	South America	Europe	Russia (USSR)	Asia	Africa	Oceania
1913	15.8	2.4	6.7	50.9	4.3	12.5	4.7	2.7
1926	20.7	3.0	6.4	42.9	1.2	18.1	4.4	3.3
1929	19.5	9.6		47.4	1.4	14.9	4.5	2.7
1932	16.3	9.1		48.8	2.3	13.7	6.7	3.1
1937	17.1	10.3		44.8	1.1	16.2	7.1	3.4
For comparison								
1947	36.1	3.9	8.8	32.2	1.0	9.7	5.5	2.9

b) Regional Share of World Imports (World = 100)

Year	North America	Central America	South America	Europe	Russia (USSR)	Asia	Africa	Oceania
1913	12.4	1.9	5.7	57.9	3.6	11.8	4.1	2.6
1926	17.6	2.2	5.5	50.6	1.2	15.3	4.4	3.2
1929	16.1	7.7		54.2	1.3	13.2	4.8	2.7
1932	14.2	7.2		53.7	2.5	13.7	6.2	2.5
1937	15.5	8.6		50.2	1.0	14.9	6.7	3.1
For comparison								
1947	26.4	4.1	8.3	38.8	2.1	11.3	6.5	2.6

c) Regional Share of Total Foreign Trade (World = 100)

Year	North America	Central America	South America	Europe	Russia (USSR)	Asia	Africa	Oceania
1913	14.1	2.1	6.2	54.5	3.9	12.1	4.4	2.7
1926	19.1	2.6	6.0	46.9	1.2	16.6	4.4	3.2
1929	17.7	8.6		51.1	1.3	14.0	4.6	2.7
1932	14.2	7.2		53.7	2.5	13.7	6.2	2.5
1937	15.5	8.6		50.2	1.0	14.9	6.7	3.1
For comparison								
1947	26.4	4.1	8.3	38.8	2.1	11.3	6.5	2.6

Source: W. S. and E. S. Woytinsky, *World Commerce and Governments* (NY, 1955), p. 45.

Table 9a European Share of World Trade

	1913	1928	1938
Intra-European trade	40.0	29.2	29.1
Imports into Europe	21.5	24.7	26.6
Imports from Europe	15.2	17.2	17.7
Trade between non-European countries	23.3	28.9	26.8

Source: M. Byé and G. Destanne de Bernis, *Relations économiques internationales* (Paris, 1977^4), p. 343.

favourable anyway in the case of Great Britain, took a turn for the worse. When confronted with powerful American competition, Britain was forced to beat a retreat as a supplier of capital and exporter of goods to virtually all substantial world markets, whether Latin America and south-east Asia, the oil fields of the Middle and Near East or even the dominions of Canada and Australia. The consequence was economic stagnation, the decay of entire branches of the economy, especially 'old' industries, and further aggravation of structural unemployment.[95] This was one of the main reasons for the deterioration of Britain's position both within the Versailles System (as a mediator or referee between France and Germany) and within the Washington System. This decline in Britain's position in the world economy and on the international political stage was grist for the mill of those who, drawing their inspiration from Chamberlain's Greater Britain movement before the Great War,[96] clung to the Empire as Britain's security net and an enduring reminder of her former power and glory.

German exports also declined substantially, especially in the first half of the 1920s. By 1928, the net domestic product had risen to 103 per cent

95. Cf. with many of M.D. Goldberg's details in 'Anglo-American Economic Competition'; contemporary information, e.g. L. Denny, *America Conquers Britain* (NY, 1930). Examples: Britain's share of the imports of twenty Latin American countries plummeted between 1913 and 1927 from 27 per cent to 16 per cent while the U.S. share rose from 24 to 38 per cent; Britain's share of Chinese imports fell from 16.5 per cent in 1913 to 10.2 per cent in 1926 while American imports rose from 6 per cent to 16 per cent; Britain's share of Japanese imports fell from 16.8 per cent in 1914 to 7 per cent in 1925 while American imports rose from 16.8 per cent in 1914 to 30.9 per cent in 1927. Statistics on this loss of market share can be found in R.H. Meyer, *Banker's Diplomacy*, p. 12 and F. Somary, *Wandlungen der Weltwirtschaft*, p. 64; cf. as well A.L. Bowley, *Some Economic Consequences of the War* (London, 1930); K. Hutchison, *The Decline and Fall of British Capitalism* (London, 1951).
96. See in this regard W. Mock, *Imperiale Herrschaft und nationales Interesse. 'Constructive Imperialism' oder Freihandel in Grossbritannien vor dem Ersten Weltkrieg* [Imperial Rule and the National Interest. Constructive Imperialism or Free Trade in Great Britain before the First World War] (Stuttgart, 1982).

Table 10 Regional Share of Exports from Selected Countries, 1913 and 1927 (as a percentage)

Country	Year	North America	Central America	South America	Europe	Asia	Africa	Oceania
USA	1913	16.4	7.7	5.9	60.4	6.2	1.2	2.2
	1927	17.4	8.4	9.0	47.5	11.5	2.2	4.0
GB	1913	10.3	1.8	9.5	34.7	25.2	9.8	8.7
	1927	10.7	1.8	8.4	34.0	22.3	11.3	11.5
France	1913	6.6	1.1	9.5	69.0	3.9	13.3	0.4
	1927	7.3	1.3	4.7	63.6	7.3	15.1	0.7
Germany	1913	7.7	1.0	6.6	75.2	6.4	2.1	1.0
	1927	7.8	1.1	6.3	74.0	7.6	2.4	0.8
Japan	1913	30.0	0.1	0.3	23.3	43.8	0.3	2.2
	1927	43.2	0.3	1.0	7.4	42.4	2.6	3.1
China	1913	9.2	0.0	0.0	25.3	65.4	0.0	0.1
	1927	13.4	0.0	0.1	19.2	67.2	0.0	0.1

Source: W.S. and E.S. Woytinsky, *World Commerce and Governments* (NY, 1955), p. 74f.

Table 11 Share of Intra-European Trade Held by Various Countries (Exports to all of Europe and Russia) (as a percentage)

1913		1928	
1. Germany	25.3	Germany	21.5
2. France	12.8	France	12.7
3. Britain	12.6	Britain	11.5
4. Russia	9.9	Belgium/Luxembourg	6.0
5. Belgium	7.8	Netherlands	5.9
6. Austria–Hungary	6.6	Czechoslovakia	5.3
7. Netherlands	5.0	Italy	4.4
8. Italy	4.3	Denmark	4.2
9. Switzerland	2.7	Sweden	3.2
10. Sweden	2.7	USSR	3.0

Source: H. Gaedicke and G. von Eynern, *Die produktionswirtschaftliche Integration Europas* (Berlin, 1933), p. 27.

of its 1913 level and imports to 102 per cent; exports, however, fell to 86 per cent of their 1913 values.[97] Germany's export ratio fell from 17.5 per cent in 1910–13 to 14.9 per cent in 1924–5, and her import ratio from 20.2 to 17 per cent. Both countries suffered particularly painful losses to the United States in the world market for finished products. While the share of North America (primarily the United States) climbed from 10.6 per cent in 1913 to 19.2 per cent in 1928, Britain's share fell from 25.3 to 21.8 per cent and Germany's from 21.3 to 16.4 per cent (1925: 13.9 per cent).[98] G. Bienstock has calculated that the four most important economies (Great Britain, Germany, France and the United States) accounted for almost three-quarters of total world exports of finished goods before the First World War and that of this amount Germany accounted for some 30 per cent in 1913, 20 per cent in 1925 and 25 per cent in 1928. However, Germany succeeded at first more than Britain in defending her position on world markets thanks to her exports of finished goods which rose from 53.3 per cent of the total in 1910–13 to 59.1 per cent in 1924–5. Machine-building, the electrical industry, precision mechanics and chemical products continued to be the main-stays. While the export index for all finished goods (1913 = 100) only once surpassed prewar levels during the 1920s (1929 = 106.7), the

97. G. Hardach, *Deutschland in der Weltwirtschaft 1870–1970*, p. 167; W.G. Hoffmann et al., *Das Wachstum der deutschen Wirtschaft seit der Mitte des 19. Jahrhunderts* [The Growth of the German Economy after the mid-19th Century] (Berlin, 1965), pp. 820–8.
98. D.H. Aldcroft, *Zwanziger Jahre*, Table 19, p. 349; somewhat different figures but the same trend in G. Bienstock, *Deutschland und die Weltwirtschaft*, p. 44 and *passim*; cf. above, Table 9.

Table 12 Proportion of the Exports of Eight Industrial Countries:[1] Market Share by Product Group (all eight countries = 100)

		GB	Germany	France	USA
Electrical and	1913	29.4	34.8	3.5	23.5
Non-Electrical	1928	23.9	28.2	5.9	31.2
Machines	1938	24.6	30.4	2.8	30.2
Transportation	1913	37.3	17.3	16.4	17.3
	1928	21.0	4.4	8.4	58.8
	1938	21.9	19.6	4.0	45.1
Chemical Industry	1913	23.4	44.0	11.9	7.6
	1928	17.4	42.8	11.7	16.2
	1938	15.7	40.7	9.7	17.4
Textiles	1913	46.8	15.4	14.6	3.2
	1928	41.7	12.9	19.6	6.8
	1938	42.2	15.3	11.1	7.7
Total Exports	1913	24.6	23.2	12.8	23.4
	1928	22.0	18.1	12.8	31.6
	1938	21.9	20.7	8.5	29.3

[1]Great Britain, Germany, France, Italy, Belgium–Luxembourg, Switzerland, Sweden, USA
Source: I. Svennilson, *Growth and Stagnation*, p. 187.

performance of machine-building alone was far more impressive: 1924 = 60.5, 1925 = 78.4, 1926 = 86.4, 1927 = 91.2, 1928 = 110.1, 1929 = 129.6, 1930 = 134.4.[99] Germany's export success in the area of mechanical engineering was especially important to her in that internal markets for these products were very soft. The German chemical industry, on the other hand, lost world market share during the 1920s, whereas it had held a virtual monopoly prior to 1914.[100] An analysis of the evolution of market share by product group (Table 12) illustrates once again the relative success of American exporters compared to Europeans, primarily in the realm of transportation but also in machine-building and chemicals.

A number of neo-Marxist authors[101] contend that the technical and

99. W. Hoffmann et al., *Das Wachstum der deutschen Wirtschaft*, Table 129, p. 531; Table 130, p. 534f.
100. Some information in J. Borkin, *Die unheilige Allianz der IG-Farben. Eine Interessengemeinschaft im Dritten Reich* [The Unholy Alliance of IG-Farben. Common Interests in the Third Reich] (Frankfurt, 1979), Chapter 2.
101. See the contributions from I. Wallerstein (see esp. Chapt. 1, note 48), G. Arrighi, 'Der Klassenkampf in Westeuropa im 20. Jahrhundert', and S. Amin et al., *La crise, quelle crise? Dynamique de la crise mondiale* (Paris, 1982), pp. 34, 69 note 4, and 172.

organisational superiority of American capitalism and, above all, its aptitude for crossing international frontiers drove other industrial nations such as Germany and Japan back into the 'semiperiphery'. They even speak of a 'Thirty Years War' from 1914 till 1945 between Germany and the United States over domination of the world economy. Such assertions are doubtless vastly exaggerated. Germany and certainly Japan did not have the slightest hope of engaging in such a competition in the 1920s. And yet there could be a grain of truth in these assertions which deserves further consideration. One of the reasons for the rise of National Socialism in Germany and of militarism in Japan may well be that the apparently irresistible economic offensive of the United States, only temporarily blunted by the Great Depression, frightened the Germans and Japanese into believing that they might be driven from the world markets on which they were both highly dependent. It must be admitted that American economic supremacy represented at the very least an extremely serious challenge. The other view, according to which the United States made Germany and Japan her privileged economic partners within the Versailles and Washington Systems, produces in the end much the same result when the striving for political revisionism and economic autonomy resulted in a highly explosive situation. Logically enough, it was the Great Depression which ultimately lit the fuse.

An examination of the ups and downs of the world economy during the 1920s demonstrates once again the extent to which it was influenced by domestic developments within the United States. The economic recovery that began in the United States in 1922 and in Europe in 1924 was less broadly based and persistent than at first assumed, as perspicacious contemporary observers quickly noted.[102] Its strength also varied greatly from country to country. Steep downturns, and occasional lasting recessions, occurred on all sides. A number of countries experienced ongoing stagnation or weak rates of growth: England, Italy, Denmark, Norway, Sweden, Austria, Australia and India. Particularly high rates of growth were recorded in the United States, Canada, some Latin American countries, Japan and South Africa. Serious and recurrent recessions, often steeper than before the war, shook the economies of the leading industrial nations. Germany and Great Britain were

---

102. D.H. Aldcroft, *Zwanziger Jahre*, Chapt. 8; C.P. Kindleberger, *Die Weltwirtschaftskrise 1929–1939*; E. Lundberg, *Instability and Economic Growth*. Some voices in Europe were extremely sceptical about the recovery. See. E. Wagemann, *Struktur und Rhythmus der Weltwirtschaft. Grundlage einer weltwirtschaftlichen Konjunkturlehre* [The Structure and Rhythm of the World Economy. Foundation of a Theory about the Vicissitudes of the World Economy] (Hamburg, 1931). Wagemann too considers the most dangerous symptom to be the mounting disparity after 1928 in the power of capital and consumers.

particularly hard hit in 1926 and the United States, France and Italy in 1927. Japan experienced a severe financial crisis in 1928, and portents of a similar crisis loomed elsewhere, especially in Germany and Poland. In the already rather short period between 1922/24 and 1929, real economic recovery only endured for a few months.

The fragility of the economic upswing was related to another of its major characteristics: inadequate demand. Prices declined too slowly – wholesale prices did not begin to fall until the first half of 1929[103] – while average wages in most countries rose only marginally. In some countries the unemployment rate between 1925 and 1929 was even higher than it had been between 1921 and 1924. As developments in the United States were duplicated elsewhere (particularly in the developed countries though to differing extents), two pernicious trends emerged, strengthening and reinforcing one another: first, a structural crisis (the decline of 'old' industries; the first wave of economic rationalisation, especially in the expanding sectors of the economy; the catastrophic state of agriculture) and secondly the imbalanced distribution of increases in income as a result of deflationary policies and the concentration and centralisation of capital.[104]

IV. The Failure of the International Economic Conference of 1927

The underlying weaknesses in the world economy and monetary system were not unknown to those countries which were eager to consolidate the 'postwar order' by means of the Versailles and Washington Systems and which realised that the economic situation posed a far greater danger than potential political or strategic events. It was by no means mere happenstance, therefore, that a Frenchman, Louis Loucheur, urged the League of Nations as early as 1925 to hold an international economic conference. After tortuous preliminary negotiations, the conference finally convened in Geneva from 4 to 23 May 1927 with the hope of reducing political tensions by addressing the most pressing economic difficulties.[105] The League Assembly had already passed a resolution at

103. H. Truchy, *La reconstruction économique de l'Europe*, pp. 15ff. contains precise indices.
104. C.P. Kindleberger, *Die Weltwirtschaftskrise 1929–1939*, p. 108f. and D.H. Aldcroft, *Zwanziger Jahre*, p. 223f. tend to obscure the phenomenon when they describe it as 'structural deflation within a boom'.
105. See in detail E. von Bastineller, 'Die Genfer Weltwirtschaftskonferenz des Jahres 1927'; E. Respondek, *Die Internationale Wirtschaftskonferenz des Völkerbundes zu Genf. Wiedergabe der Plenar- und Kommissionssitzungen* (Berlin, 1927); A. Salter, *The Economic Consequences of the League. The World Economic Conference* (London,

its regular meeting in 1925 declaring that 'economic peace will make a substantial contribution to national security'. It was therefore necessary for the League 'to study the economic problems which hinder a return to general prosperity and to determine the most appropriate means of overcoming these difficulties and preventing conflict'. The League also drew an explicit connection between 'prosperity' and 'world peace'. Forty-seven states accepted an invitation to the conference, and the appearance of both the United States and the Soviet Union caused no small sensation. The delegations comprised representatives of governments, employer associations and labour unions (though the latter were vastly underrepresented in the typical fashion of the day). In total, the meetings were attended by 194 official delegates assisted by 157 experts.

No one seriously believed of course that this unwieldy body would soon repair the profound structural flaws in the world economy. Indeed, the conference got off to a very bad start when France, the initiator of the proceedings, announced just as they were commencing that it intended to adopt extremely prohibitive tariffs. On a more positive note, the opening address of the conference president, M. Theunis of Belgium, was a masterpiece of clarity and insight into the problems of the world economy. Drawing on a host of monographs and memoranda which together drew a detailed picture of the world economy (and which still await closer analysis), the delegates decided to deal with three of the most important issues: the impediments to international trade, the problems of key industrial sectors and the plight of agriculture.

The entire course of the debates need not be outlined for the purposes of this study. It is noteworthy though that calls for a return to the prewar order were widely considered to be outmoded and of little help. Indeed, all of the 'recommendations' in the final resolution would have made a positive contribution toward resolving global economic problems. During the debates, free trade was much extolled as a means of overcoming the impediments to international trade, though everyone realised that this was a pipe dream; the final resolution therefore contented itself with encouraging the inclusion of unconditional most-favoured-nation status in trade agreements. The League of Nations was even asked to draw up fundamental principles to this end. Somewhat naively, 'exaggerated' tariffs were condemned as 'injurious' to the state that imposed them as well as to the world economy. All the participating governments were requested to draw up plans for the gradual reduction of tariffs, and the final resolution encouraged joint action by national governments in

1927); League of Nations, *La politique commerciale entre les deux guerres: propositions internationales et politiques nationales* (Geneva, 1942), pp. 33–47.

order to facilitate this process. Export levies would only be imposed 'to the extent that they are absolutely essential to national finances' or in case of particularly trying circumstances.

These points touch on only a small fraction of the numerous 'recommendations' of the conference, the economic rationale of which is immediately apparent. However there was, then as now, a long and difficult road from theoretical insight to actual policy. Contemporaries themselves criticised the vague and non-binding nature of the 'recommendations' which were always tailored to the lowest common denominator and riddled with loopholes. The conference had more in common with a 'commission of inquiry' into the reasons for crisis than an assembly empowered with decision-making abilities.[106] The difficulty was highlighted when the 'recommendations' touched on the hotly disputed topic of economic rationalisation. The battle lines were drawn along two distinct fronts, one representing competing national interests and the other the competing views of employers and labour unions regardless of nationality. Employers categorically rejected any union participation in the planning and implementation of rationalisation, steadfastly refusing even the most modest requests to take the interests of labour into account. It is a struggle that has not been satisfactorily resolved to this very day.

The debate about international industrial cartels was also very contentious, and the conference was forced to abstain from any 'fundamental conclusions'. On the other hand, there was general agreement that international cartels were unlikely to make a positive contribution toward solving the problems of the world economy; but on the other they were said to embody some advantages, at least in so far as they did not contrive to discourage technical innovation or to trample on the fundamental interests of certain social groups or national economies. The conference found itself performing a balancing act on the high wire of diplomatic compromise, and though it managed to draw up a register of proscribed activities ('artificial' price increases, for instance), any form of international enforcement was rejected. None the less, when the final vote was held on this series of resolutions predicated on nothing more than declarations of noble intent, the United States and the Soviet Union both abstained, though for opposite reasons.

The impracticality of the conference was reflected in the fact that such crucial topics as war reparations and inter-Allied debts were not discussed and even could not be discussed. None of the powers involved was about to allow these matters to enter the purview of the League of

---

106. B. Harms, *Vom Wirtschaftskrieg zur Weltwirtschaftskonferenz* [From Economic War to the International Economic Conference] (Jena, 1927), p. 334f.

Nations. In fact, the League was very ill-suited to act as a central economic institution in addition to its primary function of establishing and reinforcing collective security. It was this veiled economic agenda, discernible in the final resolutions, to which the United States and the Soviet Union both objected, along with many others who kept their feelings more guarded. And so the conference was left to wither on the vine.[107] However, the League's attempt to establish collective security in isolation from economic developments remained a highly dubious undertaking, and it is not surprising that the League met its final come-uppance in the Great Depression.

The great conference of 1927 had few practical consequences, especially as many countries experienced a downturn in their economies a few months later, though still well before the Great Depression. The showpiece of the contractual system advocated by the conference – a Franco-German trade agreement – was achieved in August 1927, but the trend toward higher tariffs reasserted itself as early as 1929, especially in the realm of agricultural products. Governments increasingly feared that tariff reductions would destroy their less competitive industries and further aggravate unemployment. The political debate in the United States made further massive increases in the American tariffs appear inevitable, sending devastating psychological signals. One year later, Washington actually enacted these tariffs under the pressure of the economic crisis, delivering the *coup de grâce* to all further efforts at tariff reduction.

---

107. Some voices in German public opinion judged the conference to be a success simply because it opposed French interests (lowest possible reduction in tariff barriers). See among others A. Feiler, *Neue Weltwirtschaft. Die Lehre von Genf.* Special publication of the *Frankfurter Zeitung*, 1927.

3
The Structural Problems of the Versailles System 1924–9

I. The Myth of an Era of 'Relative Stability'

1. The United States as the Driving Force

Though fears had abounded in late 1923 that the Versailles System would 'eventually collapse',[1] indications began to accumulate in 1924 that the chaotic condition of postwar Europe was slowly being overcome, on both the domestic and international levels. This recovery was triggered not least of all by the economic boom in the United States. In all the leading industrial countries, factory output began to rise, though at very different rates, and by 1929 it reached the level of 1913 (Table 3, p. 42). On a regional level, rising industrial production was distributed more evenly after 1924 than in the first half of the 1920s.[2] Even raw materials were affected by this upswing, though with fairly large regional variations. At the same time, world trade was expanding. It regained its prewar level in 1924 (Table 8, p. 63) and increased another 21 per cent between 1925 and 1929. All this leads Aldcroft to conclude that 'the world was richer on the whole in 1925 than in 1913'.[3]

What is more, the political atmosphere was improving. The adoption of the Dawes Plan marked a first step toward resolving the thorny reparations issue which had long envenomed international relations. The Dawes Plan owed its acceptance in large part to the election of left-leaning governments in Great Britain (December 1923) and France (May 1924). This in turn set the stage for what was termed 'the spirit of Locarno' after 1925. The new spirit rested on Germany's acceptance of the western boundary established by the Treaty of Versailles and on her

---

1. According to M. Trachtenberg, *Reparations in World Politics*, p. 334.
2. D.H. Aldcroft, *Zwanziger Jahre*, p. 216f.
3. Ibid., table 5, pp. 120ff.

apparent readiness to contribute to the system of collective security fostered by the League of Nations and based on the acceptance of international arbitration and disarmament. All these factors contributed to the development of a *modus vivendi* between the victors and the vanquished strong enough to stabilise the situation in western Europe.

In eastern Europe too, the atmosphere began to improve. France and Great Britain recognised the Soviet government, marking a first step towards the normalisation of relations with the world's foremost revolutionary power and the elimination of the 'cordon sanitaire' which had isolated her. Moscow, for its part, adopted the 'New Economic Policy' and signed the Rapallo Treaty in a limited but unmistakable gesture of opening to the West. The Soviets realised that the revolutionary tidal wave foreseen by Lenin showed no signs of emerging, and ideological tensions began to abate as well. For a time, it may have seemed as if economic and monetary developments as well as domestic and international politics were beginning to come together in support of the Versailles System.

These impressions were illusory, though they still often shape the historical view of the era. Europe was still, to be sure, the second most powerful industrial region in the world after the United States (despite substantial reductions, in some cases, in its share of global industrial output and commerce). Fully one-third of aggregate world income was earned in Europe, excluding the USSR.[4] However, Europe was stagnating, as we have seen, in respect to both productivity and per capita income, which did not make its social problems any easier to solve. What we have called the 'relative economic decline of Europe' did not change appreciably during the second half of the 1920s, especially in comparison to the United States. Furthermore, the way in which currency stabilisation was carried out actually aggravated the economic situation on both the national and international levels, though it contributed a great deal to the feeling of a 'return to normalcy'.

The single most important factor has long been underestimated, at least by European historians:[5] the impulse to save the Versailles System did not emanate from Europe itself but rather from the United States. It was Washington that intervened to rescue the system from early collapse, though the Americans had clearly withdrawn from it both politically and institutionally. This necessarily implied a fundamental change in the new order in Europe, which raises the question of whether it was strengthened or weakened by American intervention. Washington's interests on the other hand were clear: any continuation of the chaotic

---

4. W. Fischer, *Weltwirtschaftliche Rahmenbedingungen*, p. 13.
5. Apart from some exceptions, especially the works of W. Link and the French historian, D. Artaud.

situation in Europe would one day threaten America's own prosperity and notably the open-door policy, which had perforce to operate on a global scale or not at all and which Wilson had again proclaimed at the Paris Peace Conference. If this policy was to succeed, it had to include a reconstructed Europe.

The only modification to this strategy in the 1920s was that Wilson's Republican successors hoped to achieve the 'open door' without the benefit of formal agreements based on international law, which they believed would only limit their freedom of action. Buoyed by the wave of prosperity in their own country, the Republicans were all the more determined to implement their 'grand design' and to construct, as Hughes said, 'a "community of ideals, interests and purposes" together with other highly developed industrial nations, the first and foremost of which was Germany. This would be accomplished through peaceful compromise, backed up if necessary by economic pressure'.[6] This was undoubtedly the impulse behind the Dawes Plan, which formed the keystone of the Republican strategy.

In addition, the position of the United States had improved substantially after 1919.[7] Historians often claim that Washington originally disengaged from the world scene because it did not wish to assume global political and economic responsibilities.[8] But another view (first propagated by W.A. Williams and his school, notably C.P. Parrini, and later developed further[9]) provides a more likely explanation: the American withdrawal was not due to 'isolationism' but was rather a tactical measure dictated by temporary weakness. In contrast to Truman in 1947, Wilson was unable in 1919 to help put Europe back on its feet by dint of government loans. He came under heavy pressure from the Treasury Department, supported by the Federal Reserve Board, which strongly opposed any continuation of the credits granted to Allied

6. W. Link, *Die amerikanische Stabilisierungspolitik*, p. 37. The similarities between Wilson's views at the Paris Peace Conference and the Dawes Plan are pointed out by C. Parrini, *Heir to Empire*, p. 68f., and W. Diamond, *The Economic Thought of W. Wilson* (Baltimore, 1943).

7. For the following see the extended analysis of F. Luther in a paper delivered on 3 January 1975.

8. According, for instance, to K. Schwabe, *Deutsche Revolution und Wilsonfriede* (Düsseldorf, 1971), *passim*. However, Schwabe too seems inclined to think that the Americans found themselves in a weak position, p. 652.

9. See for what follows the pioneering work of D. Artaud, *La reconstruction de l'Europe 1919–1929* (Paris, 1973), p. 14; idem, 'Le gouvernement américain et la question des dettes de guerre au lendemain de l'armistice de Rethondes (1919–1920)', *RHMC* 20 (1973); above all, idem, *La question des dettes interalliés et la reconstruction de l'Europe* (Paris, 1978); P.P. Abrahams, 'American Bankers and the Economic Tactics of Peace 1919', *JAH* 56 (1969/70); R.H. Van Meter, *American Foreign Policy and the Economic Reconstruction of Europe, 1918–1921*, Topic 16 (Washington, DC, 1968).

governments during the war. Influential bankers encouraged Washington to keep the pipeline open and thereby assume its international responsibilities, but the Treasury Department together with the Congress and the bulk of the American people demanded first of all that America's former Allies pay off their war debts as quickly as possible.

This was the principal reason for the political objections to far-reaching American participation in the reconstruction of Europe (though modest amounts of capital were made available). In addition, bankers found it difficult to raise private capital for Europe on account of the political, social and economic turmoil prevailing there.[10] In the end, Washington experienced some difficulties with the open-door policy because both Britain and France fiercely resisted non-discrimination in trade as well as a settlement of the reparations issue as prerequisites for American cooperation with Europe. The failure of the United States to ratify the Treaty of Versailles, her boycott of international conferences in Brussels in 1920 and Geneva in 1922, her refusal to cooperate on the inter-Allied economic committee and her exclusive regard for domestic concerns in formulating monetary policy all resulted to a large extent from her limited margin of manoeuvre.

In view of the extensive literature available,[11] it is not necessary to examine the genesis of the Dawes Plan in detail. The crucial question from our point of view is how the United States was able to strengthen her position to such an extent that she was capable in 1923 of simply seizing control and dictating the conditions under which she would re-engage in Europe. In fact, a number of domestic and international developments were responsible for this turn of events. The economic upswing in the United States after 1922 was primarily due to the domestic economy, while international economic relations played only a marginal role.[12] By 1923 therefore, the United States was far less dependent on European markets than she had been in 1919. Her trade surpluses plummeted in these years from 4,500 million dollars to 400 million; exports plunged from 10 per cent to 4.8 per cent of domestic production, and the unemployment rate fell from 11.9 per cent in 1921 to 3.2 per cent in 1923 – all of which underscores the crucial role of the domestic market in the American recovery. The sharp reduction in the American balance of payments surplus stemmed largely from diminished demand in Europe for foodstuffs and raw materials.

The international shortage of dollars grew more and more acute, a

---

10. Not even the suggestion of presidential advisers that the War Finance Corporation guarantee private American export credits was accepted by the Treasury Department. In addition, it took some time to appreciate the full extent of Europe's economic decline.

11. Cf. W. Link, *Die amerikanische Stabilisierungspolitik*, Part II.

12. See for the following H.B. Lary et al., *The United States in the World Economy*.

situation to which the United States intentionally contributed (in all likelihood in order to compel the Europeans to stabilise their currencies on the gold standard, balance their budgets and make concessions to open-door trade). American capital exports to Europe also reached a nadir in 1923 as a result of mounting social tensions. The Europeans were scrambling for dollars; the United States was awash with cash, and it became essential for both sides to ensure a substantially increased flow of capital across the ocean. However, Washington clearly signalled that this would not be possible unless Germany settled the reparations question and stabilised her currency by immediately introducing the full gold standard. In imposing her will on Europe despite stiff resistance from France and originally Great Britain, the United States scored a decisive initial victory and prompted a return to the gold(-exchange) standard by all the European currencies – a step which coincided in any case with the wishes of the ruling classes.

A further factor was the mounting pressure from severely depressed agriculture, as well as from industry which demanded stable markets and reliable exchange rates. Fears arose in Washington that the reparations issue, among others, might lead to monopolistic cooperation among the leading interests in France and Germany, or even that a pan-European preference zone under British leadership might arise. The German–American trade agreement of 8 December 1923 was intended not least of all to obviate these real or imagined dangers to the open-door policy. The parties conceded one another most-favoured nation status for the unusually long period of ten years,[13] marking another victory for American interests. The conclusion of this agreement demonstrates that, after the economic crisis in Europe and the occupation of the Ruhr, the American government and leading economic interests had finally understood the close connection between prosperity at home and prosperity in Europe.[14]

Finally, Great Britain's attitude began to change in late 1922 and early 1923. London began to share America's concerns about mounting French claims to paramountcy on the continent and the possible emergence of a heavy industrial block led by France. Under the circumstances, London had no other choice than to cosy up to the United States. Britain therefore renounced her attempts to undermine the open-door policy and formally recognised in the conversion agreement

13. B.H. Williams, *Economic Foreign Policy*, p. 300.
14. See M. Leffler, 'The Origins of the Republican War Debt Policy, 1921–1923. A Case Study in the Applicability of the Open Door Interpretation', *JAH* 59 (1972–3), pp. 586ff.; W. Link, *Die amerikanische Stabilisierungspolitik*, Part I, Chapt. 2; idem, 'Die Ruhrbesetzung und die wirtschaftlichen Interessen der USA' [The Occupation of the Ruhr and the Economic Interests of the United States], *VfZ* (1969).

of 19 September 1923 war debts to the United States totalling 4,600 million dollars – a third victory for the United States. Repayment was to take place within sixty-two years at an interest rate of 3 to 3.5 per cent. As a nation highly dependent on exports and suffering from a stagnant home economy, Britain was extremely eager for economic recovery in Europe,[15] and she realised that such a recovery was impossible unless the United States agreed to increase capital exports.

In early 1924, France stumbled into a serious financial crisis as a result of speculation that the franc would soon be revalued upwards. Somewhat chastened by this experience, Paris agreed to show some flexibility in the reparations question, marking as S.A. Schuker has noted, 'the end of French predominance in Europe'[16] and another victory for Washington.

Conditions were now ripe for a solution to the reparations question that reflected American interests. France and Britain could no longer resist Washington's long-cherished hope of bringing about an 'economic peace' in Europe modelled along the lines of the Washington Conference of 1921–2 (Chapter 4, I). The reparations issue provided an ideal vehicle for the attainment of American goals in Europe. For instance, it provided a golden opportunity to scotch Britain's remaining pretensions on the economic and monetary front, e.g. her attempt to integrate the new German currency into the sterling block.[17] By now it appeared obvious as well that an American would be appointed agent-general of the Dawes Plan. His chief task was to oversee the German economy and finances, thus providing Washington with the influence it needed in order to attach Europe firmly to the conservative, capitalistic

15. See G. Libal, *Aspekte der britischen Aussenpolitik 1919–1922* (Göppingen, 1972). While one-quarter of total British production depended on exports before 1914, only one-fifth did so in 1924. See A.L. Bowley, *Some Economic Consequences of the Great War* (London, 1930), p. 207. The unemployment rate (percentage of the insured population) was 7.8 per cent in December 1920, 11.0 per cent in January 1921, 23.0 per cent in May 1921 (= 2.5 million), 17.7 per cent in December 1921, 12.6 per cent in December 1922, 10.5 per cent in December 1922, and 9.6 per cent in July 1924. Cf. A.C. Pigou, *Aspects of British Economic History, 1918–1925* (London, 1948); a fundamental study in D.H. Aldcroft, *The Inter-War Economy: Britain, 1919–1939* (London, 1970).

16. See the brilliant study by Schuker, *The End of French Predominance*; J.-N. Jeanneney, 'De la spéculation financière comme arme diplomatique. A propos de la première bataille du franc (nov. 1923–mars 1924)', *Relations internationales* (1979); J.C. Debeir, 'La crise du franc de 1924. Un exemple de spéculation internationale', in ibid.; for the political, economic and financial reasons for the weakening of France in the Spring of 1924, see the perspicacious analysis of C.A. Wurm, *Die französische Sicherheitspolitik in der Phase der Umorientierung 1924–1926* [French Security Policies in the Reorientation Phase 1924–1926] (Frankfurt, 1979).

17. Cf. C. Parrini, *Heir to Empire*; W. Link, *Die amerikanische Stabilisierungspolitik*, Part II, Chapt. 2.

world system and provide adequate scope for the Ford model of economic growth to prosper. The claim that the Dawes Plan turned Europe into a hostage of American high finance is therefore no exaggeration.[18]

2. German–American Relations: A Force for Stability?

Did American intervention in Europe serve to consolidate economic and hence political conditions, as many contemporaries first believed? The internal inconsistencies in the Dawes Plan soon became apparent, dispelling the original euphoria that had greeted its introduction. The plan obliged Germany to make annual payments rising from 1,000 million gold marks in the first year to 2,500 million gold marks in the fifth year of 1928–9 and then holding at this level for an indefinite period. These obligations were secured by mortgages on German railways and industries.[19] However, the Dawes Plan was marred by a fundamental flaw which soon became apparent: it did not contain a final financial settlement of the war and therefore failed to solve the fundamental problem afflicting the international economy and political system.[20] In keeping with the conservative monetary and economic doctrine prevailing in the United States and elsewhere, the Dawes Plan remained captive to a narrow budgetary approach.

The Dawes Plan was dogged by another major weakness. It fully appreciated the potential of the German economy but failed to address the key issue of how it could be put to work paying back Germany's creditors without at the same time substantially damaging their economic interests both at home and abroad.[21] In addition, a solution to the reparations problem by means of even partial debt conversion would have required a degree of international political and economic cooperation which none of the principal actors was prepared to provide. In any case, the Versailles System was supposed to curtail Germany's position on world markets, a goal to which Britain was particularly devoted.

What effect did the American intervention have on the relative strength of the European powers? Is Schuker correct in his claim that the Dawes Plan not only mitigated French domination of Europe but even went so far as to restore Germany's traditional economic para-

18. According to W.A. McDougall, 'Political Economy versus National Sovereignty', p. 21; a telling analysis by E. Trendelenburg, 'Bis zum Dawes Plan', p. 98f.
19. An overview of the numerous provisions in the Dawes Plan can be found in F.-W. Henning, *Das industrielle Deutschland 1914 bis 1972* (Paderborn, 1974), pp. 83–6 .
20. For the following see E. Trendelenburg, 'Bis zum Dawes Plan', pp. 114–39; S.B. Clough, *The Economic Development of Western Civilization* (NY, 1968), p. 440; R.E. Lüke, *Von der Stabilisierung zur Krise* [From Stabilisation to the Depression] (Zurich, 1958).
21. According already to E. Trendelenburg, 'Bis zum Dawes Plan', p. 121.

mountcy?[22] The first part of this thesis is indubitable. France lost some of the levers through which she maintained her position as champion of the Versailles System and the *status quo*. The plans of the Quai d'Orsay to use reparations in order to force the German economy to play a complementary and therefore subordinate role to the French economy were finally shattered,[23] and Paris was deprived of its economic weapon until the currency stabilisation of 1926–8. The second part of Schuker's thesis, however, is more dubious. As W. Link has shown in his pioneering work,[24] the shared interests of Germany and the United States played a major role in transforming Germany from a passive object of international negotiations into an active participant. This development certainly represented a giant step toward fulfilling Germany's ambition to regain her great power status. However, the question arises of whether she paid too high a price in the form of mounting financial dependence on the United States. This at least was the crux of the dilemma which would soon spawn mounting enmity between Washington and Berlin.

A foretaste of this was provided by the German–American trade agreement. As an intentional side effect, it curtailed future Franco-German economic cooperation in order to pressure France into granting most favoured nation status and into softening her intransigence on the question of debt repayment. In addition, the differences in the German and American tariff systems meant that the United States derived greater benefit from most favoured nation status than did Germany, which saw her freedom to set trade policy curbed by the agreement. The most important factor, however, was that the method adopted by the Dawes Plan for reintegrating Germany into the world economy (exchange of goods and capital) did not suffice to stimulate fundamental structural change in order to improve Germany's position in the international division of labour and thereby permit a more independent foreign policy.

Instead, a flood of primarily American capital poured into Germany, creating an ambivalent but fundamentally pernicious effect, as quickly noted at the time by observers ranging from the left-wing opposition to the conservative president of the *Reichsbank*, Hjalmar Schacht, as well as by modern researchers.[25] American capital became, in Lüke's words,

22. S.A. Schuker, *The End of French Predominance*, p. 386.
23. D. Artaud, *La reconstruction de l'Europe 1919–1929*, p. 20.
24. See W. Link, *Die amerikanische Stabilisierungspolitik*.
25. W. Link, *Die amerikanische Stabilisierungspolitik*, Part III, Chapt. 2; idem, 'Der amerikanische Einfluss auf die Weimarer Republik in der Dawesplanphase (Elemente eines "penetrierten Systems")' in H. Mommsen et al. (eds), *Industrielles System*; C.L. Holtfrerich, 'Amerikanischer Kapitalexport und Wiederaufbau der deutschen Wirtschaft

the 'most important factor in the economic cycle', indicating that such massive capital imports could only increase the vulnerability of the entire economy: industry, agriculture and financial institutions. In the end, the Dawes Plan did more to aggravate the structural problems of the Germany economy than to alleviate them. The main reason was that the recycling of international liquidity by means of reparations payments and loans made it possible, as Schiemann has pointed out,[26] to maintain equilibrium in the international balance of payments until the Depression without Germany being compelled to generate the necessary export surplus in order to cover the outflow of capital. Massive foreign loans intensified Germany's appetite for imports and diminished the pressure to boost exports. Furthermore, the economic interests of the Allied powers were apparently served if Germany further indebted herself through large capital imports rather than expanding exports in order to achieve an external balance.

The cardinal misfortune of the times lay more in this overall imbalance in foreign trade than in the reparations payments themselves which were not overly onerous. An export surplus would have immediately changed the situation in Germany's favour by 'reducing her appetite for huge foreign loans and generating the exchange necessary to pay off the reparations.'[27] In fact though, Germany pursued a course fraught with danger by attempting to compensate for her trade imbalance by taking out short-term loans. This not only heightened the general financial instability but also exacerbated the already difficult problem of transfer payments, that is, the annual reparation instalments in foreign currencies. During the period of 1924 to 1929, imports exceeded exports by some 9,400 million RM. Approximately 13 per cent of the total imports of 70,800 million RM were payed for with capital derived from foreign loans, which was therefore not available for reparations payments. In order to make up the difference (a total of 8,300 million RM were needed for reparations), new foreign credits were taken out. When the United States sharply reduced the flow of capital after 1928, Germany's financial position became so precarious that the Dawes Plan had to be revised.

Contemporary observers were most troubled by another aspect of

1919–1923 im Vergleich zu 1924–1929' [American Capital Exports and the Reconstruction of the German Economy 1919–1923 in Comparison with 1924–1929], *VSWG* 64 (1977); D.H. Aldcroft, *Zwanziger Jahre*, pp. 291–4; from the substantial remaining literature see W. Fischer, *Deutsche Wirtschaftspolitik 1918–1945* (Opladen, 1968); E. Wandel, *Die Bedeutung der Vereinigten Staaten von Amerika für das deutsche Reparationsproblem 1924–1929* (Tübingen, 1971).

26. J. Schiemann, *Die deutsche Währung*, p. 93.
27. F.-W. Henning, *Das industrielle Deutschland*, p. 88.

huge capital imports: the mountainous foreign debt that Germany was accumulating. As time passed, the conviction spread that these loans had created nothing more than a 'borrowed prosperity' which could not last. This impression was strengthened by the fact that public authorities, especially at the local level, had sunk the loaned capital in largely unproductive projects.[28]

The federal government and the *Reichsbank* were well aware of the repercussions of foreign loans. Measures were adopted in late 1926 to encourage long-term borrowing, but without the desired effect. All levels of government fell prey to the vicious circle which they had helped to generate: Germany needed foreign capital in order to stimulate the economy, which in turn increased tax receipts. But the increment was entirely taken up by sharply rising expenditures in the area of infrastructure, social benefits and improved salaries for the civil service. Meanwhile, the true gravity of the deficit was masked by the continuing influx of foreign capital.

Under these conditions, the debt burden of the national government, the *Länder*, municipalities, industry and agriculture swelled to menacing proportions. Between late 1923 and the summer of 1930, a total of 21,000 million RM in foreign credit flowed into Germany, of which 4,000 million went to various levels of government, 10,000 million to business and 7,000 million to the banks.[29] German foreign investment in this period reached 7,700 million RM. The difference of some 13,300 million RM equalled the total value of German exports in 1929. Henning has calculated that this could be likened, *mutatis mutandis*, 'to the Federal Republic incurring a net foreign debt of some 125,000 million DM between 1967 and 1972'.[30]

By late 1930, Germany's foreign liabilities (all levels of government as well as banks, industry and private citizens) totalled between 25,300 and 25,800 million RM, of which 14,500 million was short-term.[31] Moreover, the banking system was less liquid than it had been before the war, so that relatively small withdrawals could threaten its stability[32] – not to mention foreign obligations of some 9,700 million RM in December 1930 when *Reichsbank* reserves were running at 2,700 million, of which two-thirds were required by law to be held as covering funds. In case of a run on the mark, the *Reichsbank* had barely 1,000 million in gold and

28. Preference was given for instance to the construction of swimming pools and sporting facilities in general, such as the Nürburg Ring (1927).
29. F.-W. Henning, *Das industrielle Deutschland*, p. 86.
30. Ibid., p. 87.
31. D.H. Aldcroft, *Zwanziger Jahre*, pp. 110–12.
32. For more details see F.-W. Henning, 'Die Liquidität der Banken in der Weimarer Republik' in H. Winkel (ed.), *Finanz- und wirtschaftspolitische Fragen*.

currency to throw into the battle. Such disparities, together with the restrictive monetary policies of the *Reichsbank*, were a major cause of the financial and banking crisis of the summer of 1931.[33] This crisis in turn represented a significant step down the road leading to the final collapse of the Weimar Republic (see Chapt. 5, II). The decisive factor was not the lack of foresight on the part of the *Reichsbank* and the federal government, as is commonly asserted; instead, Germany's mountainous debts were an inevitable consequence of the Dawes Plan, implemented in an attempt to save and stabilise the Versailles System.

It is difficult to determine the exact extent to which these external factors were responsible for the relatively sluggish economic growth in Germany in the second half of the 1920s. There are not enough detailed studies on the use of capital imports. The often repeated view that the Dawes Plan initiated a period of recovery 'unprecedented in Germany in its vigour and breadth'[34] is far from true and indeed has been corrected by recent research.[35] The annual growth rate did attain 4 per cent, but this figure is inflated by extremely low initial levels of production. There were only three years of strong growth – 1924, 1925 and 1927 – and Germany's performance on average was less impressive than that of other industrialised nations, especially Japan and the United States. Neither the general standard of living nor the average real per capita income of these years reached the heights achieved immediately before the war. A particularly telling indication of the prevailing economic stagnation is the fact that the investment rate also failed to attain

33. G. Hardach, 'Reichsbankpolitik und wirtschaftliche Entwicklung 1924–31' [Reichsbank Policies and Economic Development 1924–31], *Schmollers Jahrbuch* 90 (1970), pp. 563ff.

34. According for instance to G. Stolper et al., *Deutsche Wirtschaft seit 1870* (Tübingen, 1966[2]), p. 113.

35. See for what follows D. Petzina, *Die deutsche Wirtschaft in der Zwischenkriegszeit* (Wiesbaden, 1977), pp. 14–18, 52–69; on a broad statistical basis: D. Kesse, 'Die volkswirtschaftlichen Gesamtgrössen für das Deutsche Reich in den Jahren 1925–1936' [Overall Economic Statistics for the German Reich 1925–36] in W. Conze and H. Raupach (eds), *Die Staats- und Wirtschaftskrise des Deutschen Reiches 1923–33* (Stuttgart, 1967); W. Abelshauser and D. Petzina, 'Krise und Rekonstruktion. Zur Interpretation der gesamtwirtschaftlichen Entwicklung im 20. Jahrhundert' [Crisis and Reconstruction. An Interpretation of Economic Development in the 20th Century] in idem (eds), *Deutsche Wirtschaftsgeschichte im Industriezeitalter. Konjunktur, Krise, Wachstum* (Königstein, 1981), pp. 47–93; D. Petzina and W. Abelshauser, 'Zum Problem der relativen Stagnation der deutschen Wirtschaft in den zwanziger Jahren' [The Problem of the Relative Stagnation of the German Economy in the 1920s] in H. Mommsen et al. (eds), *Industrielles System*, pp. 57–76; W. Fischer and P. Czada, 'Wandlungen in der deutschen Industriestruktur im 20. Jahrhundert' [The Changing Industrial Structure of Germany in the 20th Century] in G.A. Ritter (ed.), *Entstehung und Wandel der modernen Gesellschaft. Festschrift für H. Rosenberg* (Berlin, 1970), pp. 118–65, esp. 129, 131, 135f., 138, 154; F.-W. Henning, *Das industrielle Deutschland*, pp. 88ff.

its prewar levels. In the years between 1924 and 1929, net investment reached 45,000 million RM, but this did not suffice to enable Germany to catch up to the other leading industrialised countries in either output or industrial technique (see Table 3).[36] Modernisation was blunted by mounting taxation and other burdens, especially the high interest rates resulting from the deflationary policies adopted by the *Reichsbank* in order to help balance Germany's external accounts and attract foreign capital.

The 'normal' methods of coping with an economic crisis, especially in Germany, were concentration,[37] rationalisation[38] and the formation of cartels.[39] This spurred productivity and enhanced already existing over-capacity, but did nothing to solve the 'structural crisis running throughout German industry'. In fact, the main thrust of the research of Petzina and Abelshauser[40] has been to demonstrate that these measures exacerbated the ever-increasing disparity in the growth rates of the capital goods and consumer goods sectors of the economy. This imbalance had emerged before the war and was a primary cause of domestically-induced stagnation in both the United States and industrialised Europe, as we have seen. The slower growth of consumer demand could not be offset by exports or by expansion in other branches of the economy.

36. The figures in D. Petzina, *Die deutsche Wirtschaft*, p. 14 differ from those of the League of Nations (Table 3 in the text). Industrial production in Germany (1913 = 100; in borders at the time): 1920 = 55, 1921 = 66, 1922 = 72, 1923 = 47, 1924 = 70, 1925 = 83, 1926 = 80, 1927 = 100, 1928 = 103, 1929 = 104, 1930 = 91. These figures are bleaker than those of the League, but they reflect the same trend.

37. The best known and most important examples are the founding of I.G. Farbenindustrie A.G. in December 1925, which made this concern the largest chemical company in the world, and the United Steel Works in 1926. Already by 1926, production cartels covered 98.3 per cent of potash mining, 96.3 per cent of the paint and dye industry, 94.5 per cent of lignite mining, 90.1 per cent of hard coal mining, 86.9 per cent of the electrical industry and 85 per cent of the pig iron industry.

38. Rationalisation was undertaken primarily in basic industries such as Ruhr coal and steel. It proceeded more slowly in traditionally expanding sectors of the economy such as machine-building, the electrical industry and precision engineering. See R.A. Brady, *The Rationalization Movement in German Industry. A Study in the Evolution of Economic Planning* (Berkeley, 1933); E. Schalldach, *Rationalisierungsmassnahmen der Nachinflationszeit im Urteil der deutschen freien Gewerkschaften* [The Rationalisation Measures of the Post-Inflation Period as Seen by the Free German Unions] (Jena, 1930); R. Krengel, *Anlagevermögen, Produktion und Beschäftigung der Industrie im Gebeit der Bundesrepublik von 1924 bis 1956* (Berlin, 1958); I. Svennilson, *Growth and Stagnation*, p. 254, Table A 23; O. Dascher, 'Probleme der Konzernorganisation' in H. Mommsen et al. (eds), *Industrielles System*, pp. 127–35; A. Sohn-Rethel, 'Ökonomie und Klassenstruktur des deutschen Faschismus', pp. 41–52.

39. Especially in branches such as steel, chemicals, automobiles, ship building, etc.

40. D. Petzina and W. Abelshauser, 'Zum Problem der relativen Stagnation' in H. Mommsen et al. (eds), *Industrielles System*, pp. 66–70.

Though Germany did experience some success in foreign markets, it was insufficient to compensate for this structural defect in her economy. As a result, Germany's share of global economic activity declined.

From an economic point of view, there were no 'golden twenties' in Germany. As Petzina and Abelshauser concluded,[41] Germany and Great Britain lost most ground of all in the race among industrialised countries in the 1920s, regardless of whether their situation is described as 'relative stagnation' or 'delayed reconstruction'. The lost industrial output due to the First World War was more or less made good, but only so long as the influx of foreign capital persisted. Reconstruction of a stable economy was impossible on such fragile foundations, and the ensuing crisis was all the more serious when it finally struck.

The controls and guarantees written into the Dawes Plan accorded the United States considerable influence not only over German financial policy but also over domestic and foreign policy. The authority exercised by the American financier Parker Gilbert, as agent general and 'official trustee of the creditor nations', can scarcely be exaggerated. He was, according to Arthur Rosenberg, one 'of the most powerful men in Berlin'.[42] The extent of Germany's dependence on American politicians and financial leaders was highlighted by her attempts to cope with the severe economic crisis of the winter of 1925–6[43] – an episode which well illustrates the fundamental weakness of the Weimar Republic even in a period of relaxed tensions in so far as monetary policy and foreign affairs were concerned. The main cause of the crisis was insufficient internal demand, evident in the record number of business bankruptcies between September 1925 and the spring of 1926. Recalling the de-

---

41. W. Abelshauser and D. Petzina, 'Krise und Rekonstruktion' in idem (eds), *Deutsche Wirtschaftsgeschichte*, p. 60; an attack on the theory of the 'golden twenties' can be found in F.-W. Henning, *Das industrielle Deutschland*, p. 90.

42. A. Rosenberg, *Geschichte der Weimarer Republik*, chapter on 'Stabilisation and Stresemann 1924 to 1928' reprinted in G. Ziebura (ed.), *Grundfragen der deutschen Aussenpolitik seit 1871* (Darmstadt, 1975).

43. See for what follows D. Hertz-Eichenrode, *Wirtschaftskrise und Arbeitsbeschaffung. Konjunkturpolitik 1925/26 und die Grundlagen der Krisenpolitik Brünings* [The Economic Crisis and Job Creation. Economic Policies 1925–6 and the Foundations of Brüning's Policies] (Frankfurt, 1982); G. Hardach, *Weltmarktorientierung und relative Stagnation. Währungspolitik in Deutschland 1924–1931* [The Turn to World Markets and Relative Stagnation. Monetary Policy in Germany 1924–31] (Berlin, 1976); C.-D. Krohn, *Stabilisierung und ökonomische Interessen. Die Finanzpolitik des Deutschen Reiches 1923–1927* [Stabilisation and Economic Interests. The Financial Policies of the German Reich 1923–27] (Düsseldorf, 1974); I. Maurer, *Reichsfinanzen und Grosse Koalition. Zur Geschichte des Reichskabinetts Müller (1928–30)* [German Finances and the Grand Coalition. The History of the Müller Cabinet 1928–30] (Bern, 1973); R.E. Lüke, *Von der Stabilisierung zur Krise*.

pressed winters of 1918–19 and 1923–4, the number of unemployed in February 1926 soared to a new record of 2.1 million.

For the first time ever, the German government attempted to cope with the crisis by adopting extensive, coherent anti cyclical policies such as price reduction, reduced taxes, encouragement of exports, loans for housing, increased public contracts, improved social benefits in order to stimulate demand, and regional restructuring assistance. This response was showing definite signs of success[44] when a characteristic dilemma emerged: the government's ability to intervene in the economy was jeopardised when it began to run short of capital. This point was reached because it was unwilling to subordinate its attempts to stimulate the economy to reparations payments, even though the annual payment for 1928–9 of 2,500 million gold marks was still outstanding.

Agent General Gilbert denounced the attitude of the German government, and the fronts were clearly drawn. While the government considered its social legislation essential if Germany was to have the productive capacity to meet its obligations, Gilbert saw the legislation as endangering German fulfilment of the Dawes Plan. So far as the government was concerned, Germany was caught on the horns of a dilemma: how to make reparations payments while maintaining social stability. The only possible solution was a revision in the terms of the Dawes Plan, while ensuring that Germany's budgetary deficit did not become all too apparent lest her creditworthiness be called into question. The concurrence of a budgetary deficit, strong outflows of foreign currency and increased reparations payments for 1928–9 made a financial crisis inevitable.

In these dark days for Germany, the initiative in obtaining a revision of the Dawes Plan was seized by the United States, particularly the chairman of the Federal Reserve Board, B. Strong. The troubles in Germany, combined with the conflict between the British and French central banks, raised fears of a convulsion throughout the entire monetary system, so elaborately propped up by the Dawes Plan.[45] Strong was supported by Gilbert who viewed the influx of foreign capital into Germany with mounting apprehension and feared that the *Länder*, cities and communes would no longer be able to pay even the interest on their foreign debts, let alone the principal.

Meanwhile, the political opposition in Germany to American domination was mounting, spreading far into heavy industrial circles and reaching a first crescendo during the elaboration of the Young Plan. The

44. It was helped however by a 'stroke of luck': the miners' strike that began in Great Britain in May 1926 revived the German hard-coal mines and in their wake the iron industry.
45. W. Link, *Die amerikanische Stabilisierungspolitik*, pp. 411ff.

'Young Plan crisis' of the spring of 1929, fomented by concerns about Germany's creditworthiness, serves to underline its political vulnerability as a result of excessive dependence on short-term foreign credits. When faced with the threat, partially carried out, that these credits would be withdrawn, Berlin was forced to abandon all resistance. The *Reichsbank* had to draw on its foreign reserves in order to uphold the value of the mark and also moved, under pressure from those banks which had been the main recipients of foreign loans, to restrict credit and increase the discount rate.

The German government had nothing at all to gain by undermining the negotiations surrounding the Young Plan, especially when it turned out to contain many advantages. For instance, the total reparations bill was finally fixed, stimulating a fresh influx of foreign funds. Annual payments were reduced,[46] relieving the pressure on the budget, and transfer conditions were ameliorated. Of great importance as well was the elimination of the supervisory bodies included in the Dawes Plan, which had infringed so deeply on German national sovereignty. Reparation payments between 1929 and 1932 amounted on average to no more than 7.9 per cent of Germany's foreign earnings and did not pose an intolerable burden.[47] Finally, the creation of the Bank for International Settlements eased transfer payments and improved cooperation among the central banks, in accordance with its charter.

However, the political atmosphere in Germany had already been so poisoned that the Young Plan was deeply resented by much of the population despite its obvious advantages. The Young Plan referendum provided shocking evidence of the extent to which nationalist feeling had been aroused and the 'spirit of Locarno' had dissipated. Hertz-Eichenrode has pointed out another fateful consequence of these events:[48] Heinrich Brüning, who became the new German chancellor shortly after the Young Plan took effect in January 1930, had taken the restrictions on the Republic's ability to respond to the economic crisis of 1925–6 and his experience of the financial and reparations issues of 1929

---

46. The remainder of the reparations estimated at 109,800 million gold marks was to be paid in fifty-nine yearly instalments from 1929 to 1988: 1,300 million until 1930–1, rising to an annual payment of 2,300 million in 1965–6 and remaining at this level until the end. Each annual payment was divided in two: a deferrable 'protected' part and a non-deferrable 'unprotected' part. This last sum amounted to a total of 22,600 million, which Germany had to pay in any case. The 'protected' part of 87,000 million corresponded to the amount of inter-Allied debt to the United States. The Allies intended to renounce as much of this German debt as the United States renounced of their debts. Thus for the first time, the connection sought by France since 1919 was established between reparations and inter-Allied debt.

47. W. Link, *Die amerikanische Stabilisierungspolitik*, p. 472.

48. D. Hertz-Eichenrode, *Wirtschaftskrise und Arbeitsbeschaffung*, pp. 235ff.

as evidence that Germany should seek a final settlement of the reparations question as its highest foreign policy objective and at the same time should balance its budget in order to strengthen its hand for the future. This approach obviated of course any possibility of overcoming the crisis through an expansive economic policy. In the end, it was the combination of steep deflation and a more nationalistic foreign policy which led, under the pressures of the Great Depression, to the demise of the Weimar Republic.

The inconsistencies in the German–American alliance based on common interests began to emerge in the late 1920s. Dependence on foreign, primarily American, capital sapped Germany's ability to use her economic strength in order to force revisions in the Treaty of Versailles. This was certainly a positive consequence of the American engagement in Europe, though London and Paris were chagrined to lose control over economic, monetary and even to a certain extent political developments in Europe after Germany was integrated as a privileged ally into the world economic system dominated by the United States. However, as Link has pointed out,[49] this did not eliminate the deeper, long-term conflicts between Germany and the United States. As we have seen, American bankers were interested primarily in investing their money as profitably as possible in a secure area. The various governments of the Weimar Republic, however, viewed close German–American ties principally as a vehicle for recovering Germany's great power status and for revising the Treaty of Versailles. This explains the importance they attached to securing Allied withdrawal from the occupied territories as part of the reparations settlement. Germany did indeed derive political benefit from her close ties with the United States and tried to take advantage of them mainly to the detriment of France which was the power most intent on preserving the *status quo*. Berlin was assisted in this by a fundamental inconsistency in American policy toward Europe and Germany. The United States wished in its own interests to promote political and economic stability in Europe and a peaceful settlement of national disputes. But at the same time it insisted on bilateral agreements only, particularly in the realm of trade and international debt. This reflected Washington's deep distrust of any kind of agreement with Europe as a whole and its belief that they would be incompatible with the American national interest.

Tensions between Germany and the United States were further increased by the fact that any improvement in the Germany economy could only heighten competition on world markets, especially as the United States had penetrated many of the traditional export markets of

---

49. W. Link, *Die amerikanische Stabilisierungspolitik*, pp. 350–8; *passim*.

German industry (steel, silk, leather and chemicals, particularly dyes and paints) after the occupation of the Ruhr.[50] After 1924, the American advance met with mounting resistance from German industry, which was increasing productivity and experiencing greater pressure to export. Though competition on the American domestic market was curtailed by the protective tariff of 1922, fierce struggles did occasionally erupt (for instance in potash), which then spread to other products in third countries. However, the era between 1924 and 1929 did not last long enough for this inevitable competition to reach maximum intensity. Paradoxically, Washington's efforts to strengthen Germany politically helped lay the foundations for a German attempt to regain her previous status. For this to succeed, the economic restraints on Germany would also have to be shattered, as indeed occurred as a consequence of the Great Depression.

3. Franco-German Relations: A Force for Stability?

Did the much vaunted 'spirit of Locarno', marking a new era of compromise and rapprochement between the two main rivals in Europe, France and Germany, assist in stabilising the Versailles System? Many contemporaries certainly believed so. The improving relations between the two countries, exemplified by their foreign ministers Aristide Briand and Gustav Stresemann, seemed to signal the dawn of a new era of peace and mutual understanding. The Locarno Pact, signed in October 1925, reaffirmed Germany's western boundary and seemed thereby to lay to rest the uncertainty caused by the fact that it had been created only by the *Diktat* of Versailles, as Briand noted with some satisfaction. Britain and Italy agreed to act as guarantors of the treaty, alongside the nations directly involved – France, Germany and Belgium. In addition, Poland and Czechoslovakia were included in the complex agreement by means of arbitration agreements.

Germany's entry into the League of Nations and acceptance of a permanent seat on the Council raised the impression that the most revisionist-minded of all the nations, now recognised once again as a great power, would in turn fully support the postwar order through involvement in the system of collective security. On 10 September 1926, Briand and Stresemann both delivered compelling addresses in Geneva in which they reiterated their vision of a peaceful future, making a profound impression on public opinion. Nationalist passions abated in both countries, especially on the extreme right. Franco-German friendship even came into vogue, supported by a number of groups, committees and individual citizens.

50. Cf. W. Link, 'Die Ruhrbesetzung', p. 378.

But the Franco-German rapprochement lasted only one-and-a-half years from 1925 to 1927. In fact it simply obscured rather than really beginning to solve their conflicting interests within the Versailles System. For this reason, recent research has greatly diminished the esteem in which Briand and Stresemann were formerly held.[51] Neither man ever openly posed, let alone answered, the question of how the difficult relationship between 'stabilisation' and 'peaceful change' was going to be managed. Each of course had his own agenda: Briand emphasised stabilisation; Stresemann emphasised change, and neither lost sight of his ultimate aim throughout all the ensuing manoeuvres.

Briand knew from the outset that Stresemann saw the Locarno Pact not least as a bridgehead for obtaining revisions in Germany's eastern border. Briand therefore took steps to reinforce France's alliance system, especially the position of Poland, though without great success. France also recognised the Soviet Union in a continuation of her traditional policy of forging counter weights to Germany. But again she was disappointed with the results. After 1927 there was a strong upswing in the political fortunes of those groups within France and Germany which believed that their country had made too many concessions to her former enemy. With only some exaggeration, the situation could be compared to that prevailing after the Second World War when 'détente' was simply a continuation of the cold war by other means – a situation of which both foreign ministers were fully cognisant.

The normalisation of economic relations is usually considered the most significant achievement of Franco-German rapprochement, but even they were not free of discrepancies and imbalances. French industries, both older branches and modern growth sectors, recorded higher rates of growth than did their German counterparts during the second half of the 1920s.[52] Moreover, French exports were stimulated by the undervaluation of the franc until final stabilisation in 1926–8. All the same, France did not succeed in breaking her dependence on German capital goods.[53] Thus a traditional weakness in French economy could

51. The first half of the 1920s has been more thoroughly studied than the second. The most outstanding work is: J. Bariéty, *Les relations franco-allemandes après la première guerre mondiale, 10 novembre 1918–10 janvier 1925. De l'exécution à la négotiation* (Paris, 1977); a summary of the most important results can be found in R. Poidevin and J. Bariéty, *Frankreich und Deutschland. Die Geschichte ihrer Beziehungen 1815–1975* (Munich, 1982), Chapters 15 and 16; W.A. McDougall, *France's Rhineland Diplomacy, 1914–1924. The Last Bid for a Balance of Power in Europe* (Princeton, 1978); C.A. Wurm, *Die französische Sicherheitspolitik*, pp. 141ff., 482ff., 557ff.
52. This was already recognised by contemporary German observers. See H.J. Schneider, *Grundlagen der deutsch-französischen Wirtschaftsbeziehungen* [The Foundations of Franco-German Economic Relations] (Berlin, 1931), pp. 51ff., 61ff.
53. See J. Marsielle, 'Le commerce entre la France et l'Allemagne pendant les "années

not be repaired. The Franco-German trade agreement of 1927 certainly contributed to a normalisation of commercial relations, but the appreciation of the franc as a result of currency stabilisation had the immediate effect of reducing French exports to Germany by some 38 per cent between 1927 and 1930. At the same time, Germany became France's most important trading partner. While German imports increased by 60 per cent, British imports advanced by only 13 per cent, and American imports actually fell by 21 per cent. By 1930, 15 per cent of all French imports came from Germany, including 30 per cent of imported coal, 40 per cent of chemical products, 35 per cent of iron and steel and a crucial 52 per cent of machine tools. The industrial development of France therefore depended to a large extent on imports from Germany.

The attempt to create an economic basis for Franco-German rapprochement by forming international cartels also proved to be a two-edged sword. Paris and Berlin pushed their mutually hostile iron magnates to join forces, and after two years of laborious negotiations, iron producers in Germany, France, Belgium, Luxembourg and the Saarland united to form the International Pig-Iron Association in September 1926. It set steel production quotas of 40.45 per cent for Germany, 31.89 per cent for France, 12.57 per cent for Belgium, 8.55 per cent for Luxembourg and 6.54 per cent for the Saarland (a model on the basis of which the European Community is even now trying to solve its steel crisis). It is true that from the day the pact was signed until 1939 no further problems emerged in the realm of coal and steel to trouble relations between France and Germany.[54] But all such attempts to share the market are fundamentally flawed in that they represent a defensive, Malthusian response not at all apt to solve the underlying structural problems of the economic sector to which they are applied. Market sharing forges an armistice, but no more. It certainly did not offer a constructive solution, such as would have been provided for instance by moving to a more pronounced Franco-German division of labour. Such a policy would have been highly advantageous for both sides, though it aroused no interest at the time.[55] Similar restrictive accords such as the potash agreement and the international paint and dye cartel (1927) suffered from the same flaw. In the end, the collapse of world markets and falling production during the Great Depression rendered these cartels largely inoperative.

30"' in Deutschen Historischen Institut, Paris (ed.), *La France et l'Allemagne 1932–1936* (Paris, 1980); A. Sauvy, *Histoire économique de la France entre les deux guerres* (Paris, 1965), vol. 1: 1918–1931; T. Kemp, *The French Economy 1913–1938. The History of a Decline* (London, 1972).

54. R. Poidevin and J. Bariéty, *Frankreich und Deutschland*, p. 358.

55. See F. L'Huillier, *Dialogues franco-allemandes 1925–1933* (Strasbourg, 1971).

All these agreements were merely intended to shore up a highly unstable economic relationship, and it is therefore not surprising that they proved of little value after 1927 in checking a renewed deterioration of Franco-German relations. The wellspring of the conflict lay, as might be expected, in the unresolved tension between reinforcing the *status quo* and the desire for change. This underlying stress in the 'spirit of Locarno' grew increasingly apparent as the two main protagonists, Briand and Stresemann, slowly realised that they were not progressing any closer to the long-term aims which each had set for himself. Public opinion in France and Germany was also aware of the failure to fulfil national goals, and both Briand and Stresemann came under mounting domestic fire.

Their response only typified the problem. Briand sought to further reinforce the Versailles System by strengthening France's political and military bonds with the United States, a strategy which, if successful, would certainly have greatly bolstered France in her role as champion of the *status quo*. Briand therefore intended to conclude a full-fledged Franco-American pact. But he reckoned without Washington. Secretary of State Kellogg and the entire Republican administration were convinced that the political goals of the United States were better served by applying economic and financial pressure rather than by signing pacts and agreements. The United States therefore totally frustrated Briand's original intent by transforming his bilateral pact into a multilateral declaration repudiating war (1928) but void of all substantive content, not least of all out of concern for Washington's privileged partner, Germany. In fact, Kellogg kept Stresemann informed about all these developments from the outset.

The German foreign minister had reason to be satisfied with the final result for it provided him with grounds on which to denounce French rearmament as excessive. Although the Kellogg–Briand Pact renouncing war was eventually endorsed by over sixty countries, it was devoid of all sanctions and was therefore of little practical value.[56] The ultimate failure of Briand's policies was signalled by the 1929 conference in the Hague which called for early French evacuation of the Rhineland without any recompense. Domestic support for Briand and his policies ebbed away with the return to power in 1926 of a conservative, upper-middle-class government under Raymond Poincaré, though Poincaré himself adopted a relatively moderate stance toward Germany.

Stresemann responded in a similar way, giving German foreign policy a strongly revisionist emphasis. The famous meeting at Thoiry in

56. R. Poidevin and J. Bariéty, *Frankreich und Deutschland*, p. 360; C. Hodier, 'Aristide Briand. Apôtre oublié de la paix', *Le monde diplomatique* XI (3 October 1982).

September 1926 provided a preliminary glimpse of German intentions. In the course of a superb dinner well lubricated with wine, Stresemann and Briand worked out a global solution to the tensions between their countries. This solution, once filtered through the proper diplomatic channels, reveals the extent to which France felt her back against the wall at this time. In return for early French evacuation of the Rhineland, the return of the Saarland and the dissolution of the French military mission overseeing German disarmament, Stresemann offered only to provide the capital assistance which France desperately needed in view of another precipitous decline in the value of the franc.[57]

Nothing of this plan ever reached fruition. The United States and Great Britain objected vigorously to an exclusive Franco-German deal, and in addition domestic political support evaporated. Briand's dealings were disavowed by the French government and parliament. Poincaré soon succeeded not only in stabilising the franc but elevating France to the status of the third greatest financial power in the world, eliminating all need for the compromise of Thoiry. However, Germany gained ground even under these conditions when the League of Nations decided to withdraw the military mission. Political tensions heightened, and Franco-German cooperation and understanding receded to the point where it was still cultivated by only a few idealistic writers and small clubs.

Germany bears her full share of blame for this turn of events. Shortly before Stresemann's death in October 1929, Germany announced under the newly fashionable claim to 'equal rights' that she considered herself justified in rearming if the international movement toward general disarmament did not proceed apace. Meanwhile, the disarmament negotiations under the aegis of the League of Nations were anything but expeditious. For a time it seemed as if the Young Plan might improve Franco-German relations by coupling full evacuation of the occupied territories with a new financial package which satisfied the long-standing French demand that inter-Allied debt should be linked to German reparations – not as systematically as Paris would have liked, to be sure, but to some extent. France even proved willing to renounce some of its reparation claims if Washington cancelled an equal amount of French debt. But in Germany the Young Plan proved highly unpopular and in conjunction with the beginning of the Great Depression created an ideal climate for the National Socialists to dramatically broaden their appeal. The landslide Nazi victory in the *Reichstag* elections of 14 September 1930 naturally sent shockwaves reverberating across France.

57. H.-O. Sieburg, 'Les entretiens de Thoiry (1926)', *Revue d'Allemagne* 4 (1972); the best analysis in J. Bariéty, 'Finances et relations internationales à propos du "plan de Thoiry", septembre 1926', *Relations internationales* 21 (1980).

These developments underline the fundamental weakness in the Locarno Pact.[58] When Stresemann's attempts to turn the agreement to advantage and to obtain substantial revisions in the Versailles System did not meet with the expected success, public opinion in Germany turned against the entire policy of reconciliation, depriving it of the requisite domestic support. Meanwhile, the forces on the right which had always maintained that the Versailles System could not be changed through cooperation and understanding were given fresh impetus.

The fading of the spirit of Locarno had further baleful effects. It reinforced those voices in the realms of politics and economics which claimed that an expansionist commercial policy was essential if Germany was to regain great power status. This policy had the additional advantage, in their view, of bolstering the established social order in Germany by unifying the ruling classes which were increasingly riven by divergent interests. Berlin's strategy of drawing eastern and southeastern Europe into a German-dominated economic zone was the main reason why the old German concept of 'Central Europe' experienced a revival in the late 1920s, and indeed, German economic activity in these areas did increase.[59]

The next step in the German strategy was necessarily the formation of a customs union with Austria. Poincaré had warned Stresemann in vain against this when they met in Paris in August 1928 for the signing of the Kellogg–Briand Pact. However, it was difficult to turn economic muscle to advantage so long as it 'was largely borrowed' (Maxelon), and Germany's economic power was too limited to bolster the state significantly.[60] The Young Plan met with such resistance from a rising part of the German public because it did not appreciably alter the economic dependence on the United States, even though it eliminated Allied economic controls and contained other advantages. Since economic influence was the only instrument which Germany had at her disposal in order to work a revision in the Versailles System while observing the spirit of Locarno, Stresemann was left empty-handed at

58. For what follows see M.-O. Maxelon, *Stresemann und Frankreich. Deutsche Politik der Ost-West-Balance* (Düsseldorf, 1972), pp. 292–5.
59. From the voluminous literature see R. Berndt, 'Wirtschaftliche Mitteleuropapläne des deutschen Imperialismus (1926–1931)' [German Imperialism's Economic Plans for Central Europe] in G. Ziebura (ed.), *Grundfragen der deutschen Aussenpolitik*; H.C. Meyer, *Mitteleuropa in German Thought and Action 1815–1945* (The Hague, 1955); J. Droz, *L'Europe centrale. L'évolution historique de l'idée de 'Mitteleuropa'* (Paris, 1960); W. Schumann (ed.), *Griff nach Südosteuropa* (Berlin, 1973); R. Frommelt, *Paneuropa oder Mitteleuropa. Einigungsbestrebungen im Kalkül deutscher Wirtschaft und Politik 1925–1933* (Stuttgart, 1977).
60. K. Megerle, *Deutsche Aussenpolitik 1925. Ansatz zu aktivem Revisionismus* [German Foreign Policy 1925. The Beginning of Active Revisionism] (Bern, 1974).

the end of his life, a situation for which he himself was largely to blame.

Briand too found himself at a dead-end. In a final burst of activity, he attempted to shore up the status quo by proposing a 'European Union' in early September 1929. Briand's proposal was, characteristically, a response to a scheme advanced by Stresemann the previous March which would have had the League of Nations guarantee the rights of national minorities, of which the largest single group was Germans. This plan too represented another step in the great revisionist offensive, and Briand responded in kind. In a memorandum of 1 May 1930, he proposed a kind of confederative association of European states (with no loss of national sovereignty), combined with an extension of the Locarno guarantees to all of Europe – a clause which would have implied voluntary acceptance of Germany's eastern frontier. The underlying motive behind Briand's plan was of course to thwart the powerful German drive for revisions in the Versailles System primarily by means of the 'Central European' strategy. Stresemann's successor, Curtius, had no difficulty perceiving the French intent, and he moved to block the project, which in any case had not found much favour elsewhere in Europe.

In conclusion, the Locarno approach had run dry long before the onset of the Great Depression. When the Depression temporarily weakened Germany further, Berlin insisted even more intransigently on revisions to the Versailles System. The years 1924 to 1929 therefore stand out all the more clearly as a period of illusory rapprochement between France and Germany. The attempts undertaken in these years to stabilise the Versailles System were inevitably foiled by fundamental misunderstandings and inconsistencies which were never seriously addressed.

The supreme importance of German–American relations, and in consequence Franco-German relations, greatly overshadowed all other factors, especially Britain's attitude.[61] Between 1923 and 1926, Great Britain attempted to play the role of mediator between Paris and Berlin, but renewed tensions with the United States after 1927 greatly limited her margin of manoeuvre. Ironically, London's early efforts in this regard had the unintended effect of advancing American interests in Europe and thereby curtailing Britain's own economic, financial and military influence. London originally intended to concede France a certain ascendancy over Germany while attempting to accommodate a moderate amount of German revisionism. However, Britain's ability to pursue this strategy began to fade as her own power ebbed away, not

---

61. G. Schmidt, *England in der Krise. Grundzüge und Grundlagen der britischen Appeasement-Politik (1930–1937)* [Britain in Crisis. Basic Features and Foundations of British Appeasement Policies, 1930–7] (Opladen, 1981), pp. 52–8.

least of all as a result of her continuing economic problems. Britain's position was undermined in the late 1920s by the weakness of sterling and of the Bank of England, which, as we have seen, was struggling to compete with the central banks of France and the United States. On the whole, British policy did not really please anyone, whether the United States, France or Germany, and London tended therefore to play more of a defensive than an assertive role. Britain therefore contributed very little in the later 1920s to attempts to stabilise the Versailles System, an arrangement which in any case she had viewed from the outset with considerable misgivings.

As was previously mentioned, the Versailles System was continually being undermined by the question of inter-Allied debt.[62] The European countries consolidated their debts to the United States through so-called conversion agreements, though this raised numerous other problems, as can be seen for instance in the Mellon–Béranger agreement between France and the United States. Though the deal was concluded in 1925, it was not ratified by the French parliament for three long years during which it inflamed the domestic political situation more than once.

The Europeans continually hoped that the United States would soften her attitude toward debt forgiveness, but this was out of the question so far as the Americans were concerned, for reasons of domestic, international and financial policy. Congress was forever warning that the Europeans intended to dump all their debts on the backs of the American taxpayer, and business interests, apart from export-oriented industries, opposed any cancellation of the inter-Allied debt. Moreover, the United States benefited from the European debt because it provided her with an effective tool for limiting the economic and financial influence of Britain and France. However, the debt problem also sowed discord among the Allies and hindered the monetary and financial reconstruction of Europe.[63] It surfaced, directly or indirectly, at virtually all international negotiations, always inflaming even further the issues at hand.

---

62. See the works of D. Artaud.
63. The negative effects of American policies were far greater than what they were able to achieve. By 1931–3, when the Hoover moratorium suspended debt repayments for one year before they were cancelled altogether, the United States had received only about 2,600 million dollars of the total of some 10,000 million which she had loaned the Allies.

II. The Limits of Social and Political Stabilisation

1. Maladjustments in the Consolidation of Capital Relative to Labour

All the European countries[64] found themselves in a difficult position in the 1920s. Their ability to conduct international economic and political policy was constrained to varying extents by the global situation, especially their economic and financial dependence on the United States. This curtailed their ability to set off on foreign adventures in order to distract attention from domestic conflicts: the safety valve of 'social imperialism' no longer functioned in the same old way. Only the huge colonial empires of Britain and France still provided a buffer for domestic difficulties, at least those of an economic nature, though independence movements in the colonies were gathering steam and posing mounting political problems. Concern about foreign implications, such as those that developed after 1924, required a certain amount of discretion in handling domestic political conflicts. Certain social strata, such as industrialists and merchants, profited more from these conditions than did others.

At the same time, the interconnections among nations (and therefore the international division of labour) had not yet reached anything like the proportions attained after the Second World War. Protectionism and the trend to economic autarky and to regional monetary and trading blocs stalled the emergence of an interdependent world economy and contributed to its later collapse. This created a climate in which nationalism could flourish, encouraging the utter egotism and beggar-thy-neighbour policies that reached their apogee during the Great Depression. All this only occurred, however, in reaction to mutually reinforcing domestic and global economic difficulties, apparent even during the so-called 'stabilisation phase', which were greatly aggravating social tensions. What is more, the Bolshevik revolution had encouraged a hardening of ideological fronts around the world. The resulting interplay of integrative and divisive forces generally reached something of a balance, the precariousness of which was hidden for a few years by relative prosperity. Less successful societies took immediate refuge in authoritarianism, and even in the western democracies the number of those seeking a solution in corporatist, authoritarian or even fascist ideologies was clearly on the rise.[65]

64. For this concept, see G. Ziebura, *Frankreich 1789–1870. Entstehung einer bürgerlichen Gesellschaftsformation* (Frankfurt, 1979), Introduction.

65. See the unfortunately very disorganised book of K.J. Newman, *Zerstörung und Selbstzerstörung der Demokratie. Europa 1918–1938* (Cologne, 1965); in summary Th. Scheider, 'Europa im Zeitalter der Weltmächte, § 7: 'Der liberale Staat und seine Krise' in idem (ed.), *Handbuch der europäischen Geschichte*, vol. 7 (Stuttgart, 1979), pp.

The volatility of the social situation can be see in what unfortunately must remain a cursory examination of the conflict between capital and labour. The stages in this basic conflict were strikingly similar in all three of the large European democracies: Germany, France and Britain.

In the immediate aftermath of the war, the labour movement began to exert tremendous pressure. Widespread strikes and labour unrest carried these countries on several occasions to the brink of civil war. The sudden, almost revolutionary eruption of the working class had several causes. One of course was the Russian Revolution which many construed as a sign of great things to come.[66] Even more important, however, was the revolt against domestic conditions: exploitation during the war and, as soon as it was over, unprecedented levels of unemployment exacerbated by equally extraordinary increases in the cost of living.[67] The middle classes of all three countries were severely shaken and only managed to retain their hold on power by granting such concessions as the eight-hour day, improvements in social legislation and, notably in Germany, the full acceptance of labour unions as the representatives of the workers in wage negotiations.

In the end, however, capital gained the upper hand, despite these concessions. Both inflation and subsequent currency stabilisation through reversion to the gold standard clearly worked in favour of business interests,[68] while the working class and the lower- and middle-middle classes suffered the greatest losses. Everywhere, the 'red peril' was invoked in order to maintain social control. In this way, the United States and her upper middle-class allies in Europe fulfilled their highest aspiration: no substantive social change.[69] Their victory was certainly eased by the divisions within the international working-class movement and its national counterparts. The severest blow in this regard fell at the Sixth Congress of the Communist International held from July to September, 1928.[70] The final resolution averred, with much justifi-

201–40 (further literature indicated here).

66. For the situation of the French working-class movement see G. Ziebura, *Léon Blum. Theorie und Praxis einer sozialistischen Politik*, vol. 1: *1872–1934* (Berlin, 1963). Comparative studies are not available.

67. C.S. Maier, *Recasting Bourgeois Europe*, Chapt. 1, 'The Dimensions of Social Conflict at the End of World War I'; G.D. Feldman, 'Wirtschafts- und sozialpolitische Probleme der deutschen Demobilmachung 1918/19' [Economic and Social Problems Arising from German Demobilisation 1918–19] in H. Mommsen et al. (eds), *Industrielles System*, p. 636.

68. Well studied in Germany by G.D. Feldman, *Iron and Steel in the German Inflation, 1916–1923* (Princeton, 1977).

69. Information in W. Abendroth, *Sozialgeschichte der europäischen Arbeiterbewegung* (Frankfurt, 1969).

70. See in detail O. Bauer, 'Zwischen zwei Weltkriegen? Die Krise der Weltwirtschaft,

cation, that 'further development of the imbalances inherent in capitalist stabilisation will greatly intensify the general crisis in which capitalism finds itself'. But this was followed by the absurd conclusion that in the struggles triggered by the crisis to come, the principal enemy would not be fascism but rather the parties of the non-Communist left, which were reviled as 'social fascist' for blocking the ultimate victory of the working class.

The Communist International was convinced that a revolutionary movement would soon arise, and it was eager to induce the masses to turn their backs on other working-class parties. As in the past, the Third International was again exploited for the purposes of the Soviet leadership. Stalinisation was beginning to take root under the motto of 'socialism in one country', and the internal opposition under Trotsky and Bukharin had been liquidated. By the same token, Stalin wished to purge 'rightist elements' from communist parties elsewhere in Europe. The new tactic of 'class against class' was perfectly suited to this purpose for it accentuated the Communists' exclusive claim to be the 'avantgarde of proletariat' and widened the breach with other working-class parties. This drove these parties further to the right, again weakening their reformist impulse, as Otto Bauer correctly observed, especially when they returned to government, as they did in Germany and Great Britain in the late 1920s, only to be soon torn apart by internal differences. The French Socialist Party (SFIO) alone survived this difficult period unscathed because it refrained from entering the government.

Labour organisations inevitably declined during the so-called 'stabilisation' phase, and union membership plunged.[71] In Great Britain, it had doubled during war, but these gains were totally wiped out during the 1920s, and the peak membership of 6.6 million in 1921 fell to 3.3 million in 1933. The contraction was even more pronounced in France, which already counted the fewest organised workers (10 per cent overall and scarcely more than 5 per cent in the metal-working industry). Of a total of some 2 million organised French workers in 1919 only 0.6 million remained in 1929. The story was similar in Germany where union membership of 7.9 million in 1920 shrank to 4 million in 1926. These trends in Europe were reflected, in characteristic fashion, in the United

---

der Demokratie und des Sozialismus' [Between Two World Wars? The Crisis of the World Economy, of Democracy and of Socialism] (Bratislava, 1936) in *Otto Bauer, Collected Works* (Vienna, 1976), vol. 4, pp. 49–331, here pp. 283ff.; F. Claudin, *La crise du mouvement communiste. Du Komintern au Kominform* (Paris, 1972), vol. 1, pp. 172–81; N. Poulantzas, *Faschismus und Diktatur. Die Kommunistische Internationale und der Faschismus* (Munich, 1973).
71. See D. Demarco et al., 'Etude comparée' in D. Fauvel-Rouif (ed.), *Mouvements ouvriers et dépression économique de 1929 à 1939* (Assen, 1966), pp. 3–7.

States where the largest union, the AFL, saw its total membership rise during the war from 2 million to 4 million only to fall back to 2.9 million by 1929. Moreover, some segments of the impoverished and economically uprooted lower-middle class joined the ranks of the labour movement, curtailing its reformist zeal even more than it already had been by the lack of a clear vision, especially in Britain and Germany.

Despite the shifting balance of power in their favour, many business interests still found themselves in a difficult situation. Though they had succeeded through rationalisation in reversing some of the concessions which they had been compelled to make in the immediate postwar years, they still found it difficult to achieve the profit ratios they considered necessary. Moreover, the antagonism between various sectors of the economy was increasing. War and inflation had curtailed the ascendancy of the financial sector over industry, and the power of the banks was in decline. However, this also limited the availability of new loans for business. The economic and political influence of heavy industry had increased in all countries, often at the expense of the newer growth branches of the economy. In a climate of restrictive foreign markets and weak internal demand, the traditional friction between export- and domestically-oriented businesses grew even more intense, especially in Germany.

The flagging labour movement therefore faced employers who had not succeeded in reinforcing their position and had grown more dependent on the state, which provided constant assistance for the larger companies. In so doing, however, the state further exacerbated the sectoral imbalances resulting from the war and hence social disparities, which were already quite severe due to inadequate wealth distribution. The feeble attempts of left-wing governments to correct this situation (the 'Grand Coalition' in Germany and the Labour government in Britain in 1929) seemed anachronistic even at the time. Their instruments were very blunt, and when the economic crisis finally erupted, they were totally overwhelmed.

This short outline of international trends should not obscure the fact that class conflicts were much more intense in such 'delayed nations' as Italy and Germany than they were in Great Britain and France, whose economies were also stagnant or even in decline but which had formed unified industrial states for a longer period of time.[72] In Britain and France, the clash between labour and capital was tempered by a broad social consensus which, despite evidence of impending failure, was still firmly in place. Furthermore, the existence of colonial empires greatly

---

72. N. Poulantzas, *Pouvoir politique et classes sociales* (Paris, 1968): here a short comparison between Germany and France.

reduced the pressure to modernise the economy in order to remain competitive on world markets. The resilience of the social consensus is however rather surprising in view of the implacable hostility of employers and workers, the former insisting on their rights as owners, and the latter enjoying precious little social security. None the less, the parliamentary systems of government in France and Britain functioned far better than in Germany and Italy and contributed enormously to the maintenance of the social fabric by providing a forum where conflicts could be played out.

How different things were for the 'latecomers' of Italy and Germany. Their economies were more heterogenous (including even some traditional, even 'feudal' sectors alongside modern, rapidly expanding sectors); their peoples did not identify strongly with a central government consecrated by lengthy political tradition, and their lack of colonial preference zones meant that that they had to be continually ready to defend their position in world politics and in the world economy. All these factors required their governments to play a stronger role.

Italy solved the problem, at least superficially, through fascism while governments in eastern and south-eastern Europe also assumed more economic responsibilities.[73] Germany, however, followed an inconsistent and hence paralysing course. The state continued to intervene in the economy after the end of the war economy, though now primarily by means of social programmes. At the same time, it delegated authority to various social groups which sought with the help of corporatist measures to gain a direct share of political power even outside of democratic institutions.[74] In this way, the state was drawn directly into the struggles of competing interest groups and thereby lost some of its mediative and integrative abilities, especially in regard to shaping the relationship between capital and labour. This was the major reason why authoritarian schemes to put an end to excessive class conflict gained mounting support.

2. The 'Conservative Offensive' in Britain, France and Germany

In view of all this, it is not surprising that all three countries witnessed in the latter 1920s a general transfer of power to conservative, middle-class forces which succeeded in marginalising both mainstream working-class parties and extremists on the left and right. The communist parties of

73. See A. Teichova, 'Konzentrationstendenzen in der Industrie Mittelost- und Südosteuropas nach dem Ersten Weltkrieg' [Concentration Tendencies in Industry in Mid-eastern and South-eastern Europe after the First World War] in H. Mommsen et al. (eds), *Industrielles System*, pp. 135–53.
74. Numerous references to this in ibid. and C.S. Maier, *Recasting Bourgeois Europe*.

Britain and France shrivelled into insignificance, and the German Communist Party, which like its sister parties had suffered enormously from Stalinisation, also lost ground. Right-wing and nationalist groupings went into even steeper decline. The middle classes in Germany withdrew their support for racist parties in order not to cast any clouds over 'reconciliation' and the resulting influx of foreign capital. However, the political axis of the middle class shifted to the right, as evidenced by the entry into government of the German National People's Party. In Britain and France as well, conservative forces were dominated by rock-ribbed elements closely allied with industry and banking circles.

Furthermore, fascism strengthened its hold over Italy after 1927–8, and a welter of authoritarian regimes emerged in eastern and southeastern Europe (Lithuania in 1926, Poland in 1928, Yugoslavia in 1929 and Romania by 1930 at the latest). In all three of the great west European democracies, but most notably in Germany, parliament continually lost ground either to the executive branch (as in France through *décret-lois*) or to corporatively organised interest groups. The *Union interparlementaire*, an international body of parliamentarians, began warning of this tendency in 1928. These developments gave institutional expression to the widening cleft between 'political society' and 'economic society' as social problems grew increasingly intractable.[75] Parliaments proved less and less able to mediate between producers and consumers or between groups of producers with competing interests in order to forge a social consensus. As in so many other ways, Germany was worse off in this regard than either Britain or France. In consequence, more and more social elements felt excluded both socially and economically and were drawn in the late 1920s towards fascism or communism. As the social damage wreaked by the 'conservative offensive' mounted, extremist parties increased in popularity, especially in countries with little hope of such parliamentary alternatives as a common front or *National Union*.

Though the 'conservative revolution' in Britain, France and Germany manifested many similarities, especially in the form of orthodox economic, financial and social policies coupled with a gradual retreat from the 'spirit of Locarno', there were also some differences reflecting the peculiarities of each society. In Great Britain, a strong conservative tendency ran through all strata of society. It is symptomatic that the first Labour government in British history under MacDonald lasted barely half a year before being defeated in August 1924 in connection with diplomatic recognition of the Soviet Union. In the ensuing elections

75. See B. de Jouvenel, *D'une guerre à l'autre*, vol. 2: *La décomposition de l'Europe libérale 1925–1932* (Paris, 1941).

held in October, Labour and the Liberal Party suffered heavy losses, allowing the Conservatives to return to power with an absolute majority of 415 seats in the House of Commons.[76] The new Prime Minister, Stanley Baldwin, was an industrialist from the Midlands who incarnated the classic Conservative blend of pragmatism and social reaction. In his vague way, he promised internal peace and a 'return to normality', i.e. a return to the prewar conditions so dear to the hearts of all European conservatives. Behind this verbal smokescreen, the government proceeded to take decisions with an enormous impact on the balance of social power in Britain.

The Chancellor of the Exchequer, Winston Churchill, announced his first measure: a return to the gold standard in order to restore 'confidence and security'.[77] At the same time, the Geneva Protocol for the strengthening of collective security in Europe (which had been heavily influenced by the previous British government and which provided for those who had disturbed the peace to be summoned before the Court of International Justice in the Hague and punished if necessary with economic sanctions) was abjured on the grounds that it infringed on the British government's freedom of action. This response of the new Conservative government torpedoed the Geneva Protocol and signalled that narrow limits would be set to any collective security system in Europe.

As we have seen, Britain's economic decline was hastened by Conservative monetary policy. The overvaluation of sterling further damaged the competitiveness of British industry. This problem could not be cured by the major programme which the Conservatives introduced to rationalise and concentrate British industry through mergers. In fact, this policy tended 'to damage the structure of the private economy based on competition and multiplicity'.[78] Under the impetus of these reforms, the British economy became more concentrated and responsive to state direction. However, the foremost inconsistency in Conservative economic policy was that credit was restricted in order to curtail demand, although this also had the effect of blunting the modernisation effort so essential to many businesses and branches of the economy. The outcome was inevitable: rationalisation and concentration together with insufficient modernisation led to high structural unemployment, especially in the basic industries, which soon became the scourge of British

---

76. See in detail R. Graves and A. Hodges, *The Long Week-End. A Social History of Great Britain, 1918–1932* (NY, 1941); B.B. Gilbert, *British Social Policy 1914–1939* (London, 1970); Ch. L. Mowat, *Britain between the Wars, 1918–1940* (London, 1976²).
77. According to P. Kluke, 'Grossbritannien und das Commonwealth' in Th. Schieder (ed.), *Handbuch der europäischen Geschichte*, vol. 7, p. 374.
78. E.J. Hobsbawm, *Industrie und Empire*, vol. 2, p. 79.

society. Meanwhile, the Conservative government did all it could to postpone the development of social programmes.[79]

Out of this witches' brew arose a great social explosion in the spring of 1926. The revolt was triggered by coal miners who had suffered most grievously from Conservative policies and were led by a particularly militant union. Although they had already sustained a devastating defeat in 1921, together with railway and transportation workers ('Black Friday'), they again pressed their demand for an improvement in unemployment benefits and working conditions. A general strike was called in May by the Trades Union Council (TUC), but it was crushed by a resolute government after only nine days. Only the miners carried on the strike, before finally succumbing to the common front of government and employers. The companies advanced a simple though effective argument in defence of their position: energy consumption was falling because of the economic depression. To a certain extent, the workers were batting their heads against a brick wall.

The British labour movement never recovered from this defeat. It fell into the opposite extreme, meekly acquiescing in extensive concessions to the companies, for instance in regard to rationalisation. More than their French or German counterparts, the leaders of the British trade unions espoused the view that the age of 'organised capitalism' had truely arrived. The TUC therefore saw its foremost responsibility to be the negotiation of social improvements through compromise with management. At the same time, the working masses transferred their allegiance to the Labour Party in the hope that socialist politicians, once in power, would implement what they themselves had failed to achieve through direct action. In the elections of 1929, Labour became the largest party in the House of Commons with 287 seats compared with 261 for the Conservatives and 59 for the Liberals. The situation in Germany evolved in a similar direction. In elections held in 1928 under the cloud of a massive lock-out of metal-workers, the Social Democrats and Communists substantially increased their vote and number of seats in the *Reichstag*.

None the less, the hopes which British workers placed in the Labour Party were disappointed. The second Labour cabinet, again under MacDonald, relied on Liberal support and in the crucial realm of finance and economic policy continued the course established by the previous Conservative government. Snowden, the new Chancellor of the Exchequer, was instrumental in deciding this policy. After the onset of the Great Depression, the Labour government yielded to pressure from employers and adopted strong deflationary measures, even though

79. Ibid., pp. 78ff.

many voices within and without the party (especially J.M. Keynes and the Minister of Education, Trevelyan) urged the government to abandon the gold standard and control imports. If they had been heeded, of course, the Labour Party would have had to pursue a genuinely socialist path. In contrast to Germany, where Chancellor Müller deserted the 'Grand Coalition' in deference to the wishes of the labour unions and most of his party, MacDonald stayed the course despite mounting opposition from within the Labour Party itself.

The Labour government accordingly bears a large portion of the blame for the serious monetary and economic crisis that shook Britain in the summer of 1931. While the SPD in Germany simply 'tolerated' Brüning's presidential cabinet, MacDonald played a pivotal role in forming a 'National Government' composed of Conservatives, Liberals and a minority of the Labour Party. This government implemented the same retrenchment policies that had already failed in Germany and the United States. However, there was one key difference in the British situation, which Abendroth has pointed out:

> While the German Social Democrats adopted a policy of tolerating Brüning's emergency decrees, the British Labour Party opposed reductions in wages and unemployment relief rather than tacitly sharing the responsibility for them. This prevented the middle classes from moving closer to fascism, maintained the unity of the labour movement and thereby saved bourgeois democracy in its moment of crisis.[80]

While the first Labour cabinet was quickly overturned, the *Cartel des Gauches* which had assumed power in France in May 1924 exhibited greater staying power, though it too eventually met its come-uppance.[81] How this came to pass provides a political lesson of abiding international significance. Though the left had won the elections of 1924, it was beset by problems. The governing 'cartel' was in fact a coalition of various parties of the centre left, the Socialists and the Radical Socialists, an ideologically leftist though economically rather right-wing party of the petty bourgeoisie. It won 48 per cent of the vote, compared to 44 per cent in 1919, but this support was concentrated south of the Loire, with little from the industrialised north. In addition, the *Cartel des Gauches* was anything but homogeneous. It depended heavily on the centre because Communist support (10 per cent of the vote and 26 seats) was unreliable, and the Socialist Party (SFIO) refused to enter the

80. W. Abendroth, *Sozialgeschichte der europäischen Arbeiterbewegung*, p. 121.
81. See in detail J.-N. Jeanneney, *Leçon d'histoire pour une gauche au pouvoir. La faillité du Cartel (1924–1926)* (Paris, 1977); E. Bonnefous, *Histoire politique de la Troisième République*, vol. 4: *Cartel des Gauches et Union nationale (1924–1929)* (Paris, 1960); P. Combe, *Niveau de vie et progrès technique en France 1860–1939. Contribution à l'étude de l'économie française contemporaine* (Paris, 1956).

government for fear of losing its identity. In fact, the political pendulum had swung only from the right to the centre left, and the forces of conservatism were still strong enough to stifle much change.

This was particularly true of monetary policy, which in France as elsewhere had become the centrepiece of political decision-making and the epitome of societies and states. All other aspects of *Cartel* policy can safely be ignored as politically irrelevant, including a foreign policy inclined more towards cooperation (though it too was flawed by many errors in judgement and corroded France's position as the foremost champion of the Versailles System). So far as the crucial realm of monetary policy was concerned, the new French government both shared the general illusion about a forthcoming 'return to normalcy' and cultivated its own belief that the sickly franc would soon be cured by an infusion of German reparations. Elated by their victory in the Great War, the French were more oblivious than others to the profound disruptions it had caused.[82]

Moreover, the *Cartel* had only managed to seize political power because of the disastrous financial policies of the conservative *Bloc national*, based on retrenchment and high levels of public debt while awaiting the influx of German reparations. The franc had been left to the mercy of speculators both inside and outside France who wished for nothing more than to induce highly profitable chaos.[83] The franc depreciated rapidly in early March 1924 and panic set in at the Paris Bourse. Counter-measures adopted at the last minute by the Poincaré government with the assistance of French and American banks provided only temporary relief. The crisis stemming from the huge public debt to the Bank of France – at its peak reaching as much as 27,000 million francs, the so-called *plafond* – had not been resolved. The problem was all the more intractable in that the proportion of short- and medium-term bonds was increasing, creating a floating debt that hung over the French financial world like a sword of Damocles.

Though the *Cartel* had inherited a difficult position, it hoped to overcome the monetary crisis and stabilise the internal situation. The key, in its eyes, was to forgo any attempt to re-establish prewar parities. This meant, however, that it would be subjected to virulent attack by the wealthy classes which saw orthodox financial and monetary policies

82. Among the social changes figured most prominently the dispossession of many small and medium investors through the loss of their foreign investments, especially in Russia, as well as both the absolute and relative impoverishment of the working class, i.e. those social classes which had carried the *Cartel* to power.

83. J.-N. Jeanneney, *Leçon d'histoire*, p. 48, agrees with the view that Stresemann played an appreciable role in this by persuading German-based banks in Amsterdam, London and New York to speculate against the franc, in order that he might gain some influence over French policy.

as the best guarantee of their privileged position and which could be confident of the support of the Bank of France. In confronting this challenge, the governing coalition would have to fend off abuse not only from the right but also from the extreme left, including the left wing of the SFIO.

For this reason, the *Cartel* never could nor even dared to consider taking the critical first step of distancing itself from the Bank of France. Instead, it cleaved to traditional measures and took out a new loan, the so-called *emprunt Clémentel*, in order to restore 'confidence', i.e. in order to gain the sympathy of banking and business circles that were naturally hostile to the *Cartel*. The inevitable upshot was a double defeat at the very outset of the government's mandate:[84] the new loan campaign failed to attract much new money, simply exchanging old bonds for new, while at the same time, the financial operation benefited the wealthy who had the necessary capital and technical knowledge to take advantage of the new opportunities. The fledgling left-wing government therefore pursued right-wing policies, though with insufficient consistency. This afforded the right an opportunity to bring down the *Cartel* by attacking its Achilles' heel of monetary policy.

Supported by the staunchly conservative Senate and by the no less conservative Bank of France, the right unleashed its assault using the proven methods of capital flight and the incessant casting of doubt on the financial acumen of the new government. By the middle of December 1924, the financial and monetary policies of the *Cartel* had already clearly failed. A few comments will suffice for the purposes of this book. Basically, the *Cartel* proved bereft of effective responses when the same vicious circle reasserted itself. The Treasury's loans from the Bank of France again surpassed the legally prescribed limit ('*plafond*') in late 1924, and it was revealed that the *Cartel* had 'cooked the books' by employing a double budget to disguise the actual amount of money in circulation.

The ensuing drama was typical of the downfall of left-wing governments. The franc came under internal and external pressure and began to slide in comparison with sterling, slowly at first and then more and more rapidly after October, 1925 (May 1924 = 76; December = 86.9; March 1925 = 92.1; June = 100; October = 109; November = 123; December = 130). At the same time, the SFIO distanced itself even further from the government when it realised that its plan to introduce a tax on investment income had no hope of being adopted by the *Cartel*. None the less, this tax continued to be bitterly attacked by the right, which denounced this rather modest method of coping with the financial

84. Ibid., pp. 60ff.

crisis as the first step towards a socialist revolution.

This reaction manifested the tense internal situation in France, and the *Cartel* began to disintegrate in late March 1925. The process gathered momentum after the fall of the Herriot cabinet in early April but then dragged on for another fifteen months, while the political centre of gravity shifted continually to the right. The pressure from the Bank of France intensified, and the *Cartel*, especially Finance Minister Caillaux, sought to save the day through open compromise with the right. Another loan further aggravated the problem of the *dette flottante* and rendered the *Cartel* wholly dependent on French and especially American banks. However, Washington and the American banks were only prepared to grant further assistance if a definitive solution was found to both the war debt question and France's monetary problems. The first of these conditions was satisfied by the signing of the Mellon–Béranger Accord in April 1926; but the second evidently had to wait until the right had returned to power.

As if to underscore the seriousness of the situation, the franc went into a nose-dive compared to sterling: April 1926 = 144; 12 June = 200; and 21 July = 243. On this day, Herriot made a final, desperate bid to form a government, before yielding to a Poincaré cabinet supported by all the parties of the right. As if by a 'miracle' the parity level of the franc rose in a single day to 220 and two days later to 200, before the new government of 'National Union' (including the Radical Socialists!) had even taken office.

As was the case everywhere, the social costs of currency stabilisation were very high. Disregarding his own deepest instincts and powerful voices in the conservative camp, Poincaré stabilised the franc at only one-fifth of its prewar value in order to avoid the negative effects associated with the stabilisation of sterling.[85] But in so doing, he fell into the opposite trap of stabilising the franc at too low a level. As a result, gold streamed into Paris, strengthening France's international position to be sure but at the cost of internal stability. Government financial, domestic and social policies were all trimmed to attract French capital back home. Cuts in the budget and tax increases (11,700 million francs in 1926 and 1927 alone) hit moderate income earners above all, and wealth was redistributed in favour of the narrow-minded, authoritarian *patrons*. The heaviest losses were suffered by those who had purchased war bonds and by the many who had saved small amounts of capital only to see four-fifths of it disappear. On the whole, the major victims were those social strata that had accumulated unproductive capital, suffered heavy losses after the war and now saw their faith in the French currency

85. This was the purpose as well of the clever tactic of not carrying out *de jure* stabilisation until two years later in April/May 1928 after the Right had won the elections.

and state, in whose name all this was done, totally destroyed.

The lower- and middle-middle classes, still typically Malthusian but none the less pillars of French society, were weakened for many years to come. French social programmes, already paltry, were throttled by this brand of stabilisation. Even the most modest reforms (e.g. paid vacation) were scotched by the Senate and chambers of commerce. While the balance of power within the middle class shifted in favour of finance capital (as in Great Britain), the gulf between the middle class and the working class widened further, a process which only increased in tempo in the early 1930s. The repercussions of Poincaré's policies, especially the primacy of monetary policy over economic and social questions, were obscured for a short time by a wave of prosperity. However, they re-emerged with a vengeance to figure among the principal causes of the collapse of 1931.[86] In return, it can be said that the gold reserves of the Bank of France did rise from 32,000 million francs in 1928 to 80,000 million shortly thereafter.

In Germany too, the conservative offensive gained an enormous amount of ground between 1924 and 1928.[87] Company owners did all they could to consolidate their social and economic position *vis-à-vis* both government and the labour movement. The effects of inflation and currency stabilisation were aggravated by a wave of concentration and rationalisation, including the development of better methods for controlling workers and unions in individual factories.[88] Social programmes in Germany were well developed in comparison with the United States, Britain and France, and the conservative offensive in Germany focused on them in an attempt to cut costs, restructure the system of collective wage settlements, and generally limit the state's ability to intervene in economic affairs. Industrialists concentrated above all on state arbitration of strikes and the system of compulsory, state-sanctioned wage rates, a particularly annoying thorn in the side of manufacturers. Recent research has demonstrated that the fundamental social compromise on which the Weimar Republic was based was systematically undermined

86. C. Fohlen, *La France de l'entre-deux-guerres (1917–1939)* (Paris, 1966), pp. 87ff.
87. For what follows see H. Mommsen et al. (eds), *Industrielles System*, (several articles); L. Preller, *Sozialpolitik in der Weimarer Republik* (Stuttgart, 1949); worthy of discussion as well are the works of D. Abraham based on a neo-Marxist approach (Gramsci): 'State and Classes in Weimar Germany', *Politics and Society* 7 (1977); idem, 'Constituting Hegemony: The Bourgeois Crisis of Weimar Germany', *JMH* (1979) (with a critical discussion by D. Stegmann and T.W. Mason); idem, *Political Economy, Political Crisis and the Collapse of the Weimar Republic* (Princeton, 1980). The class model on which these works are based is doubtless too schematic. In addition, the view that a dominant class bloc formed, consisting of export industries, the working class and white-collar employees, is not convincing.
88. According to Mason in H. Mommsen et al. (eds), *Industrielles System*, p. 334.

by large business interests. Since the state also felt that it had to support German business, social policy increasingly took on a 'compensatory function' (H. Mommsen), and social tensions heightened.

A distinguishing feature of the 'conservative offensive' in Germany was the prominent role played by the Ruhr coal mining industry. This in itself is not surprising given that the coal mining industry was in decline, despite all attempts at rationalisation, while politically it was still enormously powerful thanks to its connections with iron and steel magnates in elite employers' associations, with large landowners through their time-honoured alliance promoting protectionism and last but not least with the bureaucracy and the army. Industrialists sought to advance their interests less through direct political influence (in which they were not lacking) than through claims about economic realities and the need to upgrade Germany's international competitiveness. This approach proved all the more successful in that there was a broad public consensus, even including much of the SPD, that Germany required more economic muscle in order to offset her political and military weakness.

The companies declared virtual war on the labour unions in the infamous iron industry confrontation in the Ruhr in 1928, and inflicted a bitter defeat. This episode illustrates the depth of hostility that had arisen between the classes. In discussing the worsening social climate, H. Mommsen spoke of 'class warfare from above' and D. Stegmann of the 'refeudalisation of big business'. The similarities with the 'conservative offensive' in France, Great Britain and the United States become obvious, despite all national differences, when attention is focused on the crux of the matter: the subordination of social policy and the social compromise (not to mention social justice) to the demands of the economy – even though in the end this did not solve the structural problems and even tended to aggravate them. Neither manufacturers nor bankers really appreciated the root causes of the economic problem, and they pursued only their immediate, short-term interests.

Employer associations in Germany exerted even greater influence on the government than they did in the other three large industrial nations in the West. However, their leverage was moderated by their own internal disputes. The traditional alliance of heavy industrialists and large landowners often found itself at odds with export-oriented manufacturing industries such as the electrical and chemical industries and the machine-building industry, especially in southern Germany. The latter industries tended to support Stresemann's foreign policy, harboured a certain loyalty towards the Weimar Republic and at times even supported progressive social measures. But even though these industries represented an expanding sector of the economy with an immediate impact on consumers, they still could not hope to match the political muscle of heavy industry and big agriculture. The government had no industrial policy at all, and growth sectors of the economy received no special support. World markets, as we have seen, provided few opportunities, and Germany's export offensive in south-eastern Europe was just beginning. Moreover, labour unions gave no thought to an alliance with these manufacturers. The 'Grand Coalition' might have afforded an opportunity to forge an alliance among export industries, the working class and white-collar employees, but this possibility was hardly considered by those involved. The economy was too hard-pinched to arrive at much of a consensus about the redistribution of wealth, and the coaliton finally fell apart, not unexpectedly, in a quarrel over social benefits.

The dominance of heavy industry, maintained and reinforced through political muscle, was largely responsible for the structural inflexibility of the German economy – an inflexibility which became tragically apparent in the Great Depression. The anti-parliamentary, anti-democratic groundswell that began to infect industrial circles after 1927–8 would have been unimaginable, as H. Mommsen has convincingly demonstrated, without the excessive political influence of the declining sectors of the economy whose attitudes towards reparations and foreign policy in general was largely adopted by the government.[89] At the same time, the impulse in these sectors towards concentration and monopolisation of the economy drove middle-class entrepreneurs into the political opposition.[90] Once the Depression hit, the absence of promising political and economic programmes drove large segments of the middle- and lower-middle classes into the arms of the National Socialists.

In all of the great capitalist countries, the bid of conservative forces to reconstruct the world economy and world politics in conformity with their perceived interests only paved the way, in reality, for the great collapse. Like an immense cataclysm, it annihilated conservative policies and thought. The warning voices had been ignored – another indication of how little the conservatives appreciated the ramifications of their own policies.

89. See his brilliant report in ibid., pp. 612–17.
90. See in detail H.A. Winkler, *Mittelstand, Demokratie und Nationalsozialismus. Die politische Entwicklung von Handwerk und Kleinhandel in der Weimarer Republik* [The Middle Class, Democracy and National Socialism. The Political Evolution of Artisans and Small Retailers in the Weimar Republic] (Cologne, 1972).

4
The Structural Problems
of the Washington System
1922–30

I. The Bid to Achieve a Balance of Power in South-East Asia

It was not just happenstance that the new Republican administration in Washington took immediate steps, after assuming power under President Harding in the spring of 1921, to allay tensions in the Far East. The Pacific rim had always been a major focus of the open-door policy, and it figured prominently in the Republican vision of a reconstructed world economy and political system. This had underlain the barrage of criticism directed at the Democrats for allegedly neglecting Asia in favour of Europe and thereby damaging fundamental American interests. Equally important was the fact that the war had changed the balance of power in south-east Asia. The new administration was particularly concerned by Japan's highly successful and potentially dangerous campaign to extend her strategic and economic influence in this region primarily by virtue of massive industrialisation during the war. Many Americans realised that a new regional power was arising with which the United States would have to come to terms.

At the same time, the imperial powers of Europe had lost political and strategic influence in this region, and above all economic influence. Their position was further weakened by the civil war in China and by Japan's desire to hold on, at the very least, to the territorial advances she had made during the war. In addition, the European powers had pretty well abjured any intervention in the conflict between China and Japan, which as everyone knew, was a major source of instability in the region.

The Republicans were convinced that the open-door policy could only flourish in the Far East and markets could only be held open in the long run if political stability was maintained. Washington therefore concentrated its efforts on the political and strategic restructuring of the area, with the primary intention of restraining Japan and setting clear limits to her ambitions. Had not the Republicans themselves accused President Wilson of 'capitulating' to Japanese attempts to close the markets of China, a failing which bordered on treason in their books?

Not surprisingly, the Republican administration insisted that the Anglo-Japanese alliance of 1902, which had been extended in 1911 for another ten years, be disbanded. This alliance had contributed substantially to Japan's mounting power in Asia, especially in comparison with Russia. The British in any case showed little interest in renewing the treaty because the Soviet Union discontinued all attempts to expand in the Far East, at least in the 1920s. London was also eager to ensure that the impending reconstruction of Asia was carried out under close Anglo-American cooperation, in order to maintain at least some of Britain's waning influence. The United States had evidently become the dominant stabilising power in the Pacific, and the British realised that they could only hope at best to play the role of junior partner.

The new Secretary of State, Charles Evans Hughes, had a clear grasp of the situation outlined above, and under his energetic leadership, the Washington Conference was convened from 12 November 1921 till 6 February 1922. It produced a skein of international treaties establishing the legal status of the region (the Washington System).[1] The pivotal accords will be analysed in the following pages, at least so far as necessary in order to comprehend the main principles underlying the new order. The first of these accords was the 'Four-Power Agreement' which replaced the old Anglo-Japanese alliance of 1902 and was signed on 13 December 1921 by Britain, France, Japan and the United States. It basically guaranteed the territorial *status quo* throughout the islands of

1. See most importantly of all T.H. Buckley, *The United States and the Washington Conference 1921–1922* (Knoxville, 1970); L.E. Ellis, *Republican Foreign Policy, 1921–1933* (New Brunswick, 1968); but above all the pioneering work of A. Iriye, *After Imperialism. The Search for a New Order in the Far East, 1921–1931* (Cambridge, Mass., 1965); in addition: J.B. Crowley, *Japan's Quest for Autonomy* (Princeton, 1966); R.L. Buell, *The Washington Conference* (NY, 1922); M.G. Frey, *Illusions of Security. North Atlantic Diplomacy 1918–1922* (Toronto, 1972); I.H. Nish, 'Japan and the Ending of the Anglo-Japanese Alliance' in K. Bourne and D.C. Watt (eds), *Studies in International History* (London, 1967); J. Israel, *Progressivism and the Open Door. America and China, 1905–1921* (London, 1971); W.J. Cohen, *American Response to China* (NY, 1971); E.R. May and J.C. Thomson (eds), *American–East Asian Relations. A Survey* (Cambridge, Mass., 1972) (several contributions, also on what follows); C. Parrini, *Heir to Empire*. Participating in the American delegation to the conference under the leadership of Secretary of State Hughes were E. Root, a former Secretary of State with close ties to big business, H.C. Lodge, the influential chairman of the Senate foreign relations committee until his death in 1924, and the Democrat O.W. Underwood.

the Pacific, thereby amounting in the final analysis to a non-aggression pact which tended to diminish Japan's position. The elaboration of this treaty well illustrates the balance of power at the conference table. The agenda was set by the United States, with British support. All the other participants yielded more or less willingly to the desires of this alliance of powers. This was especially true in the case of Japan, which felt threatened and defensive, particularly since the global depression of 1920–1 had had a deeper and more abiding impact on her than on any other power.

The centrepiece of the Washington System was, however, the 'Five-Power Agreement' signed on 6 February 1922 for a duration of fifteen years. In it the United States, Britain, Japan, France and Italy established the relative number of their battleships at a ratio of 5 : 5 : 3 : 1.75 : 1.75. The treaty also established a ten-year moratorium on the construction of this type of ship and appended further measures to curtail naval armament. The Five-Power Agreement was accordingly a genuine forerunner of what today would be called an arms control treaty. Its significance for the balance of power in the Pacific was evident. It abridged British sea power, or at least confirmed its abridgement, and contained a formal renunciation of Britain's traditional 'two-power standard' (i.e. the British fleet must always be as strong as a combination of the next two strongest fleets in the world). Furthermore, key stretches of water such as the Gulf of Mexico and the Caribbean Sea were abandoned to the sole control of the United States. The abjuration of the 'two-power standard' provided compelling proof of Britain's decline as the world's leading sea power.

France too did not emerge from the Washington Conference unscathed. She found herself confronted by an Anglo-American coalition which wished to relegate her to the same level as Italy. This was a particularly bitter pill to swallow in that France not ony had to divide her fleet among the Atlantic and Pacific oceans and the Mediterranean Sea but also had a vast colonial empire in Indo-China to defend. Paris managed however to torpedo any restrictions on submarines or on small and medium-sized warships.

Japan's position in the Pacific, on the other hand, was not appreciably altered. She became the only great power allowed to concentrate her entire fleet in this region. In return for signing the treaty, Tokyo also managed to extract a promise from the United States not to expand her naval bases on the Pacific islands of Guam and the Philippines. For her part, the United States achieved her major aim of putting a halt to the costly arms race in the realm of battleships. None the less, most of the Japanese military remained determined, despite strong internal resistance (see below), to engage in another arms race at some point in the future in order to offset the territorial concessions which Japan had been compelled to make at the conference.[2] From the outset, therefore, the Japanese military aimed to cast off a crucial element of the Washington System.

Of crucial concern as well to the United States was the 'Nine-Power Agreement' signed on 6 February 1922 by Britain, Japan, China, France, Italy, Belgium, Holland, Portugal and the United States. This treaty accorded China equal treatment in regard to trade, guaranteed her territorial and administrative integrity and required the signatory powers to encourage the emergence of stable government. Furthermore, all foreign powers were required to renounce their special rights and privileges (such as those acquired thanks to the infamous 'unequal treaties' of the prewar period) whenever these rights and privileges infringed on the rights of third nations. All of these clauses reflected the underlying desire to impose tighter controls on the competition among imperialist powers for the Chinese market.

This treaty is of historical significance because Washington succeeded for the first time in gaining formal acceptance of its open-door policy. It conferred clear advantages on the United States, especially in respect to her fiercest rivals for the Chinese market, Great Britain and Japan. These powers had derived most benefit from the previous practice of dividing China into zones of influence and had most to lose from the 'Nine-Power Agreement', which represented a first step in the direction of what has quite rightly been labelled 'open-door imperialism'.[3] The open-door imperialism now officially sanctioned by international law accorded all nations equal rights in the markets of China – a situation which, in the long run, would clearly benefit the strongest economic power. The penetration of China could now proceed apace without the unseemly forms of direct control which had characterised the 'unequal treaties' and which were now encouraging the emergence of national liberation movements.

The Washington Conference provides much food for thought, particularly in view of present tensions on the international stage. Its originality lay in combining global arms control (in regard to battleships, a particularly powerful naval weapon at the time) with political restructuring of the Pacific region. Never again has an attempt been made to stabilise a region permanently through a combination of arms control, a non-aggression pact and political solutions (aimed in this case at re-

2. The province of Shantung taken from Germany during the war was returned to China, and Japan also promised to withdraw her troops from northern Sakhalin island and eastern Siberia.
3. The term was coined by W.A. Williams. See in this regard A. Iriye, 'Imperialism in East Asia' in J.B. Crowley (ed.), *Modern East Asia* (NY, 1970).

straining Japan and solving the Chinese question). Each of these three elements conditioned the others and made an overall solution feasible. This outcome would never have been possible without the whole-hearted participation of the United States, which, by accident or design, thereby became the linchpin of the new Washington System.

None the less, this series of agreements succeeded for only a few short years in bringing stability to the Far East.[4] The main reason for the ultimate failure of the Washington System was that it, like the Versailles System, was flawed from the outset by internal contradictions and inconsistencies. There was indeed a period of détente in Japanese-American and Anglo-American relations, but the future remained clouded because the conference participants had been unwilling to eliminate *all* foreign privileges in China, as they had been requested to do. The guarantees of Chinese sovereignty and territorial integrity contained in the Nine-Power Agreement represented a first step in this direction, but only as a tactical measure intended to counteract the mounting Chinese resentment of foreigners, which was finding expression in boycotts of foreign goods and even open violence. In fact, many elements of the 'unequal treaties' remained in force, e.g. extra-territoriality, the presence of foreign troops, and the inability of China to set tariffs or to put foreigners on trial in her own courts. The participants in the Washington Conference agreed only to consider arranging another conference on tariff autonomy for China, though this would have had little immediate effect because it required an end to the civil war and the emergence of a stable government able to speak for the entire country. In the final analysis, the Washington System was only a slightly ameliorated version of the old imperialist system in China. The 'Chinese question' remained open, and the Washington System would eventually have to prove its worth by dealing effectively with it.

The success of the system depended to an even greater extent on whether Japan continued to cooperate. Tokyo had proved compliant in the past in order to obtain restrictions on the size of the American fleet in the Pacific; but this policy could only continue in the long run if it helped to mitigate the fundamental weakness in the Japanese economy and society: utter dependence on foreign trade, particularly with China and the United States.[5] In other words, a conciliatory foreign policy was contingent, so far as Tokyo was concerned, on intensified trade. The benefits which a cooperative policy conferred on the 'liberal' commercial and industrial interest governing Japan always had to outweigh the

4. For the following I relied on two substantial versions by F. Luther on 5 November 1973 and 15 February 1974.

5. For the supreme importance of the Chinese market to Japan see J.E. Orchard, *Japan's Economic Position* (NY, 1930), pp. 451ff.

advantages of an agrresive, expansionist posture aimed at procuring a secure source of raw materials for a country which had none. This was the critical question that pervaded Japanese political life throughout the 1920s.

This was also the Achilles heel of the Washington System, especially as certain requirements for the second alternative already existed in Japan's relatively strong naval position in the Pacific and, most importantly, in the privileges she already enjoyed in southern Manchuria thanks to the railway network which had been built there. If the cooperative option failed to satisfy Japan's internal and external needs, nothing remained but to reinforce her hold in Manchuria, even though this would inevitably aggravate the conflict with China and call the entire Washington System into question. The dominant power, the United States, held the high cards. But could she manage the difficult trick of restraining Japan by virtue of intensive economic relations while at the same time satisifying China's needs?

This fundamental dilemma goes a long way towards explaining the ambivalence and inconsistency in American policy towards the Far East.[6] On the one hand, the United States demanded an open door to China and respect for Chinese unity and sovereignty; on the other, she recognised more or less explicitly certain special rights for Japan. American support for the territorial integrity of China never went so far as to provoke a confrontation with Japan, which provided a far larger market for American goods than did China (in 1920 almost five times as large). The United States therefore gave tacit approval to Japan's efforts to expand her foothold in Manchuria, indeed with the assistance of leading American banks. As a result, the open-door policy was continually being corroded by loans to Japan while China remained on the periphery of international capital flows between 1920 and 1933.[7]

American policy suffered most of all from a lack of coordination between economic and diplomatic objectives in the Far East. This stemmed from the fact that the State Department was torn between two opposing interpretations of the Washington agreements (rooted in opposing economic interest), according to which American policy was tilted in favour of either Japan or China. This uncertainty did not facilitate the task, implicit in the Washington System, of finding a balance between the two extremes.[8] In the years immediately following the Washington Conference, the director of the East Asian department,

6. See in this regard W.L. Neumann, 'Ambiguity and Ambivalence in Ideas of National Security in Asia' in A. DeConde (ed.), *Isolation and Security* (Durham, 1957).

7. H. Feis, *The Diplomacy of Dollar*, p. 36; A. Iriye, *After Imperialism*, p. 191; J.H. Wilson, *American Business*, p. 214.

8. J.H. Wilson, *American Business*, pp. 214–18.

John Van Antwerp MacMurray, successfully imposed the following interpretation (over the objections of Secretary of State Hughes): The treaties were indeed intended to help improve China's position and they therefore required the industrialised countries to yield their remaining commercial privileges; however, these countries nonetheless retained the right, anchored in the 'unequal treaties', to defend their prerogatives, by force of arms if necessary, should the nationalist movement gather sufficient strength to threaten their property or established position. In the end, this interpretation of the treaties favoured Japan by prolonging China's subjection to foreign powers.

In the later 1920s, a pro-Chinese view gained the upper hand under Secretary of State Kellogg and his chief of the East Asian department, Nelson Johnson. Two developments were largely responsible for this change of direction. Firstly, American attempts to foster cooperation among the industrial nations in China had failed; and secondly, the middle-class, nationalist movement in China under Chiang Kai-shek seemed poised for victory. In view of this turn of events, Washington decided to seek bilateral talks with the Chinese aimed at liquidating what remained of the old imperialist system. While this would provide China's new rulers with an opportunity to develop their country, it also raised the spectre of confrontation with Japan. A striking parallel becomes immediately apparent: just as the United States failed to mediate successfully between British, French and German interests within the Versailles System, so she failed to effect a compromise between Japan and China within the Washington System. These failures threatened from the outset the stability of both systems which depended heavily on the ability of the United States to play an active role in reconciling competing interests.

II. The Dynamics of the Washington System

1. The Relationship Between Japan's Domestic, Foreign and Economic Foreign Policies

In spite of all rhetoric invoking the territorial integrity and fabulous markets of China, the American government and business circles set out, with customary solidarity, to install Japan as America's privileged partner in the Far East, especially from an economic point of view.[9] This policy tallied well with Tokyo's own resolve to steer a pro-American course, a decision based equally on domestic considerations and the global economic situation. Although Japan had already begun her

9. F.C. Adams, *Economic Diplomacy*, p. 36 and J.H. Wilson, *American Business*, p. 201 agree.

Table 13 Japan's Foreign Trade in 1913 and from 1919 to 1932 (in mill. of yen)

Year	Imports	Exports	Balance
1913	729	632	− 97
1919	2,173	2,099	− 74
1920	2,336	1,948	−388
1921	1,614	1,253	−361
1922	1,890	1,637	−253
1923	1,982	1,448	−534
1924	2,453	1,807	−646
1925	2,573	2,306	−267
1926	2,377	2,044	−333
1927	2,179	1,992	−187
1928	2,196	1,972	−224
1929	2,216	2,148	− 68
1930	1,546	1,469	− 77
1931	1,235	1,147	− 88
(Yen Devaluation)			
1932	1,431	1,410	− 21

Source: K. Glück, 'Japans Vordringen auf dem Weltmarkt' (Frankfurt, Würzburg, 1937), pp. 50, 57, 60.

Table 14 Composition of Japanese Foreign Trade by Category of Goods (as a percentage)

Year	Foodstuffs	Raw Materials	Semi-Manufactures	Finished Goods
		Imports		
1912	11.6	48.4	19.8	19.6
1914	13.2	55.2	16.2	4.6
1918	10.5	51.3	27.4	10.2
1928	13.6	53.1	17.4	15.2
1929	12.2	55.2	16.0	15.6
1930	13.4	53.6	15.3	16.5
		Exports		
1912	10.4	8.4	50.3	29.6
1914	10.8	7.7	51.8	28.4
1918	10.7	5.6	38.5	43.4
1928	7.9	4.5	41.8	41.2
1929	7.4	4.1	41.1	43.6
1930	8.8	4.4	35.7	47.0
1932	7.3	3.5	34.4	49.8
1933	8.4	3.9	28.4	55.4
1934	7.9	4.4	22.9	61.9
1935	7.9	4.4	24.5	58.6

Source: same as Table 6, pp. 51, 55, 59, 61 (the figures add up to 100 per cent if 'Miscellaneous' is included)

Table 15 Japanese Exports by Region (Average for 1925–9)

Region	Value (in thousands of US gold dollars)	Share of Total Exports (as a %)
China, Hong Kong, Kwantung	278,186	26.6
British India	84,101	8.0
Rest of Asia	87,580	8.3
All of Asia	449,867	42.9
USA	444,118	42.5
Europe	73,751	7.1
Australia, New Zealand	28,976	2.8
Other countries	49,609	4.7
Total	1,046,321	100

Source: J.E. Orchard, *Japan's Economic Position*, p. 450.

ascent to the status of a modern industrial power around 1867 under the Meiji, she had to wait until the First World War before achieving the crucial breakthrough to political and economic dominance in the Far East.[10] Japan moved resolutely to occupy former German colonies and to coerce China into recognising Japanese zones of influence in southern Manchuria, eastern Mongolia and Shantung. Even more important for the future, however, was the enormous expansion of her productive capacities, which enabled Japan to expel not only the war-weary Europeans but even the Americans from considerable segments of the

10. Main works: W.W. Lockwood, *The Economic Development of Japan. Growth and Structural Change, 1868–1938* (Princeton, 1970²), pp. 38–42; M. Takahashi, *Modern Japanese Economy since 1868* (Tokyo, 1968), pp. 92ff.; H.G. Moulton, *Japan. An Economic and Financial Appraisal* (Washington, DC, 1931); K. Ohara, *Japanese Trade and Industry in the Meiji–Taisho Era* (Tokyo, 1957); M. Shinohara, 'Economic Development and Foreign Trade in Pre-War Japan' in C.D. Cowan (ed.), *The Economic Development of China and Japan* (London, 1964); B. Masao and T. Masshiro, 'Foreign Trade and Economic Growth in Japan, 1858–1937' in L. Klein and K. Ohkawa (eds), *Economic Growth* (Homewood, 1968); G.C. Allen, *A Short Economic History of Modern Japan 1867–1937* (London, 1962); K. Ikeda, *Die industrielle Entwicklung in Japan unter bes. Berücksichtigung seiner Finanz- und Wirtschaftspolitik* (Berlin, 1970); H. Rosovsky, *Capital Formation in Japan 1868–1940* (Glencoe, 1961); for domestic policy see P. Duus, 'The Era of Party Rule. Japan 1905–1932' in J.B. Crowley (ed.), *Modern East Asia*; R.A. Scalapino, *Democracy and the Party Movement in Pre-War Japan. The Failure of the First Attempt* (Berkeley, 1953); for foreign policy see H. Kamikawa (ed.), *Japan–American Diplomatic Relations in the Meiji–Taisho Era* (Tokyo, 1958); Y.C. Maxon, *Control of Japanese Foreign Policy* (Berkeley, 1957); W.L. Neumann, *America Encounters Japan* (Baltimore, 1963).

Table 16 Japanese Trade with the United States in 1914 and 1918–29 (in million of yen)

Year	Exports		Imports	
	Value	% of Total Exports	Value	% of Total Imports
1914	196	33.2	96	16.2
1918	503	27.0	626	37.6
1919	828	39.5	766	35.3
1920	565	29.0	873	37.4
1921	496	39.6	574	35.6
1922	732	44.8	596	31.5
1923	605	41.8	511	25.8
1924	745	41.2	671	27.4
1925	1,006	43.7	665	25.8
1926	861	42.1	680	28.6
1927	834	41.9	674	30.9
1928	826	41.9	625	28.5
1929	914	42.5	654	29.5

Source: O. Keishi, *Japanese Trade and Industry in the Meiji–Taisho Era*, p. 34f.

south-east Asian market and others.[11] The western powers reacted, even then, with shock and anger.

But the deep depression triggered by the global economic crisis of 1920–1 seemed to wipe out all Japan's economic advances during the war. Her vital foreign trade plummeted (Table 13), and the price of her industrial and agricultural products fell through the floor. Japanese society was shaken by violent social conflicts, particularly between peasants and large landowners. As debts, taxes and the price of land rose, the already difficult lot of the peasantry grew even worse. Even the income they earned on the side by raising silk worms dried up when cocoon prices collapsed.[12] Japan competed on world markets by offering

11. Between 1913 and 1918 the value of Japanese exports tripled (see Table 13 in the text). The markets which Japan largely took away from the Europeans included China, British India, the Dutch East Indies, Oceania, and even Latin America and Africa. The Japanese share of the Chinese market for instance rose from 20 to 36 per cent between 1913 and 1919 while Britain's share fell from 16.5 per cent to 9.5 per cent. Cf. D.H. Aldcroft, *Zwanziger Jahre*), p. 54. While Europe's share fell from 367.5 million yen in 1913 to 332.1 million yen in 1915–18 on an annual average, Asia's share soared from 623.9 million to 1111.3 million and North America's from 192.4 million to 731.6 million. See K. Glück, 'Japans Vordringen auf dem Weltmarkt', PhD thesis, Frankfurt, 1936, Würzburg, 1937, p. 55; see in detail A. Reichelt, 'Japans Aussenhandel und Aussenhandelspolitik unter dem Einfluss des Weltkrieges' [Japan's Foreign Trade and Foreign Trade Policy under the Influence of the Great War], PhD thesis, Berlin, 1931.

12. This was the case even in the period of relative prosperity: between 1925 and 1931

relatively low prices, and the living standards of the peasantry were compressed to the subsistence level, and at times even below, in order to provide for further industrialisation and essential expansion of foreign trade.[13] The financial and economic crisis reached its peak between March and June 1921 and was not fully overcome until 1924–5.[14]

Social tensions were also aggravated by other problems, primarily the rapid rate of population growth (1910 = 50 million; 1920 = 56.7 million; 1930 = 64.6 million; 1935 = 70 million). At the same time, production of the most important foodstuff, rice, levelled off. The outcome was typical of periods of rapid growth: imports were indispensible in order to make up the shortfall in rice production (as well as in all other primary products), and they could only be paid for by increased exports, especially of finished goods. Hence, another industrialisation campaign was imperative if the structural deficit in the balance of payments was not to become further entrenched.[15] The social effects were flight from the land, run-away urbanisation and swelling armies of industrial workers (barely 1 million in 1914 against 1.8 million in 1928). The peasants were systematically exploited, while at the same time they swelled the ranks of the industrial reserve army. Japan's only other trump in the accumulation process was cheap labour, an advantage which manufacturers milked with almost unimaginable brutality. The lack of labour unions worthy of the same opened the door to starvation wages and inhuman working conditions. With the help of dumping-level prices, Japanese companies seized a mounting share of world markets, while their employees suffered exploitation to rival any in the entire capitalist world.

Success was not long in coming. Industrialisation proceeded apace with strong state support in the form of export premiums, subsidies and protective tariffs. The most rapidly expanding sector of the economy was the textile industry, whose products made up the lion's share of Japanese exports (silk as well as cotton yarns and fabrics). After 1928 the finished goods portion of total exports climbed steadily and by 1932 accounted already for about half of Japan's total export earnings (Table 14), while exports of semi-manufactures dwindled accordingly. These figures bear eloquent witness to the dynamism of Japanese industry (see Tables 3 and 4). But the economy was also becoming ever more reliant

---

cocoon prices fell by more than two-thirds while production over this same period rose by 25 per cent. W.W. Lockwood, *The Economic Development of Japan*, p. 57.

13. K. Glück, 'Japans Vordringen auf dem Weltmarkt', p. 24.

14. A serious earthquake that caused damage amounting to some 11,000 million yen led to another recession in 1923.

15. For the Japanese model of industrialisation see the basic analysis of F. Moulder, *Japan, China and the Modern World Economy* (Cambridge, 1977).

Table 17 Britain's and America's Share of the Total Imports of Selected
Countries: 1913, 1929, 1935 and 1937 (as a percentage)

	Great Britain				USA			
	1913	1929	1935	1937	1913	1929	1935	1937
Canada	21.3	15.0	21.2	18.2	64.0	68.8	56.8	60.6
Australia	51.8	39.7	42.6	41.6	13.7	24.6	15.3	14.0
New Zealand	59.7	48.7	51.0	50.2	9.5	18.6	12.0	12.0
Rep. of S. Africa	56.8	43.1	48.6	42.6	8.9	18.0	16.9	19.6
India	64.2	42.4	39.3	31.5	2.6	7.3	6.6	6.4
Denmark	15.7	14.7	36.0	37.7	10.2	13.3	5.3	5.5
Argentina	31.1	17.6	24.7	18.9	14.7	26.4	13.6	16.4
Brazil	24.5	19.2	12.4	12.1	15.7	30.1	23.4	23.0
France	13.2	10.0	7.5	8.0	10.6	12.3	8.5	9.5
Germany	8.1	6.4	6.2	5.7	15.9	13.3	5.8	5.2
Italy	16.2	9.6	7.2	3.9	14.3	16.7	11.2	10.9
Great Britain	–	–	–	–	15.2	16.6	11.6	11.1
USA	13.2	7.5	7.6	6.6	–	–	–	–

Source: Two publications of the League of Nations: *Memorandum on Balance of Payments and Foreign Trade Balances 1910–1924* (Geneva, 1925), pp. 142ff. and *International Trade Statistics 1937* (Geneva, 1938), pp. 373ff. Complied by F. Luther.

on foreign trade. If Japan was to resolve her demographic, social and economic problems, only two courses presented themselves: either enhance foreign trade, especially with the United States and China, and thereby implicate Japan more deeply in the international division of labour, or if this approach did not succeed, expand by force of arms into the Chinese hinterland in order to gain the material basis of a policy of economic autarky.

At first Japan clearly steered the first course. The industrial and commercial middle classes had clearly derived the greatest benefit from the economic upsurge during the First World War, and they had also succeeded at this time in vastly expanding their political influence in the guise of two 'liberal' parties. The heads of the employers' associations – the 'general staff of the Japanese economy'[16] – met in the 'Keizai Club' to plan their strategy. Without a hint of remorse, they financed the two great 'liberal' parties, controlled the large newspapers and did not hesitate to buy votes, if necessary, at election time. An electoral reform favouring the middle classes further reinforced their control of parliament. Together with financial and business interests, they controlled Japanese foreign policy, with only one short interruption, until 1930–1.[17]

16. P. Renouvin, *Les crises du XXe siècle* (*Histoire des relations internationales*, vol. VII), part I: 1914 à 1929 (Paris, 1957), p. 243f.
17. See O. Reischauer, *Japan. Past and Present* (NY, 1950), pp. 144, 147f. The two most

These social strata firmly opposed the strategy of territorial expansion, openly advocated by leading military officers on the general staffs of the army and navy, senior civil servants and university professors.[18] In June of 1921, a conference of chambers of commerce even demanded a reduction in the military budget. Japanese business and commercial circles were accordingly overjoyed with the Washington accords. They hoped that these agreements would stimulate trade with China and the United States and stoke the industrialisation of Japan.[19] The chief proponent of this export-oriented and therefore cooperative, outward-looking foreign policy was the Japanese Foreign Minister, Baron Kijuro Shidehara (1924–7 and 1929–31). As the son-in-law of Baron Iwasaki, the chief of the Mitsubishi group of ninety-two companies and hence one of the most powerful industrialists in the land, Shidehara maintained close ties with elite business circles. Initially therefore, the balance of power in Japan worked very much in favour of a conciliatory foreign policy compatible with the basic principles of the Washington System; however, Tokyo's willingness to cooperate was clearly predicated on increased trade with both China and the United States.

This is not at all surprising, given Japan's extreme dependence on foreign markets in China and the United States (Tables 15 and 16).[20] In the period between 1923 and 1931, China absorbed 22 per cent of Japan's total exports (which accounted in turn for 27 per cent of China's total imports). In the particularly critical years of 1925 to 1929, China even absorbed an average of 26.6 per cent. The United States, in comparison, only relied on China to absorb some 3 per cent of her total exports (equalling 18 per cent of Chinese imports). The Chinese market was therefore far more important to Japan than the United States. On the other hand, the American market was even more important to Japan, absorbing on average an incredible 42.5 per cent of her total exports between 1925 and 1929. This highly dangerous concentration on only two foreign markets was the Achilles' heel of the Japanese economy.

Japan's most important exports were raw silk (some 40 per cent of

important 'liberal' parties were the Minseito and Seiyukai. They clearly do not deserve the adjective 'liberal' in the European understanding of the term because they, like the rest of Japanese society, espoused the ideology of the strong leader supported by his underlings.
18. The chief ideologue was Kita Ikki with his book published in 1919, *The Foundations of the Reconstruction of Japan*, which went so far as to advocate expansion even at the cost of the European powers.
19. A fundamental analysis in A. Iriye, *Across the Pacific* (NY, 1967); also J.B. Crowley, *Japan's Quest for Autonomy*.
20. Fundamentally J.E. Orchard, *Japan's Economic Position*, pp. 424–52; H.G. Moulton, *Japan*; M. Shinohara, 'Economic Development and Foreign Trade in Pre-War Japan.'

Table 18 Share of Colonies or Zones of Economic Influence in the Total Trade of Selected Countries (as a %)

Country	Colonies or Zones of Economic Influence	Imports				Exports			
		1929	1932	1935	1938	1929	1932	1935	1938
Great Britain	a) Commonwealth, Brit. Colonies, Protectorates, etc.	30.2	36.4	39.0	41.9	44.4	45.4	47.6	49.9
	b) Countries of the 'Sterling Block' not included under a[1]	12.0	13.2	12.5	12.8	7.4	9.8	11.5	11.7
France	Colonies, Protectorates, Mandates	12.0	20.9	25.8	27.1	18.8	31.5	31.6	27.5
Italy	Colonies, Ethiopia	0.5	1.1	1.9	1.8	2.1	3.6	14.3	23.3
Germany	Six Countries of South-Eastern Europe[2]	4.5	5.5	10.1	12.0	5.0	3.9	7.7	13.2
	Latin America	12.2	11.2	14.5	15.6	7.8	4.3	9.5	11.5
Japan	Korea, Formosa, Kwantung, Manchuria[3], rest of China	26.0	36.9	34.9	45.0	35.0	37.2	41.1	62.7

[1]Sweden, Norway, Finland, Denmark, Egypt, Estonia, Latvia, Portugal, Siam, Iraq
[2]Bulgaria, Greece, Hungary, Romania, Turkey, Yugoslavia
[3]For the Manchurian share see below p. 162
Source: Société des Nations, *Aperçu général du commerce mondial 1938* (Geneva, 1939), p. 36f.

Table 19 Japanese Raw Silk Price Indices and Exports 1923–31

Year	Index of Average Annual Prices on Yokohama Market	Index of Total Exports of Raw Silk		Percentage of Exports to the United States
		Value	Amount	
1923–5	100	100	100	90
1926	82	103	123	97
1927	69	104	146	94
1928	67	103	152	94
1929	66	110	161	97
1930	44	59	131	96
1931	30	50	155	96

Source: K. Ohara, *Japanese Trade and Industry*, Table 19, p. 297.

average annual exports between 1924 and 1927) and cotton textiles (25 per cent). In contrast to cotton textiles, the production of silk did not require any imports of raw materials and all export earnings could be used to reduce the deficit in the balance of payments. Raw silk therefore played a crucial role in Japan's export economy – which hung, according to the leading expert in the field, by 'a silken thread'.[21] In the 1924–9 period, an astounding average of 95.6 per cent of Japanese raw silk exports were shipped to the United States. Of the 35 million kilograms that the United States imported in 1928–9, 28.8 million came from Japan. Some 85 per cent of Japanese export earnings in the United States derived from raw silk. Japan exported approximately 78 per cent of her total raw silk production and upgraded the rest into fabrics also intended by and large for export. The potential catastrophe resided primarily in the fact that silk was utilised in the United States to produce luxury goods, which were normally very hard hit by economic downturns. This problem was compounded by the development of synthetic fibres which began to cut into sales of raw silk. The 'silken thread' on which Japanese exports to the United States hung was therefore very tenuous. Raw silk was not supplanted as Japan's leading export until 1932 when industrial production grew more diversified.

Asia provided the major outlet for all other Japanese exports, absorbing between 60 and 70 per cent of them. China alone purchased 40 per cent of these exports. The most important of these goods were cotton textiles which accounted for 40 per cent of total sales to China. All in all, it is obvious that thriving foreign trade was essential to the Japanese economy.

21. W.W. Lockwood, *The Economic Development of Japan*, p. 320.

In so far as capital was concerned, Japan was not nearly as dependent on the United States. By 1931, Japan had poured 81.9 per cent of all her foreign investment into China. The 'opening' and development of Manchuria (railways, mines, industrial installations) had swallowed 1,750 million yen by 1930, i.e. before military expansion began.[22] American capital, on the other hand, represented only 1.3 per cent of total foreign investment in China. However, one still cannot exclude the possibility that access to American capital markets was a major consideration in the Japanese decision to adopt a conciliatory posture towards the United States, especially as Tokyo's reserves of foreign currency were being rapidly depleted in the 1920s by the high trade deficit (Table 13, p. 124).

It has been calculated that exports accounted for 39 per cent of Japan's economic growth between 1921 and 1938. It was therefore labelled 'export-led growth',[23] in reference to the same kind of growth which was experienced after the Second World War by so-called newly industrialising countries such as Brazil and Korea, though the latter enjoyed an incomparably better international economic climate. Significantly, it was not so much the 1920s as the 1930s that laid the foundations for Japan's economic take-off of the 1950s and 1960s which propelled her far beyond the level of these countries to the status of an economic superpower alongside the United States and western Europe.

2. The 'Chinese Question'

As we have seen, the second critical element in the Washington System was the agreement among the imperialist powers (The Nine-Power Agreement) to cooperate in implementing an 'open-door' policy towards China. This included endeavours to transform the Chinese revolution into a moderate reform movement without infringing on the fundamental interests of the capitalist countries. However, this proved impossible to achieve. The first period in relations with China between 1922 and 1925–6 was marked by the failure, particularly on the part of France, Britain and the United States, to agree upon a common policy. One of the reasons for this failure can be found in internal developments within China. The traditional method of penetrating China by means of 'unequal treaties' had given the imperialist powers full extraterritoriality and the right to bring in troops to defend their own nationals, property

22. See E. Meyn, 'Die japanische Wirtschaftspolitik in der Mandschurei' [Japanese Economic Policy in Manchuria], dissertation at the Leipzig College of Commerce, 1938, p. 29.

23. B. Masao and T. Masshiro in L. Klein and K. Ohkawa (eds), *Economic Growth*, p. 179; M. Shinohara, 'Economic Development and Foreign Trade in Pre-War Japan', pp. 220–48.

and investments. They were thus able to exploit China's raw materials and forestall the emergence of competing local industries; but these tactics also fuelled a nationalist revolutionary movement, which found expression not least of all in mounting hostility to foreigners.

The inspiration and chief ideologue of this movement was Sun Yat-sen. He had reorganised the Kuomintang Party, the nucleus of the movement, in 1923 and inspired it with precepts laid out in his book, *The Three Principles of the People* (1924). The party planned to attack foreign domination by nationalising key industries, though it respected private land holdings. The political regime it sought was not so much a democracy as rule by the elite, first and foremost the intelligentsia and the leadership of the party, which numbered 1.6 million members in 1927.[24] To this extent, the Kuomintang was a middle-class, nationalist movement.

The Communist Party was founded at about the same time. It began to gather support among the peasantry after 1924 and to build a base of its own. In the spring of 1922, the Kuomintang and the Communists agreed to form a provisional alliance aimed at fomenting 'national revolution' and freeing China from the 'unequal treaties'. Sun Yat-sen died on 12 March 1925, and his successors, notably Chiang Kai-shek, the future leader of the Kuomintang and a scion of the upper bourgeoisie, jettisoned this policy out of fear of mounting Soviet influence. In December 1927 Chiang crushed with considerable bloodshed a Communist uprising in Canton, rooting out the Communist Party for some years and prompting Moscow to break off relations with nationalist China.

By this juncture, both parties had contributed enormously to stirring up hostility towards foreigners and intensifying the civil war. During the first half of the 1920s, China was effectively divided into three parts. Two governments squared off against one another: a northern government consisting of a group of generals headquartered in Peking, controlling at most three or four provinces and officially recognised by the western powers, and a southern 'revolutionary government' headquartered in Canton where Sun Yat-sen again presided after 7 May 1921 as president of the 'Republic of China' (though with frequent interruptions). The southern government controlled two provinces at most, and both it and the northern government were repeatedly shaken by *coups*. The twelve wealthiest provinces were ruled by generals, the so-called 'war lords', who concerned themselves most of all with deriving as much personal benefit as possible from the prevailing chaos. As the civil war spread, atrocities against foreigners multiplied. Many brutal excesses

---

24. P. Renouvin, *La question d'Extrême-Orient 1840–1940* (Paris, 1946), p. 339.

were recorded in Nanking in March 1927 after the city was captured by the Kuomintang, including attacks on the consulates of the United States, Britain and France. Numerous foreigners were murdered, injured and robbed. Armed confrontations and boycotts of foreign products became more and more frequent.

These events should have prodded the western powers to fulfil as quickly as possibly the goals which they had established at the Washington Conference, even though this task was rendered very difficult by the lack of a central Chinese government. The two most important tools for making progress in this regard were the Peking Tariff Conference and an international bank consortium founded in 1918. But all attempts to concede China the right to set her own tariffs and take out loans came to nought. The bank consortium was prevented from granting further loans by the insistence of one power after another that China should first be compelled to fund her existing foreign debt. In this way, the various western powers impeded one another and stalled the joint penetration of China which they had originally planned to carry out primarily by means of Anglo-American capital.

The tariff conference originally planned for 1922 was delayed until October 1925. When the parties finally convened, they agreed to concede to China the right to set her own tariffs beginning on 1 January 1929, but then the conference was forced to disband in April 1926 by the broadening civil war. The conference would likely have miscarried in any case due to the conflicting positions adopted in regard to a number of important issues mainly by the United States, Britain and Japan.[25] The commission that was supposed to deal with the question of extraterritoriality was also postponed until 12 January 1926. Even then it found itself unable simply to sweep away this anachronistic privilege, and instead proposed ways and means of reforming it. Imperialism would remain, though in watered-down form. Thus, by early 1926, the old imperialist system in China was crumbling on all sides, but no new system had been agreed upon to take its place. As a result, the western powers began to seek bilateral agreements with China.

This marked the onset of the second stage in the evolving 'Chinese question', which lasted until the Manchurian crisis. While Britain and the United States temporised, because of the uncertain internal situation, Japan set out to conclude bilateral treaties with China which would eventually play a role in Tokyo's long-term plans for a 'coexistence and co-prosperity' zone[26] including China and other countries of south-east Asia. In the elaboration of this plan, both approaches to the Japanese dilemma outlined above were essayed, though neither with

25. According to A. Iriye, *After Imperialism*, p. 85.
26. Here a persistent theme of Japanese foreign and foreign economic policy can be seen

much success.[27] The first approach, advocated by Shidehara, encouraged Japanese exports to China and peaceful economic penetration, while downplaying Japanese rights in Manchuria and not even considering military attack. The second aproach was championed by General Tanaka, who governed Japan between April 1927 and July 1929. Under the impulsion of another economic downturn in 1927,[28] Tanaka insisted on the preservation and extension of Japanese rights in Manchuria and on an 'investment oriented' foreign policy aimed at building up efficient heavy industries in this region. Tanaka sought thereby to assuage the vulnerability of the Japanese economy, due in no small measure to dependence on foreign trade, through territorial expansion. Thrice he dispatched troops to Shantung in total disregard of American interests. Shidehara soon returned to power, however, and the pendulum swung back to an 'export oriented' foreign policy.

But this approach too faced altered, more difficult circumstances. Shidehara naturally hoped to maintain the traditional division of labour between Japan and China, but it was increasingly threatened by the slow but steady industrialisation of China. Though this process suffered some reverses in the late 1920s,[29] the Japanese had seen enough to remember with some trepidation the steep decline in British trade with them as a result of their own industrialisation. The Chinese textile industry was expanding rapidly, and Japanese yarn exports to China had been contracting since 1915. In order to choke off these developments, Japan decided to insist that China grant her most favoured nation status.

Despite protracted negotiations, China remained obdurately opposed to such a request. As a result of this setback in his export-oriented policy, Shidehara was accused of a lack of firmness in dealing with China and was eventually replaced by General Tanaka. Japan then succeeded in concluding a treaty with the 'independent' Manchurian warlord, Chang-tso-lin, allowing the construction of five (!) new railway lines in order to open up Manchuria's mineral wealth. At the same time, armed clashes began to erupt in this area. Although they were most likely

continuing into the present, except that all of south-east Asia has now supplanted China alone.

27. Insufficiently studied. Information in S.N. Ogata, *Defiance in Manchuria* (Berkeley, 1964), pp. 7–13; M. Vié, 'Points de vue sur la politique extérieur du Japon entre les deux guerres mondiales', *Relations internationales* (1980), pp. 141–52, for Shidehara's foreign policy pp. 144–8 in particular. Vié points out the remarkable fact that Shidehara returned to government again in 1945 after the war and played a key role in draughting article IX of the new Japanese constitution forbidding the formation of armed forces.
28. See M. Beckmann, *The Modernization of China and Japan* (NY, 1962), p. 552; R. Storry, *Geschichte des modernen Japan* (Munich, 1962), p. 172.
29. See J.K. Chang, *Industrial Development in Pre-Communist China. A Quantitative Analysis* (Edinburgh, 1969), pp. 60ff.

inspired by the Kwantung army and not by Tokyo, these clashes strained relations with China, the United States and other western powers by undermining the open-door policy and the entire Washington System. Since Japan had first broken ranks to engage in bilateral negotiations with China, she bore much of the blame for the flagging spirit of cooperation among the western powers.

There were other reasons as well why Japan's position in south-east Asia was beginning to weaken. Chiang Kai-shek prevailed in the civil war in 1926–7 and extended his authority over virtually all of China. In spite of the excesses of the Nationalist forces, Britain and the United States decided to treat with the new government in Nanking and broke off relations with the phantom government in Peking in the spring of 1928. When these powers began to compete with one another for the favour of the new government, China's strategic position underwent a sudden improvement.[30] This was one consequence of the pro-Chinese strategy advocated by Kellogg and Johnson, which had been held in abeyance at the height of the civil war in 1925–8 but was now being fully implemented. A new series of negotiations led to the tariff treaty of 25 July 1928, which gave China the right to establish her own tariffs and awarded United States the cherished status of most favoured nation. This spawned a spate of further treaties, and by early 1929 eleven of fifteen foreign powers, including Britain and France, had accorded tariff autonomy to China.

These developments, especially the planned 'modernisation' of China with the help of Anglo-American capital (as compensation for renunciation of the 'unequal treaties'), obviously posed a severe threat to Japan. While actively collaborating with the two mightiest economic powers on earth, the leaders of the Kuomintang felt able to stiffen their opposition to Japanese interests, insisting on Chinese sovereignty in Manchuria and increasing their resistance to Japanese penetration. By 1929, the potential was building for an armed conflict between Japan and China, which would determine the ultimate fate of the new nationalist government. But first Japan took another stab in the summer of 1928 at a conciliatory approach towards China so as not to be outshone by Britain and the United States. Tokyo too sought to conclude a tariff treaty with China and attempted to enhance its influence

---

30. See D. Borg, *American Policy and the Chinese Revolution 1925–1928* (NY, 1947), pp. 392ff., 421ff.; F. Joyeux, '"Question chinoise" ou "Politique chinoise". La Chine sur la scène internationale de 1919 à 1931', *Relations internationales* (1980); J. Chesnaux and F.L. Barbier, *La Chine. La marche de la Révolution* (Paris, 1975). These two authors emphasise on p. 82 the congruity of interests between the imperialist powers and 'the modern, new political class' (Kuomintang) in connection with the granting of tariff autonomy to China.

with the western powers by returning to the former spirit of cooperation. Japan deferred construction of the railways in Manchuria, so as not to aggravate relations with China, and, in a reversal of earlier policy, even agreed to political union between China and Manchuria (December 1928). Finally, a one-year tariff agreement was signed with China in January 1929 according Japan favourable conditions.

In July 1929 Shidehara assumed the post of foreign minister in the new Hamaguchi cabinet. He carried on the export-oriented approach to China and the cooperative posture towards the other powers. By early 1930, he was still cleaving to this course, despite the onset of the Great Depression. On 6 January 1930, Japan and China reached another tariff accord running for three years. It conceded China full tariff autonomy while freeing 40 per cent of Japanese exports from any further increases in Chinese tariffs. Another accord was reached in the matter of debt consolidation. The final flourish in this cooperative approach occurred in January 1930 when Japan returned to the gold standard in order to gain easier access to foreign capital markets. Tokyo demonstrated a similarly conciliatory attitude in regard to armaments when it joined the London naval agreement (April 1930), even though this provoked screams of outrage in Japanese military circles and widened the gulf between export-oriented light industries which supported Shidehara's posture and the military-heavy industrial complex which championed a policy of territorial expansion, primarily in Manchuria.

But the Great Depression undid many of the assumptions on which Shidehara's cooperative policies were based (see Chapter 5, III), and Japan reverted to a more aggressive foreign policy. Conflict with China became inevitable, and with it, the destruction of the foundations of the Washington System. This cleared the way for a more militant Japanese foreign policy of which General Tanaka had already provided a certain foretaste.

5

The Great Depression
and the Collapse of
the Postwar Order 1930–1

I. The Decline of the United States
as the World's Foremost Economic Power

The foregoing analysis has shown that the postwar order established in
Europe and south-east Asia between 1919 and 1922 was predicated on
successful economic reconstruction. It alone – not strategic or military
policies – could have engendered the social stability essential for 'peaceful change' and the creation of a flexible, adaptable international system. We have seen that the United States had clearly taken over as the
leading economic power in the world and as such had a pivotal role to play.
It was the hinge between the Versailles and Washington Systems, an
early version of the superpower role she would later play (though her
position in the 1920s was attained and reinforced almost exclusively
through economic means).

We have also seen that America's new role was entirely consistent
with her own best interests. The Ford model of economic growth
required that the world be opened to American products and capital in
order to keep the domestic economy flourishing (hence the 'open-door'
policy and most favoured nation status). It is therefore not surprising
that the political and economic elite, including a great many Democrats,
was far more convinced than before the war that America's 'economic
borders', in the telling phrase of the times, encompassed the whole
world.[1]

1. W. Link, *Die amerikanische Stabilisierungspolitik*, p. 598f.; H.-J. Schröder, *Deutschland und die Vereinigten Staaten 1933–1939. Wirtschaft und Politik in der Entwicklung des
deutsch-amerikanischen Gegensatzes* [Germany and the United States 1933–1939. Economics and Politics in the Development of German-American Antagonism] (Wiesbaden,
1970), p. 15.

It is also evident, however, that the United States discharged her new role in an inconsistent and at times even counter productive fashion. It thereby helped to aggravate the structural flaws already inherent in the world economy as well as in the Versailles and Washington Systems. Misguided American policies included not only high tariffs but above all her attempt to control the world economy and the restructuring of Europe and the Far East by relying on the privileged partners of Germany and Japan. Washington failed to give adequate consideration to the political implications of this policy, namely, the encouragement of German revisionism and the absence of a clear American posture towards any potential conflicts between Japan and China.

All of this leads to the conclusion that the part played by the Great Depression in dismantling the postwar order can scarcely be exaggerated. It was largely responsible for the destruction of all the underpinnings on which this order rested. But the Depression would never have been so devastating if the gathering economic problems on the domestic and international levels had not been allowed to intensify in the second half of the 1920s beneath surface appearances of 'relative stability'. It is therefore all the more remarkable that a systematic study of all these factors has never been undertaken – nor ever can be undertaken so long as the approaches of political and economic historians continue to drift apart.[2] A study that would meet such high aspirations cannot be attempted, moreover, in what follows. We shall therefore content ourselves with formulating a number of questions stemming from our previous analysis which may open new vistas for research.

The origins and repercussions of the Great Depression[3] illustrate much more clearly than the phase of 'relative stability' the extent to which the world economy 'had become chained for better or worse to

2. Typical of this are J. Becker and K. Hildebrandt (eds), *Internationale Beziehungen*. The classic study by K.-D. Bracher of the 'dissolution of the Weimar Republic' fails to ascribe to the Great Depression the role it actually played in the collapse of the Weimar Republic.

3. From the abundant literature see above all the multi-authored volume: 'The Great Depression', *JCH* (1969), dealing with the economic effects of the crisis in Germany, Britain, France, Italy, eastern Europe and the Soviet Union; for the causes and course of the Great Depression see C.P. Kindleberger, *Die Weltwirtschaftskrise 1929–1939*; H.B. Lary et al., *The United States in the World Economy*; the classic and still worthwhile book of A. Sturmthal, *Die grosse Krise* (Zurich, 1937); J.K. Galbraith, *The Great Crash, 1929*; R.F. Himmelburg (ed.), *The Great Depression and American Capitalism* (Boston, 1968); M. Friedman and A.J. Schwartz, *The Monetary History of the United States 1867–1960* (NY, 1963), Chapt. 7: 'The Great Contraction'; L.V. Chandler, *America's Greatest Depression 1929–1941* (NY, 1970); of fundamental importance for the discussion about the origins of the Great Depression: H. van der Wee (ed.), *The Great Depression Revisited. Essays on the Economics of the Thirties* (The Hague, 1972).

the American economy' after the war.[4] Despite the fashionableness of neo-conservative monetarism, researchers seem generally to agree that monocausal explanations are not sufficient. The Depression had its origins in the totality of structural weaknesses within the American model of economic growth, weaknesses which took on a universal significance because of America's dominance of the world economic system. The United States sought, as we have seen, to reinforce her economic leadership by encouraging the emergence of a monetary system based on the gold(-exchange) standard. But when the American economy collapsed, it was paradoxically this system of fixed exchange rates that contributed enormously to carrying the Depression throughout the world system.

A majority of economic historians believe that structural under-consumption, i.e. weak demand, was the most important of the many causes of the Depression. This leads logically to the conclusion that the Ford model of economic growth, the most advanced form of capitalist production, had reached its outer limits. At least two serious consequences inevitably resulted: first, the United States began to slip as the dominant economic power in the world and as the hinge of the Versailles and Washington Systems; and secondly, the entire world economy, based on the vast economic power of the United States, began to crumble.

The crisis in the United States had immediate negative effects in Europe, Japan and countries which exported raw materials. This rebounded on the United States herself, precipitating the worldwide depression from which no land was spared. The collapse hit its nadir in mid-1932 – apart from France whose economy was not much affected until the summer of 1931 but which then did not begin to recover until 1935, later than most countries. It is not necessary for the purposes of this book to elaborate on the effects of the crisis: simultaneous, mutually reinforcing downturns in the prices of raw materials and of industrial and agricultural products; a decline in industrial production (see Table 3); shrinking world trade;[5] the collapse of the gold standard; a slump in national income; and mass unemployment. Historians agree that attempts to cope with the crisis through deflation (a strategy adopted at

4. D. Junker, *Der unteilbare Weltmarkt. Das ökonomische Interesse in der Aussenpolitik der USA 1933–1941* [The Indivisible World Market. Economic Interest in the Foreign Policy of the United States 1933–41] (Stuttgart, 1975), p. 36.

5. The publications of the League of Nations recording monthly developments in the volume of world trade disclose the rapid and continuous deterioration of world trade. For instance, the total imports of seventy-five countries (monthly value in millions of dollars before devaluation) show a decline from their zenith of 3,039.1 in April 1929 to their nadir of 944.0 in February 1933. See the graph version in the form of the celebrated 'spider's web' in C.P. Kindleberger, *Die Weltwirtschaftskrise 1929–1939*, pp. 179, 180.

first by all governments and which in most cases simply required a tightening of the economic policies already in place during the second half of the 1920s) eventuated in what Petzina has called 'a devaluation competition'[6] which only deepened the crisis.

The intensifying rivalry in international trade induced national governments to install steadily mounting controls, thereby hastening the collapse of the world economy.[7] Foremost among these measures were massive increases in tariff rates, led by the poor example of the United States. The Smoot–Hawley tariff of June 1930 touched off a chain reaction of tariff hikes around the world, aggravating the protectionism that already existed, especially in the realm of agricultural products.[8] As a result, domestic prices rose relative to world prices, further isolating national markets from one another.

World trade was hampered by a host of further measures. Import quotas became widespread, especially in Europe. After the international credit and financial crisis of 1931, ever more countries resorted to foreign exchange controls. Experts at the League of Nations pointed out the particularly harmful effects of such controls,[9] which not only restricted credit and reduced world trade but also caused prices to rise in the country applying them and thereby diminished its own ability to export. Foreign exchange controls therefore contributed more than any other instrument of economic policy to the 'nationalisation' or, more appropriately, the 'politicisation' of the world economy through the destruction of what remained of the market system (supply and demand). By managing and allocating foreign currencies in short supply, states gained control over foreign trade to varying extents and harnessed it to serve their own economic and political purposes.

Governments then inevitably came under pressure to replace traditional commercial treaties with so-called clearing agreements designed to promote a trade balance between two countries, thereby circumventing the currency problem. This led to further erosion of the

---

6. In H. Mommsen et al. (eds), *Industrielles System*, p. 937.

7. What follows is based on a paper by R. Mayer delivered on 28 August 1974; see as well W. Greiff and A. Bergsträsser, *Der Methodenwandel der europäischen Handelspolitik während des Krisenjahres 1931* [The Change in European Trade Policy in the Year of Crisis 1931] (Berlin, 1932).

8. See in detail J.M. Jones, *Tariff Retaliation. Repercussions of the Hawley–Smoot Bill* (Philadelphia, 1934); H. Liepmann, *Tariff Levels and Economic Unity of Europe* (NY, 1938), pp. 413–15.

9. League of Nations, *Report on Exchange Control* (Geneva, 1938), p. 37; J.B. Condliffe, *Reconstruction of World Trade* (NY, 1940), p. 242.; for what follows see the further publications of the League: *Enquiry into Clearing Agreements* (Geneva, 1935), *Commercial Policy in the Interwar Period* (Geneva, 1942), *Network of World Trade* (Geneva, 1942).

multilateral trade system in favour of bilateral agreements which increasingly fragmented the world market. Although by 1937 only 12 per cent of world trade had been affected by such agreements (which were especially prevalent in central, eastern and south-eastern Europe), their effect was far more chilling than would otherwise have been the case because it was reinforced by numerous other restrictive measures.

Under these conditions, international treaties began to move in the direction of de-liberalised trade. A study of 510 commercial agreements signed betweeen 1931 and 1939 shows that most favoured nation status, the centrepiece of the liberal, multilateral world trading system, was accorded in only 42 per cent of all agreements and even then usually in limited form.[10] The sharp reduction in the lifespan of these agreements speaks volumes about the atmosphere of scepticism and uncertainty surrounding the future of world trade.

Almost every national government, save that of the United States, had recourse to various combinations of these measures for controlling foreign trade in order to protect its deflationary attempts to cope with the crisis. When a general economic upswing commenced in 1932–3, the expansion of world trade was accordingly much more sluggish than that of world industrial production. Although this trend had already been apparent during the 1920s, it was now far more pronounced. The contrast between the quickening pace of domestic economic production and stagnating imports bore eloquent witness to the decline of the world economy.

There were other signs as well that the world market was being fractured into national sub-markets. A rising share of production was absorbed by domestic markets,[11] a situation which many peripheral countries turned to advantage by pursuing a policy of import substitution. The trend to bilateral trade made it more difficult to pay foreign debts and choked off the supply of foreign exchange. This in turn aggravated the plight of countries lacking in raw materials and fuelled the trend toward expansionism and economic autarky. The decay of the world economy not only hobbled international trade but also damaged creditor nations as well as those countries desperate for capital imports.

The United States was not only the fountainhead of these changes in the world economy but also their main victim. Washington's reaction now directly contradicted everything which Republican administrations had done throughout the 1920s in order to open up the world economy

10. R.C. Snyder, 'Commercial Policy as Reflected in Treaties from 1931 to 1939', *AER* 30 (1940).
11. For the evolution of world export quotas for manufactured goods see S. Helander, *Das Autarkieproblem in der Weltwirtschaft* (Berlin, 1955), p. 23f.; League of Nations, *World Economic Survey 1937–8* (Geneva, 1938).

and expand markets for American products. Everything that the United States had gained in the international arena during the 1920s was lost between 1930 and 1932.[12] A few statistics will suffice to indicate the extent to which the economic crisis shook the foundations of America's export economy.[13] According to M. Dobb, the production of finished goods fell by 1932 to the level of 1913 and even after four years of recovery in 1937 only reached levels previously attained in 1929. Foreign trade fell through the floor. Imports, primarily of raw materials, sank from 4,400 million dollars in 1929 to 3,100 million dollars in 1930, 2,100 million dollars in 1931 and finally 1,300 million dollars in 1932. America's status as the leading market in the world was thereby curtailed even more sharply than it already had been by its high tariff policies. The United States to be sure remained the second largest importing nation in the world after Great Britain, but its position in trade negotiations was much weaker because, unlike Britain, it lacked the leverage of a negative trade balance.

Even more significant, for the purposes of this book, was the plight of American exports. They reached a crest of 5,240 million dollars in 1929 before plummeting to 1,610 million dollars in 1932, a level far below the previous trough of 1922. American exports looked even worse in comparison with the general evolution of world trade which declined by 30 per cent between 1929 and 1939 while American exports tumbled a full 48 per cent. America's share of world exports dipped from 15.6 per cent in 1929 to 12.4 per cent in 1932. The United States also lost ground to other countries in regard to volume, and numerous markets had to be forsaken. When the global economy began to improve after 1932, the United States succeeded only in recovering its previous share of the Asian market. Its market share failed to reach previous levels in all other regions, including the leading industrialised countries with the notable exception of Japan, where American imports increased from 29.5 per cent of the total in 1929 to 35.6 per cent in 1932.

Exports of American products to the most industrialised countries declined considerably therefore in the 1930s, more steeply on average than the exports of other countries (with the exception of Japan). The fundamental contradiction in American policy, which had begun to emerge during the 1920s, wreaked its vengeance in the Great Depression. Though the United States dominated the world economy, it had adopted a high tariff policy which inhibited full participation in the international division of labour and now resulted in a severe drag on

12. See in detail H.-J. Schröder, *Deutschland und die Vereinigten Staaten 1933–1939*; H.B. Lary et al., *The United States in the World Economy*; J.K. Galbraith, *The Great Crash, 1929*; and in addition a paper by R. Mayer delivered on 24 September 1974.

13. M. Dobb, *Studies in the Development of Capitalism*, p. 329.

American exports. When capital exports dried up under Depression conditions and dollars fell into short supply on international markets, American exports became directly dependent on the volume of American imports. These, however, had suffered greatly from the reduction in national income. America's ability to export no longer hinged on the superior productivity of her industry but rather on her capacity to import, which was relatively weak.

Interestingly, it was her old rival, Great Britain, which derived the greatest advantage from America's faltering position on world markets.[14] Britain succeeded in largely regaining the ground she had lost to the United States during the 1920s (Table 17, p. 128). Britain benefited greatly from the fact that it had participated more fully in the international division of labour and provided a huge market for imported goods. Demand for its exports remained relatively firm and its import markets suffered less than those in the United States. The depression of the early thirties seemed relatively mild in Britain because of the structural crisis it had endured ever since the end of the war, and it soon yielded to an economic upturn. F. Luther has pointed out that Britain's share of world exports therefore remained relatively constant. The losses she suffered to Germany and Japan were offset by gains at the expense of the United States, especially in the Dominions. The economic power of the United States was further diminished by the system of preferential agreements within the British Empire which served to reduce price competition. This held true as well for the other economic blocks that began to emerge. Neither the devaluation of the dollar in 1933 nor Secretary of State Cordell Hull's strategy for reintegrating the United States into world markets proved very effective. In consequence, competition between Britain and the United States heated up. All this does not mean that Britain experienced any more success in the 1930s in solving her structural problems. Quite to the contrary: unemployment, which had lain slightly below 10 per cent in the 1920s, rose to 22.9 per cent in 1932 before receding to 12.6 per cent in 1936 and then holding firm at 9.1 per cent even in 1937 at the height of the economic recovery. It was not mounting exports that fuelled the upswing but rather the unleashing of deferred investment.

The sharp reduction in American capital exports after mid-1930 was another important reason for the decline in America's economic and hence political position in the world. No new foreign loans were extended during the 1930s because of the insolvency of the recipients, political uncertainties and foreign exchange controls. Direct investment

14. See H.W. Richardson, *Economic Recovery in Britain, 1932–1939* (London, 1967); D.H. Aldcroft, *The Interwar Economy*; A.E. Kahn, *Great Britain in the World Economy* (NY, 1946).

overseas also fell to very low levels. In consequence, investment income was sharply curtailed. As dollar exports dried up, the United States began to lose not only her position as a great creditor nation but also her financial clout, which had been a mainstay of her ability to dominate the world economy.

The United States seemed confronted once again with the same old conundrum in regard to international economic relations and hence foreign policy.[15] One response to the collapsing world economy would have been to withdraw inward, accept the new international conditions and attempt to adapt the American economy to them. This would have entailed of course a policy of political and economic isolation and the sacrifice of all the progress that had been achieved in the direction of international economic integration. It was clear that attempts to overcome the Depression through this kind of restructuring would have exacted a high social and economic cost and would have damaged the standard of living. It also would have struck a stunning blow at the Ford model of economic expansion. This response to the Depression would necessarily have entailed de-industrialisation, especially among America's export industries, and a radical reduction of agricultural production. Not surprisingly, this strategy was only given brief consideration immediately after the onset of the crisis.

The other possible response, which gained impetus from the economic upswing, was to carry on the previous policy of economic internationalism and worldwide expansion. As in the early 1920s, this only afforded a viable alternative if the United States again did everything in its power to prevent further erosion of the world economy. However, even the most modest liberalisation of the world economy was only possible if the post-1932 upswing led to an abiding period of general prosperity. This in turn required that the huge 'dollar gap' be closed, which is to say that American tariffs had to be reduced in order to enable foreign countries to earn sufficient dollars on American markets to pay for imports from the United States.[16]

This was the strategy which Washington finally adopted in the guise of the New Deal. The first step was the passing of the Trade Agreements Act of June 1934 which enabled the president to accord tariff reductions of up to 50 per cent when concluding trade agreements. Another important measure was the return to most favoured nation trading status, which the United States demanded and in return was willing to concede.

The record of the debates on the neutrality laws shows that some Democrats even argued that an updated open-door policy would help

15. For what follows see R. Mayer, paper of 24 September 1974, pp. 12ff.
16. H.W. Arndt, *The Economic Lessons*, pp. 87ff.

to check Japan and the fascist countries of Europe which were increasingly turning to aggression in order to gain enough territory to essay a policy of economic autarky. The American strategy did succeed in expanding export markets, but it failed in its political ends. For this, a confrontation with the Axis powers would have been necessary, which was out of the question so long as the United States was fully absorbed with her own economic difficulties.

In the meantime, the Great Depression was sweeping away the remaining pillars of the Versailles and Washington Systems which had served to restrain the revisionist powers. The Hoover administration contributed decisively to the collapse of both systems when it resorted to increased protectionism and deflation in order to cope with the crisis. Great Britain, the classic home of free trade, found herself compelled in the autumn of 1931 to introduce tariffs and to devalue sterling. When she also set about devising a system of preferential tariffs within the Empire (Ottawa Conference of 1932) and distancing herself from the problems of continental Europe and Asia,[17] the stage was set for other powers such as Germany, France, Italy and Japan to follow her example and attempt to create their own zones of economic influence (Table 18, p. 130).

Contemporaries were already aware of the causal connection between the disintegration of the world economy and mounting international tensions on both the political and economic levels.[18] By a tragic stroke of fate, the collapse of American hegemony and hence of the core of the international economy had the effect of magnifying the economic and political latitude of other nations. With the help of high tariffs, devaluation and exchange controls, some succeeded before the United States in freeing themselves from the deflationary spiral and reverting to expansionist policies. The 'race to devalue' was therefore rather paradoxical in its impact: on the one hand it aggravated the global depression, but on the other it afforded national economies greater freedom of action, including even the possibility of modernisation. However, this expanded leeway was exploited with mounting chauvinism, and national strategies for overcoming the crisis were accorded absolute priority over international cooperation. This occurred at a time when the Great Depression had severely attenuated the ability of the

17. J.-B. Duroselle, *Histoire diplomatique de 1919 à nos jours* (Paris, 1978[7]), p. 139.
18. See for instance O. Leibrock, *Weltwirtschaft oder Grossraumwirtschaft? Eine kritische Studie* [A World Economy or an Expanded National Economy? A Critical Study] (Leipzig, 1933); F. Fried, *Autarkie* (Jena, 1932); K.A. Herrmann, *Autarkie und Kapitalgüterexport* [Autarky and Exports of Capital Goods] (Berlin, 1933); K.C. Thalheim, *Autarkie – weder Ziel noch Schicksal* [Autarky – Neither our Goal nor our Destiny] (Leipzig, 1933); H. von Beckerath and F. Kern, *Autarkie oder internationale Zusammenarbeit?* [Autarky or International Cooperation?] (Berlin, 1932).

Hoover administration to bring even political pressure to bear on the Europeans and the Japanese. The totality of these circumstances greatly assisted those who were keen to burst the bonds of the Versailles and Washington Systems.

The collapse of traditional patterns of trade had the effect of drawing the great arch-enemy, the Soviet Union, into the international division of labour dominated by the capitalist countries. For instance, German exports to the Soviet Union rose from 2.6 to 7.9 per cent of the total between 1929 and 1931. In 1931, 55 per cent of American exports of machine tools went to the Soviet Union. In 1932 Great Britain shipped 81 per cent of its machine tool exports to the Soviet Union, and Germany shipped 74 per cent of its.[19] Hence the theory that Stalin's ambitious industrialisation programme was only possible thanks to the Great Depression.

II. The Collapse of the Versailles System

1. The Dissolution of the Special Relationship between Germany and the United States

The Versailles System rested, as we have seen, on rather shaky foundations, even during the era of relative stability. But it may well have endured considerably longer, despite mounting difficulties, if not for the Great Depression. As late as 1929, the system had demonstrated its ability to assuage at least temporarily the tense political situation occasioned by German reparations. The United States, Germany, France and Great Britain were again able to achieve a minimal consensus with the help of the Young Plan. However, a crucial effect of the Great Depression, with all its national and international ramifications, was that it eradicated this minimal consensus and thereby destroyed the Versailles System. There was an inseparable connection between the collapse of the world economy and monetary system and mounting hostility in international relations, both between Germany and the United States and between the former Allied powers.

The slide of the United States into the grip of the Depression led inevitably to a loss of economic and, most important, financial clout in Europe. This weakened those forces that had played an essential role in ensuring the survival of the Versailles System after 1924. Henceforth,

19. Figures from: *Statistisches Handbuch der Weltwirtschaft*, prepared by the Statistisches Reichsamt (Berlin, 1936); A. Gerschenkron, *Economic Relations with the USSR* (NY, 1945); see in this regard as well P.G. Fileue, *Americans and the Soviet Experiment, 1917–1933* (Cambridge, Mass., 1967); especially J.H. Wilson, *Ideology and Economics. U.S. Relations with the Soviet Union, 1918–1933* (Columbia, 1974).

the United States left Europeans to their destiny, not least of all because of disgust with their attitude towards war debt. Germany of course was most severely affected by the decline in American influence for, according to one of Link's major conclusions, it had served as a kind of 'beachhead' for American economic penetration of the old continent.[20] We further deduced from this that the German–American relationship played a crucial role in reconstruction and therefore in the stabilisation of the Versailles System.

Of at least equal significance was Germany's own fervent desire to bring about a sharp reduction in American influence in Europe, as a result of the shift to the right on the domestic political scene. This sea change in German politics could also be traced to the Great Depression, which was most severe in Germany in addition to Japan and the United States. The Grand Coalition had collapsed when internal strife tore apart its mainstay, the Social Democratic Party. The infighting within the SPD was indicative of the party's inability to elaborate an effective strategy for overcoming the crisis, let alone to command a majority in Parliament. The Social Democrats had always championed the new German republic, and when the party was torn asunder in the spring of 1930, the political pendulum swung far to the right. Henceforth, it was the 'conservative offensive' that was gaining momentum, especially in as much as many elements of society including business, the army, the middle classes and to some extent the working class had lost confidence in the republic.

After 30 March 1930, the new German government under the Centrist politician Heinrich Brüning executed sharp policy reversals in three interrelated areas. Since the government was unable to muster a reliable parliamentary majority, it depended on the power of the *Reichspräsident* to issue emergency decrees under article 48 of the Weimar constitution. In this way, a fateful first step was taken down the road to authoritarian rule. Secondly, Brüning attempted to cope with the economic crisis by further accentuating the austerity policies of the previous government. This impoverished broad masses of the population and redistributed wealth in favour of the rich. Finally, Brüning established as a major goal of his deflationary policy a 'final solution to the reparations question' (i.e. cancellation of the Young Plan) as part of a grand revisionist programme supported by mounting segments of public opinion. The high social and economic costs of such a step, including the loss of foreign and especially American credits, was disregarded.

20. W. Link, *Die amerikanische Stabilisierungspolitik*, pp. 351ff., 517ff., 553; idem, 'Der amerikanische Einfluss auf die Weimarer Republik', pp. 497ff.

The shift in German government policy had a devastating impact in both the domestic and international realms. Besides advancing a battery of legal and economic arguments aimed at avoiding reparations, the government decided not to devalue the mark out of fear that an economic upswing would only encourage the Allies to renew their demands. The president of the *Reichsbank*, Hans Luther, supported Brüning's view that the 'final solution of the reparations question' took precedence over all other considerations,[21] even though he was fully cognisant of the pernicious effects which the failure to devalue the mark would have on the German economy and balance of payments, especially if sterling was devalued. In consequence, Germany suffered worse deflationary woes[22] than were perhaps necessary. The German economic policy also necessitated foreign exchange controls, hastened the decline of the international monetary system, and thereby 'led directly to the economic autarky of the Nazi era'.[23]

In pursuing these policies Germany was cutting off its nose to spite its face. There was an intimate connection between its financial position and a conciliatory foreign policy, as practised by Stresemann, though with mounting ambivalence. The comments of G. Hardach in this regard are very well taken:

21. See the statements of those involved: H. Brüning, *Memoiren 1918–1934* (Stuttgart, 1970), esp. p. 193f.; H. Luther, *Vor dem Abgrund. Reichsbankpräsident in Krisenzeiten* [Before the Abyss. President of the Reichsbank in Times of Crisis] (Berlin, 1964); W.J. Helbich, *Die Reparationen in der Ära Brüning* (Berlin, 1962).

22. H. Irmler, 'Bankenkrise und Vollbeschäftigung, 1931–1936' [Bank Crisis and Full Employment] in Deutsche Bundesbank (ed.), *Währung und Wirtschaft in Deutschland 1876–1975*, p. 308.

23. G. Hardach, 'Währungskrise 1931' [The Currency Crisis of 1931] in H. Winkel (ed.), *Finanz- und wirtschaftspolitische Fragen*, p. 128. J. Schiemann in *Die deutsche Währung* has convincingly demonstrated that a devaluation of the German mark was rejected primarily for reasons of foreign policy. It was feared that an economic upswing prompted by devaluation would diminish the willingness of Germany's creditors to revise the Young Plan. 'The logic of the Brüning government in employing an economic crisis as a tactical weapon and exploiting mass deprivation, gold parity and economic depression in order to achieve a revision of the reparations agreement seems incomprehensible from the point of view of today' (p. 285). There were additional legal and economic arguments, especially the not unjustified assumption that a devaluation of 20 per cent would not produce a stable situation. It is noteworthy that in this realm as well there was strong continuity between Brüning's policies and those of Hitler. The Nazi regime continued the policy of foreign exchange controls introduced in 1931 and finally perfected it to such an extent that it became not only a method of managing foreign economic relations but also 'an instrument for more efficient political control and internal disciplining and coordination' (p. 292). See in this regard D. Doering, 'Deutsche Aussenwirtschaftspolitik 1933–1935. Die Gleichschaltung der Aussenwirtschaft in der Frühphase des national sozialistischen Regimes' [German Foreign Economic Relations 1933–5. The Coordination of Foreign Economic Relations in the Early Phase of National Socialism], PhD thesis, FU Berlin, 1969.

From the point of view of Germany's monetary position, it is hard to imagine a worse course than Brüning's attempt to shore up his domestic political support by means of an assertive foreign policy. The adoption of a more nationalistic policy beginning with demands for a revision of reparations in October 1930 and with the proposal for an Austro-German tariff union early in that year caused foreign creditors to lose confidence and reduced Germany's ability to appeal, if necessary, to the international solidarity of central banks. The blame for this attaches first and foremost to the federal government, but also to the *Reichsbank* which failed to deliver the appropriate warnings.[24]

The German government was caught, none the less, on the horns of a frightful dilemma. Acceptance of the Versailles System and therefore of continuing reparations would have curtailed the government's ability to deal with the Depression; but attempts to remedy this situation through revisionism undermined the government's ability to deal with the financial crisis of the summer of 1931 when strong international support alone could have saved the situation. By introducing foreign exchange controls, the German government aggravated the international monetary crisis and helped to deepen the Depression, thereby paving the way for the even more radical revisionists waiting in the wings.[25]

The United States was no longer anticipating or leading events, only reacting to them, by the time of the Hoover Moratorium, the final cancellation of reparation payments and the formal concession of military 'equality' to Germany in fulfilment of Berlin's most immediate foreign policy objectives. America's most effective weapon, namely her financial and commercial clout, no longer carried the same weight. It was not used, for instance, when attention focused on the *political* aspect of the reparations question as one aspect of Germany's comprehensive plan for revisions. In this way, another key element of the Versailles System crumbled away.

24. G. Hardach, 'Währungskrise 1931,' p. 133f.; see also the pioneering work of E.W. Bennett, *Germany and the Diplomacy of the Financial Crisis 1931* (Cambridge, Mass., 1962).
25. In 1931 an anonymous but highly competent author published a book entitled *Der Kampf um die deutsche Aussenpolitik* [The Struggle Surrounding German Foreign Policy] (Paul List Verlag, Leipzig). The future goals of German foreign policy are elucidated very plainly here, and with great clarity and determination (p. 410f.): abandonment of Locarno; rapprochement with Italy; a reactivated policy in eastern Europe in order to increase pressure on Poland with the help of the Soviet Union and surrounding states; renewed activity in 'Central Europe', but rejection of the 'pan-European policies' advanced by France in order to consolidate the status quo; attempts to maintain good relations with the United States; changes in the Young Plan and, combined with that, insistence on Germany's claims to her lost territories in the east.

After the reparation issue was settled, it grew increasingly apparent that the congruence in German and American policies had been but 'a temporary stage on the path to more sweeping revisionism' (Link). This was particularly true in regard to armaments. When speaking out in favour of disarmament, Berlin wished merely to give the appearance of aligning its policies with those of the United States. In reality, German rearmament had already been decided upon as a long-term goal, and the way was 'even being prepared, in a grotesque twist, with the assistance of the United States Department of War' (Link). The gulf between German and American policy became fully apparent only a little later when the Papen and Schleicher governments began to rearm in total disregard of existing treaties. But by now, the decay in the Versailles System had created such scope for the mounting tide of German revisionism that it could not be stemmed by either France, the supposed nucleus of the system, or even the United States.[26]

2. Heightened Tensions among the Allies

The Great Depression was also responsible for greatly magnifying the already considerable discord between the former Allied powers. In this regard as well, the rot in the Versailles System and the downward trend in the economy seemed mutually reinforcing. The economic, financial and political motives of nations became inextricably intertwined. The two leading economic powers, Britain and the United States, disagreed fundamentally on the best way of coping with the crisis.[27] Britain hoped that liberal policies would stimulate global economic activity sufficiently to arouse her own economy, though she had no clear concept of how this would happen. The United States, on the other hand, withdrew behind even higher tariffs. In 1931 London encouraged the United States to waive war debts, reduce tariffs and attempt to stabilise currencies again by means of an international agreement. But Hoover rejected these proposals, one after the other, with the argument that Congress would never agree. This greatly impeded the ability of the two powers to cooperate, even after Roosevelt became president.

Under these conditions, another crucial element in the Versailles System, namely Britain's attempt to mediate between France and

---

26. See the contributions of G. Ziebura and R. Höhne in K. Rohe (ed.), *Die Westmächte und das Dritte Reich 1933–1939. Klassische Grossmachtrivalität oder Kampf zwischen Demokratie und Diktatur?* [The Western Powers and the Third Reich 1933–9. Classic Great Power Rivalry or Struggle between Democracy and Dictatorship?] (Paderborn, 1982).

27. Parker, 'Probleme der britischen Aussenpolitik' in J. Becker and K. Hildebrandt (eds), *Internationale Beziehungen*, p. 8f.

Germany, began to fade.[28] When London discovered that it could not count on the support of American banks in order to maintain the international liquidity of sterling, it was deprived of an essential weapon in the struggle to withstand the mounting pressure of the French franc, which had become the strongest European currency in 1930–1. This posed a major problem for Britain. The deterioration in Anglo-American relations and the unwillingness of their central banks to join forces in order to deal with the monetary crisis greatly undermined not only Britain's financial strength but also its political position *vis-à-vis* France, whose long-term ambitions it feared. All major international occurrences in 1930 and especially in the fateful year of 1931 manifest the sharp deterioration in the ability of the international community to cope with any crisis. Much of the responsibility for this can be ascribed to the discord between Britain and France.

This worsening of relations commenced in September 1929 when Briand launched his idea of a European Union, with the backing of an already failing Stresemann. The plan was fleshed out in a memorandum of 1 May 1930 which was forwarded to all European governments.[29] Briand wished at bottom to extend the security network adopted at Locarno to all of Europe. European-wide institutions would be created, within the framework of the League of Nations, though they would not infringe on national sovereignty. This project was clearly aimed at reinforcing the shaky Versailles System and satisfying French security needs. However, most European governments were unwilling to accept another dose of French hegemony, even in the guise of a pan-European project, apart from the fact that it did nothing to solve the pressing economic and monetary problems which they were confronting.

The rejectionist front was led by Germany and Britain. The former feared for its revisionist ambitions, especially in regard to its eastern frontiers; the latter was more concerned with protecting its Commonwealth interests and in any case was deeply suspicious of pan-European institutions. The meetings at the League of Nations in the autumn of 1930 made it obvious that the Briand plan had failed, and with it the final attempt to develop and extend the Versailles System. The negative response of other governments to Briand's memorandum as well as rising domestic opposition to the 'weakness' of his response to mounting nationalism in Germany indicate the degree to which the Versailles System had already deteriorated.

But there was much more to come. German revisionism took its first

28. G. Schmidt, *England in der Krise*, pp. 55ff.
29. W. Lipgens, 'Briands Europaplan im Urteil der deutschen Akten' [Briand's Plan for Europe as Seen in the German Documents], *HZ* 203 (1966); P. Renouvin, *Les crises du XXe siècle*, Part I, p. 343f.

concrete steps when Foreign Minister Curtius and Chancellor Schober agreed in early March 1930 on an Austro-German tariff union. To the Germans, this was the beginning of an intensified 'Central European' policy which, if successful, would have spelled the definitive end of the Versailles System. Not surprisingly, the Austro-German plan met with fierce resistance from France and her allies. Britain's reaction, on the other hand, was much more cautious, and there was even obvious sympathy for the project within the governing Labour Party and public opinion.[30] The French were still virulently opposed to the project in May 1931 when a sudden turn of events enabled them to dictate their point of view: the bankruptcy of an Austrian bank, the *Credit-Anstalt für Handel und Gewerbe*, on 12 May. This was another sign that the world economy was continuing to spiral downward and had reached new depths in the guise of an international banking and financial crisis which would eventually cause the gold standard to collapse. Henceforth, monetary policy was strongly affected by political ambitions on the international stage, throwing the Versailles System into total chaos.

By the early summer of 1931, the Bank of France had accumulated vast reserves of gold. Only the French therefore were in a position to save the staggering *Credit-Anstalt* and prevent the financial crisis from spreading. But the Bank of France sat on its hands, even when German and British banks were drawn into the financial vortex.[31] Indeed, the Bank of France took this occasion to demand repayment of its loans, thereby compounding the crisis and infuriating the Bank of England.[32] When the *Credit-Anstalt* tumbled into bankruptcy, German securities on Wall Street crashed, prompting withdrawals of foreign capital from Germany and a rash of insolvencies among German banks.

The law of the jungle prevailed in the hectic days that followed. At the end of June, *Reichsbank* president Hans Luther travelled to London and Paris in search of financial support, but without success. In a response that exemplified the temper of the times, Norman felt forced to refuse out of fear that the Bank of France would launch an assault on the pound. At the same time, President Hoover announced a moratorium on intergovernmental debt running from 1 July 1931 to 20 June 1932; but he failed to consult France which stood to loose 2,000 million

30. For a detailed analysis of Britain's attitude towards Briand's plan for Europe and the projected German–Austrian tariff union, see H.H. Rass, *Britische Aussenpolitik 1929–1931: Ebenen und Faktoren der Entscheidung* (Bern, 1975), pp. 33–55.
31. For an extensive analysis of this see K.E. Born, *Die deutsche Bankenkrise 1931. Finanzen und Politik* (Munich, 1967).
32. See in detail V.O. Clarke, *Central Bank Co-operation 1924–1931*, p. 220; U. Andersen, *Das internationale Währungssystem zwischen nationaler Souveränität und supranationaler Integration* (Berlin, 1977), p. 25; see also A. Dauphin-Neunier, *La Banque 1919–1935: Allemagne–Angleterre–France* (Paris, 1936).

francs. It goes without saying that relations between the two powers cooled considerably. On 7 July France agreed to accept the moratorium under certain conditions. The Bank of England then undertook to refloat the *Credit-Anstalt*, but the French refused to help unless the plan for an Austro-German customs union was dropped.

Brüning in the meantime introduced stiff foreign exchange controls in Germany in order to offset the impact of the banking crisis. A conference was held on Germany's foreign liabilities, and it brought temporary relief by arranging to convert short-term into long-term debt. But the pound sterling was coming under heavy pressure from the Bank of France. It is generally assumed that the French were seeking revenge for the fact that Britain had opposed them in every international confrontation since 1929–30.[33] Many British banks had in fact run up debts in France, not least of all in order to extend credit to Germany, and were now vulnerable to attack. All in all, it seemed as if the central banks of the United States, France, Britain and Germany were fairly flaunting their inability to join forces in order to cope with a serious international crisis and their determination to fight one another even more bitterly than they already had since 1925–6.[34] They thereby hastened the collapse of the gold standard, which required a minimal amount of international cooperation in order to function. This too dealt a heavy blow to the Versailles System.

The staggering British pound suffered the *coup de grâce* on 31 July with the publication of the May Commission report commissioned by the Labour government. This report established the budgetary deficit at 120 million pounds and suggested that it be reduced by cutting back state expenditures (especially social benefits) and hiking taxes, i.e. more austerity. In a celebrated remark, Keynes denounced the report as 'the stupidest document that I have ever had the misfortune to read'.[35] It destroyed the last shreds of confidence in the British currency, which was already hard hit by the diminished competitiveness of British industry. Day after day, gold valuing 2 million pounds fled the country. The monetary crisis reached its climax in mid-August. Both the Bank of

33. The thesis that the Bank of France exercised decisive influence is disputed in the literature. In favour: K.E. Born, *Die deutsche Bankenkrise 1931*, p. 66 and E.W. Bennett, *Germany and the Diplomacy of the Financial Crisis 1931*, p. 152; rather sceptical: C.P. Kindleberger, *Die Weltwirtschaftskrise 1929–1939*, p. 166 and D. Landes, *The Unbound Prometheus*, p. 346f. and note 19, p. 563f. Abundant material in: *Akten zur deutschen Auswärtigen Politik 1918–1945* [Documents on German Foreign Policy], Series B: 1925–1933, vol. XVII: 1 March–30 June 1931 (Göttingen, 1982).

34. See in this regard K. Gossweiler, *Grossbanken, Industriemonopole, Staat*; F. Seidenzahl, *Hundert Jahre Deutsche Bank 1870–1970* (Frankfurt, 1970).

35. See the informative (and anonymous) article: 'The Last Great Depression and the Next', *International Currency Review* 4 (1979).

England and the American banks of J.P. Morgan refused to accord the government any further credits unless it sharply reduced its expenditures. In order to enforce this policy over mounting opposition from the trade unions, three parties in parliament joined forces to form a 'National Union' government which replaced Labour in September. The new government promptly announced the devaluation of the pound as its first major measure. Henceforward, the economic foreign policy of all countries was taken over by nationalism.

The Bank of France certainly played a major role in all these developments. The Austro-German customs union collapsed when France brought her full financial power to bear. Fully occupied with her own crisis, Britain was unable to stop the French financial offensive. Paris took quick advantage of the banking crisis to attempt to pressure Germany into political concessions, including reparations. But Brüning, given the whole logic of his foreign and domestic policy, was more determined than ever to resist[36] (though all the experts agreed in any case that Germany was incapable of resuming reparations payments even after expiration of the moratorium). Britain therefore proposed that all reparations be cancelled – in a step that was opposed by France but supported by Italy. Such a cancellation was then formally approved at a conference in Lausanne in June and July of 1932. At the same time, the conference decided to cancel the inter-Allied debt, further aggravating the rift between Europe and the United States.

There were more deep-rooted reasons as well for the discord between France and Britain. Britain believed it could only achieve its major aims – preservation of the peace and an end to the Depression – by allowing German revisionism a certain rein while simultaneously satisfying France's increased security needs. The old dilemma of British policy towards the continent now became particularly acute. In order to satisfy France, the Labour government made some proposals, often halfhearted, about strengthening collective security within the framework of the League of Nations, and it tried to play the role of mediator in disarmament negotiations. In this, Britain seemed to be continuing the impulses given by the lapsed Geneva Protocol of 1924, though it still refused to assume any clear obligations in case of conflict along the German-Polish border. However, France did not feel reassured, especially after 1930 when international tensions heightened considerably. All the major countries, with the exception of Britain and Japan, were drastically increasing armaments expenditures, and the hostility between the revisionist countries and those that championed the status quo were mounting. The extent of the discord was accentuated by the

36. K.E. Born, *Die deutsche Bankenkrise 1931*, pp. 92ff.; 135ff.

final session of the preparatory disarmament commission in November and December 1930, when the parties failed to achieve a compromise on the limitation of land-based forces.

They also failed to reach additional agreements on naval disarmament after the Washington Conference. At the Geneva naval conference of 1927 the parties sought to establish limits on cruisers but failed to achieve a consensus on parity levels for cruisers of contrasting tonnages and armament (a problem which still seems to present insoluble difficulties in disarmament and arms control negotiations). Another attempt at arms control was undertaken after Hoover was elected president and the Labour Party took power in Britain.[37] Negotiations between the United States, Great Britain, France, Japan and Italy commenced in London in January 1930, but in the end only the United States, Britain and Japan agreed to set naval limits. An overall agreement was blocked when France refused to accord Italy parity with her. After successfully scotching the plans for an Austro-German customs union, Paris continued its drive for additional security. Germany in turn felt justified in demanding abolition of the discriminatory restrictions on her armaments. The last vestiges of collective security, predicated on arms control, disappeared in this sort of atmosphere, carrying with them another pillar of the Versailles System.

A memorandum prepared by the Foreign Office in connection with the disarmament negotiations and dated 25 June 1931 provides one of many indications that contemporaries were fully cognisant of the gravity of the situation.[38] The memorandum states that the possibility of large-scale military conflict could no longer be excluded, unlike the situation just one year before. The French, according to the memorandum, could no longer maintain hegemony on the continent, which in any case was incompatible with British interests. Germany could no longer be left in a subordinate position because the economic crisis was raising emotions and radicalising political opinion. For these reasons, Germany should gradually be accorded equality with France in the framework of the disarmament conference negotiations and discussions about the further development of the peaceful dispute settlement mechanism. In addition, reparation payments should be reformed and Germany's eastern borders adjusted. If this were not done, according to the memorandum, Europe would once again become a powder keg.

This document reveals the full extent of the discord between Britain and France in regard to fundamental policy – and at a time when a

37. See H.H. Rass, *Britische Aussenpolitik 1929–1931: Ebenen und Faktoren der Entscheidung* [British Foreign Policy 1929–1931: Levels and Factors in Decision-Making] (Frankfurt, 1975), pp. 129–61.
38. In detail, ibid, p. 126f.

cooperative effort to establish new forms of European stability was more essential than ever in view of the collapsing Versailles System. But the British government discounted even the possibility of systematic cooperation with the French. Each country went its own way, in regard to both national security and the economic crisis. This sealed the fate of the Versailles System and throttled the emergence of another order in its place. This crucial political error was not realised until long afterwards, in late 1936. Even then, when it was already too late, only half-hearted efforts were made to correct the mistake.

III. The Collapse of the Washington System

1. Japan's Shift to Militarism and Territorial Expansion

The key to the Washington System, as we have seen, was Japan's willingness to pursue a peaceful foreign policy (especially towards China and the United States) in return for access to the foreign markets and sources of raw materials that were essential to her economic growth. With a practised eye for its own best interests, the 'liberal' majority in parliament, representing the industrial and commercial middle classes, was prepared to cooperate in such other areas as arms control and monetary policy, so long as the other signatories of the Washington agreements showed equal regard for Japanese interests.

Japan steadily maintained this course through the first few months of 1930, despite the onset of the Great Depression. Her return to the gold standard in January and endorsement of the London naval agreement in April (which extended the Washington agreement of 1922 to other ships, especially cruisers) indicate that Japan was more intent than any other industrialised country on upholding the world monetary system, despite the crisis, and on continuing the disarmament process. On the basis of this programme, the moderate Prime Minister Hamaguchi once again won the parliamentary elections held in February.

But beneath the surface, a fundamental shift in Japanese policy was under way. It was fuelled primarily by the fact that Japan was harder hit by the Great Depression than any other industrialised country because of her extreme dependence on imported raw materials (90 per cent). The economic crisis greatly benefited all those forces, especially the military, which doubted the ability of the 'liberal' economy to weather the storm. They championed a policy of territorial expansion in order to secure 'vital Japanese interests' and brought mounting pressure to bear on the foremost advocate of 'liberalism', Foreign Minister Shidehara. The Japanese government did sign the London naval agreement, but only over the bitter opposition of the military, especially the navy.

A few months later, Japan's orientation shifted abruptly and became increasingly radicalised throughout 1931. Three mutually reinforcing factors underlay this development: 1) the political victory of the military over the 'liberal' alliance; 2) the mounting confrontation with China over Manchuria; 3) the steep decline in economic relations with the rest of the world as a result of the Great Depression. These developments led to the deed generally seen as signalling the turning point in Japanese policy: the invasion of Manchuria on 19 September 1931. In a fortuitous but symbolic twist of fate, the invasion was launched only days before Britain devalued sterling and abandoned the gold standard. The Japanese invasion of Manchuria exposed the total collapse of the Washington System. The lack of international consequences in the wake of the attack also spelt the beginning of the end of the League of Nations and hence of collective security. These effects were felt in Europe as well, and the Versailles System was further undermined.

1) Social tensions were greatly heightened by the Depression, in Japan as in all the industrialised countries. First and foremost among these were the tensions between Japanese industrial and banking interests on the one hand and the great mass of peasants on the other, whose already parlous economic condition was growing even more difficult because of the catastrophic decline in silk exports.[39] The situation was all the more explosive in that the peasantry was more closely identified with the traditional Japanese way of life than the middle classes deeply involved in industrialisation. The military was also at odds with the middle-class industrialists and financiers because they refused to raise taxes and increase defence spending. The military, typically, was convinced that the population should be prepared to make sacrifices in the 'national interest', by which it meant the preparations for the invasion of Manchuria. The military therefore decided that the moment had come to attempt to exploit the discord between the peasantry and the middle classes, and it even went so far, though in vain, to attempt to enlist peasant support for a fascist party.

The bond between the military and the peasantry was further reinforced by the cumulative effects of a law first passed in 1927 which enabled non-commissioned officers who rejoined the armed forces to be promoted to officer rank. As a result, new cadres of junior officers with peasant backgrounds began to emerge. Similar to some European countries, these junior officers espoused a confused but highly explosive ideology compounded of both anti-capitalist and anti-Communist feelings directed against unruly workers and commercial interests alike. These social forces received mounting support from fledgling heavy industry, which feared the loss of its source of raw materials and wished

39. P. Renouvin, *La question d'Extrême Orient 1840–1940*, p. 354f.

the state to take action. The leading figure in the emerging military-agrarian-heavy industrial alliance was General Araki, who did everything in his power to curtail the influence of parliament and lead Japan back to what he and many others called 'the old ways'. The alliance was held together primarily by its esteem for traditional Japanese values, which the industrial middle classes allegedly wished to destroy.

In the meantime the 'patriotic societies', the militant spearhead of the new political coalition, carried out numerous assassination attempts on the leaders of the so-called liberal parties, an indication of the mounting radicalisation of domestic politics. In November 1930, Prime Minister Hamaguchi was severely injured in one of these attacks and was forced to step down several months later. The pressure from the right continued to mount, and Foreign Minister Shidehara was dropped from any position of power in the cabinet formed in December 1931. The new political strongman was General Araki, who entered the cabinet as Minister of War and immediately widened military operations in Manchuria. The transformation of Japan's domestic politics was thereby complete.

2) The situation in Manchuria deteriorated substantially after 1929–30. Japan had greatly strengthened her hold on southern Manchuria, administering the zone along railway lines, purchasing land and exploiting raw materials, introducing Japanese colonists, investing considerable sums in the industrialisation of the province and maintaining a garrison of 25,000 to 30,000 men on the Liao-Tung peninsula which she had leased for ninety-nine years.[40] All of this was done without formal infringement on Chinese sovereignty. The situation changed, however, after the victory of the Kuomintang which began to pursue a more assertive policy in northern Manchuria. China tightened up the administration, built a parallel railway to the south Manchurian line dominated by the Japanese, encouraged much more Chinese immigration and began to make capital investments. All this caused great unease in Japan, which was further heightened when the Kuomintang opened an office in Mukden to spread patriotic propaganda, much of it directed against the Japanese. A Sino-Japanese war – which the Washington System had been designed to prevent – began to loom on the horizon. The Japanese general staff certainly envisaged only one solution to Japan's problems: military conquest of all Manchuria, possibly as just the first step towards eventual occupation of Mongolia and northern China as well. In any case, the military was able to provide a persuasive rationale for the attack on Manchuria. When Chinese resis-

40. For the Manchurian crisis in detail see T. Yoshihashi, *Conspiracy at Mukden. The Rise of the Japanese Military* (New Haven, Conn., 1963); L. Chong-sik, *Counter-insurgency in Manchuria. The Japanese Experience 1931–1940* (Santa Monica, 1967).

tance finally collapsed at the end of February 1932, the Japanese proclaimed the puppet state of Manchukuo.

3) The Great Depression also destroyed the connection that had existed during the 1920s between Japan's foreign economic needs and a conciliatory foreign policy – a fact which was not lost on contemporaries.[41] Japan's successful export offensive had been one of the few bright spots in an otherwise cloudy and difficult economic picture.[42] On the whole, trade with the United States expanded more quickly than trade with China, giving rise to some feelings of disappointment. But the Depression devastated whatever gains the Japanese had managed to achieve. Foreign trade, so vital to Japan, was especially hard hit. Volumes fell by 50 per cent between 1929 and 1931 (see Table 13, p. 124). Exports to the United States sank from 914.1 million yen in 1929 to 506.1 million in 1930 and 425.3 million in 1931, accounting respectively for 42.5 per cent, 34.4 per cent and 37.1 per cent of total Japanese exports. This decline can largely be ascribed to collapsing prices, particularly of raw silk. According to Ohara, a pound of silk brought $6.00 in New York in 1929 but only $1.20 to $1.50 between 1930 and 1932[43] (see Table 19, p. 131).

The impact of the economic crisis on the Japanese economy and society can be easily appreciated if one considers that the United States absorbed 96 per cent of Japanese exports of raw silk in 1930 and 1931, and even more significantly, that the proceeds from foreign sales of raw silk paid for no less than 40 per cent of all Japanese imports of raw materials and machinery.[44] Silk, as mentioned above, was the only product which Japan exported in significant quantities whithout first having to import the raw materials. The 'silken thread' on which Japan's entire economy hung, in Lockwood's phrase, was ruptured. What is more, the value of Japan's exports to her second largest partner, China, plummeted by more than 50 per cent. Not surprisingly, many Japanese concluded that the material basis of the Washington System no longer existed.

Japan had no alternative but to carve out a new place for itself in the world economy, and this by the last six months of 1931 at the very latest.

41. P. Renouvin, *Les crises du XXe siècle*, vol. II, p. 31f. Renouvin relies on an investigation by the League of Nations (Lytton Report) undertaken after Japan's aggression (pp. 48, 51f.).

42. In detail see H.T. Patrik, 'The Economic Muddle of the 1920s' in J.W. Morley (ed.), *Dilemmas of Growth in Pre-War Japan* (Princeton, 1971); G.C. Allen, *A Short Economic History of Modern Japan 1867–1937*; A. Lewis, *Economic Survey 1919–1939* (London, 1949), pp. 115–23; for what follows see as well the paper given by F. Luther on 15 February 1974.

43. K. Ohara, *Japanese Trade and Industry*, p. 46.

44. W.W. Lockwood, *The Economic Development of Japan*, p. 94.

Fortunately, the key elements of an alternative strategy were already in place, the most important of which was the industrialisation of Manchuria, which had already begun in 1927–8 under the government of General Tanaka. In order to push this programme ahead as quickly as possible despite Chinese opposition, military conquest would be necessary. Indeed, tremendous strides were made between 1932 and 1939 in the 'opening' of Manchuria. The railway network was expanded to a total of 4,000 km and the extraction of raw materials leapt ahead.[45] Manchuria absorbed 16 per cent of total Japanese exports in 1933, 18.5 per cent in 1936 and more than 30 per cent in 1938 (see Table 18, p. 130). Japanese capital investment in Manchuria doubled in seven years. Meanwhile, Chinese markets diminished in importance, not least of all due to a boycott of Japanese goods after the occupation of Manchuria. Japan's share of total Chinese imports fell from 25.5 per cent in 1929 to 9.9 per cent in 1933, before recovering somewhat, though it never regained the previous levels.[46] The Great Depression and the shift it prompted in Japanese policy in the direction of territorial expansion marked the end of the Japanese fixation on Chinese markets and to a lesser extent on American markets.

Japan unleashed an export offensive aimed primarily at the countries of the yen-block (primarily Korea and Formosa in addition to Manchuria). This accorded perfectly with her strategy of bringing an extensive economic zone under Japanese domination. Japan's export offensive began with the abandonment of the gold standard and the devaluation of the yen on 21 December 1931, which was even steeper than that of the British pound. This further improved the competitiveness of Japanese products, which were already highly competitive with those of the other industrialised countries thanks to the steady downward pressure on wages after 1929.[47] These factors account for the extraordinary initial success of the export offensive ruthlessly carried out by the *zaitbatsu* – the large Japanese firms – a success which was all the more remarkable in view of the fact that aggregate world trade was in decline in 1932 and 1933.

Japan's competitors had every reason for grave concern. Her share of international markets rose from 3.5 per cent in 1930 to 5 per cent in

45. E.B. Schumpeter (ed.), *The Industrialization of Japan and Manchukuo, 1930–1940. Population, Raw Materials and Industry* (NY, 1940); W.W. Lockwood, *The Economic Development of Japan*, p. 535.
46. League of Nations, *International Trade Statistics 1935* (Geneva, 1936), p. 311.
47. For the decline in real wages see K. Glück, 'Japans Vordringen auf dem Weltmarkt', pp. 72ff.; G.C. Allen, *Japanese Industry. Its Recent Development and Present Condition* (NY, 1940), p. 97f.; M. Shinohara, 'Economic Development and Foreign Trade in Pre-War Japan', p. 245.

1935. The quality of Japanese exports was also improving. Finished goods had accounted for only 43.6 per cent of total Japanese exports in 1929, but this proportion rose steadily attaining 61.9 per cent already by 1934 (Table 14, p. 124). Moreover, Japan's leading exports began to change. Exports of raw silk plunged from 38.3 per cent of the total in 1928 to 14.9 per cent in 1936, and silk was replaced by cotton fabrics as the most important export item. Metal industry exports had been insignificant in 1932, but they were mounting steadily. Glück wrote in 1937 that 'in the years since 1932, Japanese exports have grown more varied and therefore less vulnerable to fluctuations in price and demand on specific markets. More and more, the "new industries" in the import and export trade are creating a counterpoise to textiles which used to dominate'.[48]

This cursory summary demonstrates the initial success of the new orientation in Japanese policy beginning with territorial expansion and devaluation. The military strengthened its hold over political life, and social tensions eased. Rural areas benefited from mounting industrial activity in as much as it helped to absorb surplus labour. Increased emigration to the conquered territories had the same effect. No longer did agricultural and industrial interests disagree on the principle of territorial expansion, only on the modalities.[49] The bounties showered on the arms industry as a result of this policy helped to stimulate the entire economy, as happened as well in many European countries. Even more important, the close cooperation between industry and the Japanese state assisted the process of concentration and rationalisation and helped Japanese industry to restructure and modernise.[50]

It was clear from the outset that Tokyo's new expansionist policy had a strong anti-British and anti-American component which considerably heightened the potential for war in south-east Asia. However, Japanese policy had only shifted after it became equally clear that the policies of conciliation and cooperation pursued during the 1920s were no longer practicable because a crucial prerequisite, namely a fairly vigorous world market, no longer existed to help pull the Japanese economy out of the doldrums.

2. The British and American Response

The collapse of the Washington System was occasioned not only by the Great Depression and Japanese aggression in Manchuria. The United States, the mainstay of the system, as well as Great Britain must bear

48. K. Glück, 'Japans Vordringen auf dem Weltmarkt', p. 62.
49. P. Renouvin, *Les crises du XXe siècle*, vol. II, p. 33f.
50. See B. Martin, 'Aggressionspolitik als Mobilisierungsfaktor. Der militärische und wirtschaftliche Imperialismus Japans 1931 bis 1941' [Aggressive Policies as a Mobilising Force. Japan's Military and Economic Imperialism 1931–41] in F. Forstmeier and H.-E.

considerable responsibility as well. The London naval conference achieved further success in imposing limitations on Japanese armaments, but it also marked the final attempt of these powers to arrive at a joint policy in East Asia. Thereafter, Britain and America went their separate ways.

The fundamental incoherence in Washington's East Asian policy was brought to the fore by the Japanese invasion of Manchuria.[51] As we have seen, the United States failed during the 1920s to coordinate her economic and political policies in the Far East in such a way as to achieve the most important goal of the Nine Power Agreement, the stabilisation of China. Moral and verbal support for Chiang Kai-shek was not sufficient. The inadequacy of American policy became evident at the time of the Manchurian crisis when Washington did nothing to prevent Japanese aggression or to assist China. America's unwillingness to take a firm stand belied the logic of the Washington System and corroded its very foundations. This hesitation between Japan and China greatly weakened the ideal of the open door long before the Manchurian crisis dealt it the *coup de grâce*. Washington's belated decision to withhold diplomatic recognition from the new puppet state of Manchukuo did nothing to change the outcome.

The sources of America's indecision lie much deeper. By the 1920s, American business interests had already become so oriented towards Japan that an 'open door' to China was no longer of major concern. Moreover, the United States had very few economic interests of her own in Manchuria. Business circles were therefore quite prepared to recognise Japanese aspirations in south-east Asia, especially China, as equally legitimate as their own in Canada or Latin America. American business was far more interested in rapidly modernising, capitalist Japan than in China, which continued to be shaken by revolutionary convulsions.

Not surprisingly under the circumstances, the president, his cabinet, the State Department, the Department of Commerce and a majority in the Senate all spoke out against collective or prejudicial sanctions against Japan, whether economic and/or military. When Britain and

Volksmann (eds), *Wirtschaft und Rüstung am Vorabend des Zweiten Weltkrieges* (Düsseldorf, 1975); see as well the Japan chapter in B. Moore, *Social Origins of Dictatorship and Democracy* (London/Boston, 1967).

51. For what follows see R.E. Ferrell, *American Diplomacy in the Great Depression. Hoover–Stimson Foreign Policy, 1929–1933* (New Haven, 1957); J. Doenecke (ed.), *The Diplomacy of Frustration: The Manchurian Crisis of 1931–1933 as Revealed in the Papers of S.K. Hornbeck* (Oxford, 1981); M. Schaller, *The United States and China in the Twentieth Century* (NY, 1979); for the economic background: J. Hutmacher and W.I. Susman, *H. Hoover and the Crisis of American Capitalism* (Cambridge, Mass., 1973).

France proved very reserved in their responses, Hoover and Secretary of State Henry L. Stimson realised that the League of Nations was highly unlikely to adopt sanctions against Japan, though Stimson had originally considered offering to participate in such measures.[52] Eventually he even refused to appoint an official American representative on the investigatory commission which the League sent to Manchuria, maintaining that nothing should be done without Japanese consent. The State Department had decided simply to acquiesce. The only consequence for Japan was the so-called 'Stimson doctrine' which contented itself with a moral condemnation of the invasion and a refusal to extend official recognition to Manchukuo, though even this went too far in Hoover's view.[53] Such a reaction was not likely to make much of an impression on Tokyo.

The Manchurian crisis also sounded the hour of truth so far as Britain was concerned. Still debilitated by the financial crisis, she suddenly found herself facing global realities which called into question the very foundations of the foreign policy she had pursued in the 1920s:[54] firstly, the enormous challenge Japan now posed to Britain's substantial political, strategic and economic interests in the Far East; and secondly, a situation in Europe that was moving further from a solution than ever after 1930–1 and in which Germany too seemed likely to revert to a far more nationalistic and militaristic course. The British felt incapable of responding to both threats at once, and an endless and seemingly absurd debate arose over whether Germany or Japan posed the greatest danger. The response would determine the direction that British armaments policy would take, though the question itself was never clearly answered and probably could not be.

The British government sought to circumvent this dilemma by pursuing what Schmidt has appropriately termed a 'two-track strategy' towards Japan and later towards Germany. First, Britain adopted a policy of *attentisme* in order to gain enough time to implement appropriate military measures and to win over a public that was little inclined towards a military build-up; secondly, she encouraged international negotiations in the hope that the situation could perhaps be moderated. Thus the 'appeasement' policy was born. However, Britain could not

---

52. Details in J.-B. Duroselle, *Histoire diplomatique de 1919 à nos jours*, pp. 225–31; S.R. Smith, *The Manchurian Crisis. A Tragedy in International Relations, 1931–1932* (NY, 1948); J.W. Christopher, *Conflict in the Far East. American Diplomacy in China, 1928–1933* (Leyden, 1950); for the role of the League of Nations see the pioneering work of W. Willoughby, *The Sino-Japanese Controversy and the League of Nations* (NY, 1935).
53. See R.N. Current, 'The Stimson doctrine and the Hoover Doctrine', *AHR* (1954).
54. G. Schmidt, *England in der Krise*, pp. 97ff.

count on American support,[55] and even the Dominions would not necessarily defer to her strategic interests. She scarcely had any other choice therefore than to attempt to feel her way through the minefield of competing interests in Europe, America and the Far East. This task was especially difficult in that Britain, as so often in the past, was reluctant to undertake firm commitments to either France or the United States in order to maintain a modicum of her former freedom of action. This resulted, at the time of the Manchurian crisis, in a free hand for Japan, at least temporarily. However, it was clear that the collapse of both the Versailles and Washington Systems would leave Britain with very little political leeway in both Europe and Asia.

---

55. The best analysis of this is Ch. Thorne, *The Limits of Foreign Policy. The West, the League and the Far Eastern Crisis of 1931–1933* (London, 1972).

6
Final Observations:
1931 – 'Annus Terribilis'

1. We set out to discover how it was that the attempt to reconstruct a world shattered by war and social upheaval not only failed but catalysed a global depression that opened the gates to far more destructive and malevolent forces than were ever witnessed during the First World War. Was reconstruction a Pyrrhic victory only? An illustration of the sense-lessness of human endeavour and the ultimate futility of politics? The period between 1924 and 1931, when the groundwork was laid for war or peace, now seems quite remote; but the passage of the years does little to reassure the observer. Though historical eras are unique and can never be repeated, this one presents sufficient parallels with the present that we should be particularly concerned about the reasons for its failures.

Firstly, we are struck by the mounting inappropriateness of the policies adopted in order to deal with the salient problems of the time, even during the phase of 'relative stability'. The cure did not work because the diagnosis (at least that which was politically admissible) failed to recognise the underlying sources of the problem. This reminds us once again of the historical maxim that those who are concerned with maintaining political power tend to underestimate the necessity of change, especially when it could threaten their own position.

Nothing is so likely to obscure the need for change as calls for a 'return to normalcy'. This rallying cry became the measure of all things, to the great advantage of those social strata which eagerly anticipated a return to the old days and opposed significant change, let alone revolution. The trend was apparent in all the capitalist, industrialised countries, regardless of differences in the manner in which it found expression. These social strata (by no means innocent of all responsibility for the First World War) felt that their interest lay in undoing the effects of the war and in reversing its repercussions on their life style. By

167

a 'return to normalcy' they meant little more than the restoration of prewar conditions. They were assisted in this aspiration by the myth of a prewar 'Golden Age,' propagated by none other than them themselves. It helped to create an ideological and social atmosphere that was difficult to combat – even though this alleged 'Golden Age' had given rise to the most destructive war in human history. Cries for a 'return to normalcy' were doubly effective in that they soothed the conscience of conservatives while freeing them from any need to analyse the reasons for the crisis. This movement found quintessential expression in the restoration of the gold(-exchange) standard.

Those social classes in Europe and Japan which aimed to reconstruct society and the economy in the image of a 'return to normalcy', on both the national and international levels, found strong if rather unexpected support from the only power really capable of doing so: the United States. Leading figures in business, politics and high finance were in fundamental agreement that America's prosperity depended on stability in both Europe and south-east Asia (despite their many domestic differences of opinion which often served to confuse and weaken American foreign policy). The United States accordingly plunged into world affairs, drawing up a series of formal treaties which established a new order in the Far East and attempting to gain influence in Europe primarily through the exercise of financial and economic leverage. Both these approaches helped to consolidate American domination of the world economy. The fundamental contradiction in American policy, as many contemporaries realised, was that while Washington insisted that other countries should open their markets to American goods, it simultaneously adopted formidable tariffs of its own in order to limit foreign access to the world's most highly developed capitalist economy. This prevented the global marketplace from responding in its natural way in order to help solve the problems besetting the various national economies, as it was later allowed to do in the 1950s and 1960s.

In order to reinforce her economic hegemony, the United States developed various strategies to deal with the differing circumstances in Europe and south-east Asia. In Europe, she avoided any overt political or legal engagements for fear they might draw her into the intra-European squabbles she so much abhorred. Moreover, this sort of involvement would tie the United States to France, the most important regional advocate of the status quo. Finally, she might be forced to mediate between Britain and France – a most unlikely role for the country which derived the greatest benefit from their disputes.

The situation in south-east Asia was quite different. Here, the new order depended for the most part on striking a balance between the often antagonistic interests of China and Japan as well as of the United

States and Great Britain, the traditional dominant powers in the region. The best foundation and lasting assurance of a balance of power was an armaments agreement which would assuage a major source of conflict, the arms race in battleships, and act as a 'confidence-building measure', in the modern parlance, by establishing definite armaments ratios. The resulting Washington Treaties bound all the signatory powers to contribute to the preservation of the new order.

However as Washington set about implementing these two strategies on a daily basis, it lost sight of its ultimate aims, as so often happens in history. This caused further inconsistencies and imbalances to appear, and in the end American influence tended to have a rather destabilising effect in both Europe and Asia. The main reason was a striking fixation in both regions on a privileged partner: Germany in Europe and Japan in the Far East, i.e. those powers which shortly thereafter would unleash the Second World War. While some degree of stabilisation was achieved with the help of these partners in the 1920s, quite the opposite was the case in the 1930s. The significance of this paradox cannot be exaggerated. Those historians who tend to divide the 'interwar period', in the truest sense of the term, into two discrete parts, in response to the enormous impact of the Great Depression, forgo an opportunity to analyse the reasons for these developments. Those historians, however, who seek the origins of later developments in the stabilisation policies of the 1920s, as rooted in the 'conservative offensive' especially in the second half of the decade, begin to approach a solution.

In pursuing the latter course, we first outlined the extremely restrictive brand of stabilisation which was adopted, in no small measure at the urging of the United States. The key to this kind of stabilisation was the return to the gold(-exchange) standard, which the United States made a prerequisite for her financial involvement in Europe. This measure had far-reaching consequences. It compelled governments around the world to accord highest priority to monetary policy and to deflate their economies, which was entirely consistent with America's interests as by far the largest creditor nation, the currency of which had become the primary medium of international exchange. The return to the gold (-exchange) standard carried with it other social consequences as well, ranging from income redistribution in favour of the wealthy to delayed or inadequate economic restructuring. Though the conservative political elite in Europe expressed some fears about the consequences of such a policy, it was by and large willing to accommodate American demands because they reinforced many of its own aspirations.

In fact, this brand of stabilisation proved to be a strait-jacket which fatefully limited the scope of social and economic policy, especially in Germany and Japan. In addition, as we have seen, the world economy proved unable to contribute substantially to stabilisation, and Germany and Japan failed to achieve the position in the international division of labour which they deemed essential for the further development of their economies. All these factors worked to the great disadvantage of those social forces in Germany and Japan which hoped that world trade would make an important contribution to domestic and international accommodation and which opposed the nationalist circles advocating an expanded internal market. This, much more than reparations, was *one* major reason why political and economic stabilisation in Germany failed to achieve the necessary success. Far more study remains to be made of these matters than can be undertaken here.

Most importantly for the failure of stabilisation, however, was the fact that America's two privileged partners became highly dependent on her, more so than any of the other industrialised countries. The more or less premeditated decision of the Republican administrations in Washington to carry out reconstruction by working through the two strongest economies in their respective regions turned out to be a fateful error. An early form of what would later be dubbed 'trilateralism' in the early 1970s began to emerge. At first, this dependence stimulated reconstruction, but then as now, at the cost of a high price in the long run. The danger mounted (as many contemporaries pointed out) that the German and Japanese economies would not only be unduly influenced by developments in the United States but would ultimately be forced to play whatever role was ascribed to them in an international division of labour dominated by the United States. This would inevitably drive Germany and Japan towards the periphery of the world economy. By the late 1920s, domestic critics were hurling this accusation at the governments of both nations, which were still attempting, in spite of everything, to pursue relatively moderate policies within the framework of the Versailles and Washington Systems. Those who criticised the pro-American slant of German and Japanese policy necessarily called both these systems into questions as well as the postwar order which they embodied.

2. The Great Depression focused attention on all the negative effects of postwar stabilisation policies and at the same time dramatically augmented them. What had become little more than a house of cards during the second half of the 1920s finally collapsed altogether. The conservative political elites which had advocated this brand of stabilisation were left bereft of all inspiration and vision, though they continued to deny or misunderstand this fact, to the great detriment of their peoples. Self-righteously convinced of their own wisdom, they fled further into the

past and attempted to deal with the crisis by intensifying deflationary measures. However, the obvious failure of these policies finally sealed the fate of the 'conservative offensive' for a time. In the industrialised nations of western Europe and North America, democracy itself did not collapse. These countries either summoned the strength to attempt an alternative economic strategy (Roosevelt's New Deal and the Popular Front in France), with mixed success, or at the very least, forced conservatives to give up some of their hoary ideals (devaluation of sterling).

These alternatives were not available however in Germany or Japan. In the former, the Grand Coalition had just collapsed, and in the latter no significant political parties existed to the left of the governing liberal–conservative regime. The only remaining alternative in both countries was authoritarian government, a fact which greatly boosted the fortunes of the champions of nationalism and militarism. In Germany all that was needed was a further lurch to the right within the conservative, German-National bloc; in Japan, the military was already poised to seize power.

The most significant result of this study is evidence that the reorientation of both countries was greatly facilitated by the concurrent disintegration of the Versailles and Washington Systems. In fact, these developments encouraged one another and were inextricably connected. The entire process was triggered by the economic decline of the United States, which, in selecting Germany and Japan as her privileged partners, had assumed the role of hinge between the two systems, whether wittingly or not. When the Great Depression destroyed the economic foundations of this role, both systems disintegrated. The United States was naturally far more concerned about overcoming the internal economic crisis than about the resulting consequences for the world economy and political system, and in particular for her previously privileged partners of Japan and Germany. However, this attitude limited America's ability to steer foreign events and eased the way for other countries, led by Germany and Japan, to attempt to cope with the crisis by adopting aggressive, nationalistic policies.

The events of 1931 marked, as we have seen, the final demise of the attempt to reconstruct the world economy and political system. Everything that had been gained during the 1920s was lost. The extent of the general disintegration became apparent as the financial and banking crisis reached its climax in the summer of 1931. The United States had already shed its role as the hinge of the international system, and the last vestiges of coordination and cooperation between the central banks disappeared. The world economy split into various monetary and economic blocs, and foreign trade policy became a tool of national political and strategic policies. The issue of German reparations had kept the world on edge for more than ten years, but their abrupt termination did not seem to have any positive effects on the international economy and monetary system, not even in Germany itself.

France was able to take advantage of its financial strength in 1931, but it too was gradually being drawn into the vortex of the global depression. It destroyed the economic foundations of France's alliance system and rendered it impossible for the leading power in Europe to fulfil her role as the guarantor of the status quo. The grimness of the situation moved even such an admired and perspicacious observer as Arnold Toynbee to remark in the foreword to the 1932 edition of the *Survey of International Affairs* that the *annus terribilis* of western civilisation was not 1914 or even 1917 – but 1931. Not since the Turkish siege of Vienna in 1683 had the West been in such peril. Subsequent events more than confirmed Toynbee's sombre assessment.

3. In conclusion, we shall return once again to the question raised at the outset about similarities with the contemporary global situation. The most striking parallel with the years 1930 to 1932 is that the leading capitalist industrialised countries (the United States, Great Britain and Germany) are again seeking to cope with an economic crisis by means of a 'conservative offensive'. However, contemporary aims and methods have changed considerably: Ronald Reagan is no Hoover, Helmut Kohl is no Brüning, and Margaret Thatcher is not the National Union. They have retained, to be sure, some elements of the traditional conservative, deflationary approach of the pre-Keynesian era ('austerity' in the form of reduced wages and salaries; reduction of the national debt through limitations on social programmes; a balanced budget; a restrictive financial policy). But they are also taking measures to improve supply and to encourage capital in order to evade a major cause of the Great Depression: the decline in productive investment. Policies of this kind were largely absent in 1930–2. In the final analysis, what we are witnessing today is an attempt to encourage with all available means a process of national economic restructuring and adaptation to changed global conditions. This is intended to ensure competitiveness on international markets, particularly in the realm of modern growth industries on the leading edge of the 'third technological revolution.' To this extent, the conservative governments have drawn the consequences of the fact that what we face today is a crisis of capital utilisation.

This brings us to the critical difference with the Great Depression of 1929, which quickly invalidates all comparisons. What the world confronted then (and what the United States still faces in the end) was a crisis in the extensive model of economic growth. The problem was exemplified by the fact that company profits were rising faster than consumer income. 'Conversion' difficulties were the result: demand could not keep pace with increasing productivity, which led inevitably to the overproduction and speculation which triggered the crisis. This occurred first in the United States where the contradictions in the economic system were most acute. The United States was slowly outgrowing the extensive model of economic growth, but the leap to the next economic stage – intensive growth in the form of widespread 'Fordism' – had not yet been taken.

This stage was finally reached during the long expansionary phase of the 1950s and 1960s. In the economic model that now triumphed in all the leading capitalist countries, growth was supported, in contrast to the interwar period, by mounting wages due to increased productivity. Capitalist production in the welfare state underwent a sea change thanks to better distribution of income, more efficient organisation of labour, certain forms of labour–management cooperation, reductions in sectoral disparities and, most importantly, the mounting international division of labour within a steadily expanding world economy. The underlying flaw in this economic model (which was already apparent towards the end of the 1960s, well before the drastic increase in the price of oil) lay in the danger that the profitability of capital might go into steep decline. This is precisely what transpired, not least of all because of the mounting cost of labour and fringe benefits, especially during the period when nominal wage rates were rising faster than increases in productivity.

This contradiction in the system was compounded by the fact that production in the consumer goods sector of the economy was rising more quickly than in the capital goods sector, while other sectors such as construction and the tertiary sector were adapting rather sluggishly to intensive production. As a result, mean productivity and hence profit rates declined, which in turn had a chilling effect on investment. The first signs of a 'new international division of labour' increased the pressure exerted by imports on traditional economic sectors in the advanced industrialised nations. They responded by steadily heightening competition among themselves (i.e. the economic blocs of western Europe, Japan and the United States) for an enlarged share of world markets.

As in 1929, the first signs of crisis appeared in the United States, the most advanced of the capitalist economies. In contrast to earlier times, the situation was further complicated by political and strategic developments (Vietnam, mounting tensions with the Soviet Union), which called into question America's role as the leading power in the world. The 'conservative offensive', pursued with utmost determination by the Reagan administration, aims to restore this position of dominance in all realms of endeavour. As in the 1920s, America's domestic interests have clear priority, to the detriment of her allies and particularly of the Third World. In contrast to the New Deal of the 1930s, which eventually took into account the international aspect of the Depression, the conservative revolution in the United States of today does not seek to restabilise the world economy and political system but rather to subordinate them to the economic and political-strategic measures necessary in order for the United States to regain her leadership role.

The attempt of the leading western power to surmount the economic crisis by means of neo-conservative policies and to respond to the international security crisis with massive rearmament programmes (these strategies being two sides of the same coin) heightens the danger of destabilisation on two fronts. In this the contemporary world is unique. A neo-conservative approach to structural adaptation necessarily entails a high social cost and heightened social tensions, especially in those countries where adaptation to the world economy requires enormous sacrifices. The tendency grows for each country, and especially the United States, to consider only its own immediate interests and to disregard the international effects of its economic policies (e.g. the impact of a highly overvalued dollar). Less developed nations, especially in the Third and Fourth Worlds, suffer the consequences. The resulting exacerbation of regional and sectoral disparities has heightened the tensions in the existing model of economic growth. On the other hand, and in contrast to the 1930s, there is no practical alternative to conservatism or obsolete Keynesianism in dealing with the crisis. For this to occur, profound changes would be necessary in the existing balance of political power. At the same time, the superpower confrontation and the arms race tend to lock in place those domestic and international factors that are fomenting the crisis.

One should remember that the economic and political crisis of the 1930s was never overcome by government policies of any ilk. The world economy headed downward again in 1937–8, especially in the United States. The revisionist powers of Germany and Japan sought to solve their mounting problems through rearmament and military expansion, and the democratic countries of the west were forced to increase their arms expenditures as well. But this too did nothing to vanquish the Depression. The sombre conclusion from those years is that it took the Second World War to overcome the global economic and political crisis and to pave the way for the expansionary phase of the 1950s and 1960s. At the same time, the war set the stage for new international conflicts between East and West and North and South.

Select Bibliography

1. The World Economy and International Politics

Adler, S., *The Uncertain Giant: 1921–1941. American Foreign Policy between the Wars* (New York, 1965)

Aglietta, M., *A Theory of Capitalist Regulation. The US Experience* (London, 1979)

Aldcroft, D.H., *From Versailles to Wall St, 1919–1929* (London, 1977) (trans. as *Die Zwanziger Jahre: Von Versailles zur Wall Street 1919–1929*, Munich, 1978)

Angermann, E., *Der Aufstieg der Vereinigten Staaten von Amerika. Innen- und aussenpolitische Entwicklung 1914–1957* (Stuttgart, 1966, 1973³)

Angricht, H., *Guide to the League of Nations Publications* (New York, 1951)

Ashworth, W., *A Short History of the International Economy 1850–1950* (London, 1952)

Aubrey, H.G., *The Dollar in World Affairs: An Essay in International Financial Policy* (New York, 1964)

Bassett, R., *Nineteen Thirty-One: Political Crisis* (London, 1958)

Bauer, O., *Zwischen zwei Weltkriegen? Die Krise der Weltwirtschaft, der Demokratie, des Sozialismus* (Bratislava, 1936); also in *Collected Works*, vol. 6 (Vienna, 1976)

Becker, J., and K. Hildebrand (eds), *Internationale Beziehungen in der Weltwirtschaftskrise 1929–1933* [International Relations in the Great Depression] (Munich, 1980)

Brandes, J., *Herbert Hoover and Economic Development. Department of Commerce Policy, 1921–1928* (Pittsburgh, 1962)

Brendan, B., *Monetary Chaos in Europe* (London, 1987)

Brinkmann, C., *Weltpolitik und Weltwirtschaft der neuesten Zeit* (Berlin, 1936) (especially the introduction)

Brown Jr., W.A., *The International Gold Standard Reinterpreted, 1914–1934*, vols I and II (New York, 1940)

Chandler, L.V., *Benjamin Strong. Central Banker* (Washington, 1958)
——, *America's Greatest Depression, 1929–1941* (New York, 1970)
Clarke, St., V.O., *Central Bank Co-operation, 1924–1931* (New York, 1967)
Craig, G.A., and F. Gilbert (eds), *The Diplomats 1919–1939*, vols I and II (Princeton, 1953)
DeConde, A. (ed.), *Isolation and Security. Ideas and Interests in Twentieth-Century American Foreign Policy* (Durham, NC, 1957)
Duroselle, J.-B., *De Wilson à Roosevelt. Politique extérieur des Etats-Unis, 1913–1945* (Paris, 1960)
——, *Histoire diplomatique de 1919 à nos jours* (Paris, 1978[7])
Elliot, W.Y. (ed.), *The Political Economy of American Foreign Policy* (New York, 1955)
Ellis, L.E., *Republican Foreign Policy, 1921–1933* (New Brunswick, NJ, 1968)
Falkus, M.E., 'United States Economic Policy and the "Dollar Cap" of the 1920s', *EHR* 24 (1971)
Feis, H., *The Diplomacy of the Dollar. First Era 1919–1932* (Baltimore, 1950)
Ferrell, R.H., *American Diplomacy in the Great Depression. Hoover –Stimson Foreign Policy, 1929–1933* (New Haven, 1957)
Fischer, W., *Die Weltwirtschaft im 20. Jahrhundert* (Göttingen, 1979)
Fleming, D.F., *The United States and World Organization 1920–1933* (New York, 1938, 1966[2])
Grotkopp, W., *Die grosse Krise. Lehren aus der Überwindung der Wirtschaftskrise 1929/32* [The Great Depression. Lessons from Coping with the Economic Crisis 1929–32] (Düsseldorf, 1954)
Haber, L.F., *The Chemical Industry 1900–1930, International Growth and Technological Change* (London, 1971)
Hawley, E.W., *Herbert Hoover and the Crisis of American Capitalism* (Cambridge, Mass., 1973)
Helander, S., *Das Autarkieproblem in der Weltwirtschaft* [The Problem of Autarky in the World Economy] (Berlin, 1955)
Himmelberg, R.E. (ed.), *The Great Depression and American Capitalism* (Boston, 1968)
Jones, K.P. (ed.), *US Diplomats in Europe, 1919–1941* (Oxford, 1983[2])
Kenwood, A.G., and A.L. Lougheed, *The Growth of the International Economy 1820–1960. An Introductory Text* (London, 1971)
Kindleberger, C.P., *The World in Depression* (London, 1973)
Kuznets, S., *Economic Growth of Nations. Total Output and Production Structure* (Cambridge, Mass., 1971)
——, *Modern Economic Growth. Rate, Structure and Spread* (New Haven, 1966)

Lary, H.B., et al., *The United States in the World Economy. The International Transactions of the United States during the Interwar Period* (Washington, 1943) (a publication of the US Department of Commerce)

Levy, H., *Der Weltmarkt 1913 und heute* [The World Market in 1913 and Today] (Leipzig, 1926)

Maizels, A., *Industrial and World Trade* (Cambridge, 1963)

Meyer, R.H., *Banker's Diplomacy. Monetary Stabilization in the Twenties* (New York, 1970)

Néré, J., *La crise de 1929* (Paris, 1968)

Parrini, C., *Heir to Empire. United States Economic Diplomacy, 1916–1923* (Pittsburgh, 1969)

Predöhl, A., *Aussenwirtschaft. Weltwirtschaft, Handelspolitik und Währungspolitik* [Economic Foreign Policy. The International Economy, Trade Policy and Monetary Policy] (Göttingen, 1949)

Rostow, W.W., *The World Economy. History and Prospects* (Austin, 1978)

Sering, M., *Agrarkrisen und Agrarzölle* [Agricultural Crises and Agricultural Tariffs] (Berlin, 1925)

Soule, G.H., *Prosperity Decade: From War to Depression, 1917–1929* (New York, 1947)

Sternberg, F., *Kapitalismus und Sozialismus vor dem Weltgericht* (Hamburg, 1951)

Triffin, R., *Our International Monetary System: Yesterday, Today and Tomorrow* (New York, 1968)

Varga, E., *Die Krise des Kapitalismus und ihre politischen Folgen*, ed. E. Altvater (Frankfurt, 1969)

Warren, H.G., *Herbert Hoover and the Great Depression* (New York, 1959)

Williams, W.A., *The Tragedy of American Diplomacy* (New York, 1962), revised and extended edition

Wilson, J.H., *American Business and Foreign Policy, 1920–1933* (Lexington, 1971)

——, *Herbert Hoover: Forgotten Progressive* (Boston, 1975)

Winkel, H. (ed.), *Finanz- und wirtschaftspolitische Fragen der Zwischenkriegszeit* [Financial and Economic Policy Questions of the Interwar Period] (Berlin, 1973)

Winkler, H.A. (ed.), *Die grosse Krise in Amerika. Vergleichende Studien zur politischen Sozialgeschichte 1929–1939* (Göttingen, 1973)

Woodruff, W., *America's Impact on the World. A Study of the Role of the United States in the World Economy, 1750–1970* (London, 1975)

Woytinsky, W.S. and E.S., *World Commerce and Governments. Trends and Outlook* (New York, 1955)

177

Yates, P.L., *Forty Years of Foreign Trade* (London, 1959)

2. Versailles System

Abelshauser, W., and D. Petzina (eds), *Deutsche Wirtschaftsgeschichte im Industriezeitalter. Konjunktur, Krise, Wachstum* [German Economic History in the Industrial Age] (Königstein i.T., 1981) (esp. the contributions of the editors and A. Predöhl)

Abendroth, W., *Sozialgeschichte der europäischen Arbeiterbewegung* (Frankfurt, 1965)

Aldcroft, D.H., *The Inter-War Economy: Britain 1919–1939* (London, 1970)

Alford, B.W.E., *Depression and Recovery? British Economic Growth, 1918–1939* (London, 1972)

Artaud, D., *La reconstruction de l'Europe 1919–1929* (Paris, 1973)

——, 'L'impérialisme américain en Europe au lendemain de la première guerre mondiale', *Relations internationales* 8 (1976)

——, *La question des dettes interalliés et la reconstruction de l'Europe* (Paris, 1978)

Bariéty, J., *Les relations franco-allemandes après la première guerre mondiale. 10 novembre 1918–10 janvier 1925. De l'exécution à la négociation* (Paris, 1977)

Barnett, C., *The Collapse of British Power* (London, 1972)

Bassett, R., *Nineteen Thirty-One. Political Crisis* (London, 1958)

Bennett, E.W., *Germany and the Diplomacy of the Financial Crisis 1931* (Cambridge, Mass., 1962)

Bettelheim, C., *Bilan de l'économie française 1919–1946* (Paris, 1947)

Bienstock, G., *Deutschland und die Weltwirtschaft* (Berlin, 1931)

Bonnefous, E., *Histoire politique de la Troisième République*, vol. IV: *Cartel des gauches et Union nationale, 1924–1929* (Paris, 1960)

Born, K.E., *Die deutsche Bankenkrise 1931. Finanzen und Politik* (Munich, 1967)

Carlton, D., *MacDonald versus Henderson. The Foreign Policy of the Second Labour Government* (London, 1970)

Chastenet, J., *Histoire de la Troisième République*, vol. V: *Les années d'illusions 1918–1931* (Paris, 1960)

Conze, W., and H. Raupach (eds), *Die Staats- und Wirtschaftskrise des Deutschen Reiches 1929/31* (Stuttgart, 1967)

Costigliola, F.-C., 'The United States and the Reconstruction of Germany in the 1920's', *Business History Review* 50 (Winter, 1976)

Deane, Ph., and W.A. Coale, *British Economic Growth 1688–1959* (Cambridge, 1967)

Drummond, I.M., *British Economic Policy and the Empire, 1919–1939*

(London, 1972)

Fischer, W., *Weltwirtschaftliche Rahmenbedingungen für die ökonomische und politische Entwicklung Europas 1919–1939* [The World Economic Conditions for the Economic and Political Development of Europe 1919–1939] (Wiesbaden, 1980)

Fohlen, C., *La France de l'entre-deux-guerres* (Paris, 1966)

Gilbert, M., *Britain and Germany between the Wars* (London, 1962)

Hardach, G., *Weltmarktorientierung und relative Stagnation. Währungspolitik in Deutschland 1924–1931* [The Turn to World Markets and Relative Stagnation. Monetary Policy in Germany 1924–31] (Berlin, 1976)

——, *Deutschland in der Weltwirtschaft 1870–1970. Eine Einführung in die Sozial- und Wirtschaftsgeschichte* [Germany in the World Economy 1870–1970] (Frankfurt, 1977)

Hardach, K., *Wirtschaftsgeschichte Deutschlands im 20. Jahrhundert* [German Economic History in the Twentieth Century] (Göttingen, 1976)

Helbig, W.J., *Die Reparationen in der Ära Brüning. Zur Bedeutung des Young-Plans für die deutsche Politik 1930–1932* [Reparations in the Brüning Era. The Impact of the Young Plan on German Policy] (Berlin, 1962)

Hoffmann, S. (ed.), *In Search of France* (New York, 1965²)

Hoffmann, W., et al., *Das Wachstum der deutschen Wirtschaft seit der Mitte des 19. Jahrhunderts* [The Expansion of the German Economy after the mid-19th Century] (Berlin, 1965)

Ingham, G., *Capitalism Divided? The City and Industry in British Social Development* (London, 1984) (Chapters 7 and 8)

Jacobson, J., *Locarno Diplomacy. Germany and the West 1925–1929* (Princeton, NJ, 1972)

James, H., *The German Slump. Politics and Economics 1924–1936* (Oxford, 1986)

Jeanneney, J.-N., *Leçon d'histoire pour une gauche au pouvoir. La faillité du Cartel (1924–1926)* (Paris, 1977)

Jones, K.P. (ed.), *US Diplomats in Europe, 1919–1941* (Oxford, 1983²)

Kemp, T., *The French Economy, 1913–1939. The History of a Decline* (London, 1972)

Kindleberger, C.P., *Economic Growth in France and Britain 1851–1950* (Cambridge, 1964)

Landes, D., *The Unbound Prometheus: Technological Change and Industrial Development in Western Europe from 1750 to the Present* (Cambridge, 1969)

Leffler, M.P., *The Elusive Quest. America's Pursuit of European Stability and French Security, 1919–1933* (Chapel Hill, NC, 1979)

179

Lévy-Leboyer, M. (ed.), *La position internationale de la France. Aspects économiques et financiers XIXe–XXe siècles* (Paris, 1977)

Link, W., *Die amerikanische Stabilisierungspolitik in Deutschland 1921–1932* [American Stabilisation Policies in Germany] (Düsseldorf, 1970)

Lüke, R.E., *Von der Stabilisierung zur Krise* [From Stabilisation to the Great Depression] (Zürich, 1958)

Maier, C.S., *Recasting Bourgeois Europe. Stabilisation in France, Germany and Italy in the Decade After World War I* (Princeton, 1975)

Marks, Sally, *The Illusion of Peace: International Relations in Europe, 1918–1923* (London/New York, 1976)

Maxelon, M.-O., *Stresemann und Frankreich. Deutsche Politik der Ost-West Balance* (Düsseldorf, 1972)

Moggridge, D.E., *The Return to Gold, 1925: The Formulation of Economic Policy and its Critics* (Cambridge, 1969)

——, *British Monetary Policy 1924–1931. The Norman Conquest of $4.86* (Cambridge, 1971)

Mommsen, H., et al. (eds), *Industrielles System und politische Entwicklung in der Weimarer Republik* [The Industrial System and Political Development in the Weimar Republic] (Düsseldorf, 1974)

Mowat, G.L., *Britain Between the Wars 1918–1940* (London, 1955)

Néré, J., *The Foreign Policy of France from 1914 to 1945* (London, 1975)

Petzina, D., 'Grundriss der deutschen Wirtschaftsgeschichte 1918–1945' [Outline of German Economic History 1918–45] in *Deutsche Geschichte seit dem I. Weltkrieg*, vol. 2 (Stuttgart, 1973)

Pohl, K.H., *Weimars Wirtschaft und die Aussenpolitik der Republik 1924–1926. Vom Dawes-Plan zum Internationalen Eisenpakt* [The Weimar Economy and Foreign Policy 1924–1926. From the Dawes Plan to the International Iron Pact] (Düsseldorf, 1979)

Pollard, S., *The Development of the British Economy, 1914–1967* (New York, 1969²)

——, *The Gold Standard and Employment Policies between the Wars* (London, 1970)

Preller, L., *Sozialpolitik in der Weimarer Republik* (Stuttgart, 1949)

Rosenberg, A., *Geschichte der Weimarer Republik*, ed. K. Kersten (Frankfurt, 1961)

Sauvy, A., *Histoire économique de la France entre les deux guerres*, vol. 1: *De l'armistice à la dévaluation de la livre (1918–1931)* (Paris, 1965)

Schmidt, G., 'Der gescheiterte Frieden. Die Ursachen des Zusammenbruchs des Versailler Systems' in Hartmut Elsenhans et al. (eds), *Frankreich, Europa, Weltpolitik. Festschrift für Gilbert Ziebura* (Opladen, 1989), pp. 174–96. This important essay further develops my own arguments as presented in this book.

—— (ed.), *Konstellationen internationaler Politik 1924–1932: Politische und wirtschaftliche Faktoren in den Beziehungen zwischen Westeuropa und den USA* [International Political Constellations 1924–1932: Political and Economic Factors in the Relations between Western Europe and the United States] (Bochum, 1983)

Schmölders, G., *Frankreichs Aufstieg zur Weltkapitalmacht. Diplomatie und Strategie des französischen Geldes seit 1926* [The Rise of France to a World Financial Power. The Diplomacy and Strategy of French Finance after 1926] (Berlin, 1933)

Schuker, S.A., *The End of French Predominance. The Financial Crisis of 1924 and the Adoption of the Dawes Plan* (Chapel Hill, NC, 1976)

Skidelsky, R., *Politicians and the Slump. The Labour Government of 1929–1931* (London, 1967)

Solverman, D.P., *Reconstructing Europe after the Great War* (Harvard, 1982)

Soulié, M., *La vie politique d'Edouard Herriot* (Paris, 1962)

Stücken, R., *Deutsche Geld- und Kreditpolitik 1914–1963* [German Monetary and Credit Policies 1914–1963] (Tübingen, 1953)

Sturmthal, A., *The Tragedy of European Labour, 1918–1939* (London, 1944)

Svennilson, I., *Growth and Stagnation in the European Economy* (Geneva, 1954)

Timm, H., *Die deutsche Sozialpolitik und der Bruch der Grossen Koalition im März 1930* [German Social Policy and the Collapse of the Great Coalition] (Düsseldorf, 1952)

Timmons, B., *Portrait of an American: Charles G. Dawes* (New York, 1953)

Trachtenberg, M., *Reparations in World Politics. France and European Economic Diplomacy, 1916–1923* (New York, 1980)

Trendelenburg, E., *Amerika und Europa in der Weltwirtschaftspolitik des Zeitabschnitts der Wirtschaftskonferenzen*, Part I: *Bis zum Dawes Plan* (Berlin, 1943)

Vagts, A., *Deutschland und die Vereinigten Staaten in der Weltpolitik*, 2 vols, (New York, 1935)

Winkler, H.A., *Mittelstand, Demokratie und Nationalsozialismus* [The Middle Class, Democracy and National Socialism] (Cologne, 1972)

——, 'Extremismus der Mitte? Sozialgeschichtliche Aspekte der national-sozialistische Machtergreifung' [Moderate Extremism? Social Aspects of the Nazi Seizure of Power], *VfZ* 20 (1972)

Wolfe, M., *The French Franc Between the Wars, 1919–1939* (New York, 1951)

Wolfers, A., *Britain and France Between Two Wars. Conflicting Strate-

gies of Peace since Versailles (New York, 1940; repr., 1963)

Woodruff, W., *Impact of Western Man. A Study of Europe's Role in the World Economy* (London, 1966)

Wurm, C.A., *Die französische Sicherheitspolitik in der Phase der Umorientierung 1924–1926* [French Security Policies in the Reorientation Phase 1924–26] (Frankfurt, 1979)

Ziebura, G., *Léon Blum. Theorie und Praxis einer sozialistischen Politik*, vol. 1: *1872–1934* (Berlin, 1963)

3. Washington System

Allen, G.C., *A Short Economic History of Modern Japan, 1867–1937* (London, 1946)

——, *Japan's Economic Expansion* (London, 1965)

Battistini, L.H., *The United States and Asia* (New York, 1956)

Beasley, W.E., *Japanese Imperialism 1894–1945* (Oxford, 1987)

Beckmann, M., *The Modernization of China and Japan* (New York, 1962)

Bergamini, D., *Japan's Imperial Conspiracy* (London, 1971)

Borg, D., *American Policy and the Chinese Revolution, 1925–1928* (New York, 1968)

Buckley, T.H., *The United States and the Washington Conference 1921–1922* (Knoxville, 1970)

Buhite, R., *Nelson T. Johnson and American Policy toward China, 1925–1941* (East Lansing, Mich., 1969)

Cheng, Y.K., *Foreign Trade and Industrial Development of China* (Washington, 1956)

Cohen, W.I., *America's Response to China. An Interpretative History of Sino-American Relations* (New York, 1971)

Crowley, J.B., *Japan's Quest for Autonomy. National Security and Foreign Policy 1930–1938* (Princeton, 1966)

—— (ed.), *Modern East Asia. Essays in Interpretation* (New York, 1970)

Dulles, F.R., *China and America* (Princeton, 1946)

Fairbank, J.K., *The United States and China* (Cambridge, Mass., 1971³)

—— (ed.), *Republican China 1912–1949.* Part I of *The Cambridge History of China* (Cambridge, 1983) (the best introduction to China's internal development during the 1920s)

Feuerwerker, A., *The Chinese Economy 1912–1949* (Ann Arbor, 1968)

Glück, K., 'Japans Vordringen auf dem Weltmarkt' [The Japanese Advance on World Markets], PhD thesis, Frankfurt, 1936; Würzburg, 1937

Halliday, J., *A Political History of Japanese Capitalism* (New York, 1975)

Iriye, A., *After Imperialism. The Search for a New Order in the Far East, 1921–1931* (Cambridge, Mass., 1965)

——, *Across the Pacific: An Inner History of American–East Asian Relations* (New York, 1967)

——, *Japan's Foreign Policies between the World Wars: Sources and Interpretations* (London, 1971)

Israel, J., *Progressivism and the Open Door. America and China, 1905–1921* (London, 1971)

Lockwood, W.W., *The Economic Development of Japan. Growth and Structural Change, 1868–1938* (Princeton, 1955)

Marshall, B.K., *Capitalism and Nationalism in Prewar Japan. The Ideology of the Business Elite* (Stanford, 1968)

Maxon, Y.C., *Control of Japanese Foreign Policy. A Study of Civil-Military Rivalry 1930–1945* (Berkeley, 1957)

May, E.R., and J.C. Thomson (eds), *American–East Asian Relations. A Survey* (Cambridge, Mass., 1972)

Meyn, E. 'Die japanische Wirtschaftspolitik in der Mandschurei' [Japan's Economic Policies in Manchuria], PhD thesis, Handels-Hochschule Leipzig, Leipzig, 1938

Morley, J.W. (ed.), *Dilemmas of Growth in Prewar Japan* (Princeton, 1971)

Moulder, F., *Japan, China and the Modern World Economy* (Cambridge, 1977)

Rappaport, A., *Henry L. Stimson and Japan 1931–1933* (Chicago, 1963)

Rosovsky, H., *Capital Formation in Japan, 1868–1940* (Glencoe, 1961)

Schaller, M., *The United States and China in the Twentieth Century* (New York, 1979)

Schumpeter, E.B. (ed.), *The Industrialization of Japan and Manchukuo, 1930–1940* (New York, 1940)

Wheeler, G.E., *Prelude to Pearl Harbor. The United States Navy and the Far East, 1921–1931* (Columbia, 1963)

Williams, W.A., 'China and Japan. A Challenge and a Choice of the Nineteen-twenties', *Pacific Historical Review* 26 (1957)

Index

190